Communication Across Cultures

COMMUNICATION ACROSS CULTURES

The Linguistics of Texts in Translation

Basil Hatim

REVISED AND EXPANDED EDITION

First published in 2020 by
University of Exeter Press
Reed Hall, Streatham Drive
Exeter EX4 4QR
UK
www.exeterpress.co.uk

© Basil Hatim 2020

The right of Basil Hatim to be identified as author of this work has been asserted by him in accordance with the Copyright, Designs and Patents Acts 1988.

British Library Cataloguing in Publication Data
A catalogue record for this book is available from the British Library.

ISBN 978-1-905816-30-9 (Hardback)
ISBN 978-1-905816-31-6 (Paperback)

Typeset in Meta Serif and Scala Sans
by BBR Design, Sheffield

Contents

List of Figures		vii
Foreword by R.R.K. Hartmann		ix
Arabic Transliteration System		x
A New Introduction: Textual Rhetoric—The Missing Dimension		1
1.	Translator Decision-Making Informed by Textual Competence	6
2.	Deeper Text Processing	17
3.	The Myth of the Single Register: A Discourse Perspective on Linguistic Variation	28
4.	Argumentation: A Contrastive Text-Type Perspective	41
5.	A Model of Argumentation from Arabic Rhetoric	54
6.	Globalization, Academic Writing, Translation: A New Perspective on Culture	62
7.	Cultures within Cultures: Commodification Discourse	82
8.	On Purpose	98
9.	The Status of the Paragraph as a Unit of Text Structure	113
10.	Signalling Background Information in Expository Texts	124
11.	On the Interface Between Structure and Texture: The Textual Progression of Themes and Rhemes	135

12.	A Text-Type Solution to a Problem of Texture: Translating Cataphora	148
13.	Degree of Explicitness as a Distinctive Feature of Texture	160
14.	Emotiveness and Its Linguistic Realization in Texts	170
15.	Translating Direct and Indirect Speech and the Dynamics of News Reporting	185
16.	A Text-Type Perspective on the Pragmatics of Politeness	201
17.	Cultures in Contact and What People Do with Their Texts: An Applied-Linguistic Perspective	220
18.	The Discourse of Alienation and Its Linguistic Realization in a Modern Arabic Novella	238
19.	The Translation of Irony: A Discourse Focus on Arabic	251
20.	The Other Texts: Implications for Liaison Interpreting	268

Glossary of Contrastive Text: Linguistics and Translation Terms   281
References   295
Index   302

Figures

1	Strands of text in context	2
1.1	Register membership	9
1.2	Register and beyond	11
1.3	The semiotic triad	15
2.1	Register macro-structure	18
2.2	Layers of interaction	23
2.3	The structure of the counter-argument	26
3.1	Tenor vs field and mode	33
3.2	The semiotics of field, mode and tenor	36
4.1	Basic text types	45
4.2	Order of preference of argumentation type, English and Arabic compared	51
6.1	Text in context	64
6.2	The semiotic triad	69
6.3	Register membership	70
7.1	From register to macro-functions I	86
7.2	From register to macro-functions II	86

7.3	The discourse–genre–text triad	87
8.1	A typology of context and purpose	100
9.1	The negotiation of text structure	115
10.1	Exposition	125
10.2	Add-on background information	127
10.3	Three levels of narration	130
10.4	Main and subordinate texts	133
11.1	Simple linear TP	140
11.2	TP with a continuous theme	140
11.3	The tone-setter and the scene-setter	142
12.1	Argumentation and exposition	151
12.2	Cataphora in argumentation	153
12.3	Cataphora in exposition	154
15.1	Text structure of Sample 1	196
15.2	Text–discourse–genre chain	197
16.1	From discourse to text forms	202
16.2	Text type, power and distance	219
20.1	Intertextual retrieval	271

Foreword

Both contrastive linguistics and text linguistics are now truly in their prime; witness the numerous conferences held on the subject in various parts of the world, and the numerous handbooks and textbooks filling up the shelves in every university library. However, the combination of the two perspectives (the contrastive and the textual), for which some of us have been pleading for many years (I suggested the term 'contrastive textology' in 1980), and whose computational implementation is now feasible, is only just beginning. A further development, the application of contrastive text linguistics to translation studies, is long overdue.

Basil Hatim's book not only addresses all these issues and controversies, but exemplifies them through the prism of Arabic, a language that has enjoyed a long and distinguished rhetorical tradition, but not the benefit of much modern theoretical work. The author is well qualified to undertake this difficult but exciting task. Ever since the days of his Exeter PhD he has explored the relevance of contrastive discourse analysis to English–Arabic translation and demonstrated it in his practical teaching.

We are gratified to be able to present Dr Hatim's ideas in our Exeter Linguistic Studies in the hope that they will enrich the debate and aid instruction in a growing interdisciplinary field.

R.R.K. Hartmann
Exeter, October 1996

Arabic Transliteration System

Using material in Arabic has been kept to an absolute minimum, and English glosses are almost always provided. However, when it is felt that a particular form needs to be reproduced in the original, Arabic transliteration is used. The following system has been consistently employed:

Letter	Transliteration	Pronunciation
ا	aa	Like a in *car*
ب	b	Like b in *baby*
ت	t	Like t in *tree*
ث	th	Like the th in *theory*
ج	j	Sometimes like the g in *girl* or like the j in *jar*
ح	H	Like the h in *he* yet throaty, husky, in pronunciation
خ	kh	Like the ch in the name *Bach* or Scottish *loch*
د	d	Like the d in *dad*
ذ	z	Like the th in *the*
ر	r	Like the r in *ram*
ز	z	Like the z in *zoo*
س	s	Like the s in *see*
ش	sh	Like the sh in *she*
ص	S	Like the s in *sad* yet heavy in pronunciation

ARABIC TRANSLITERATION SYSTEM

Letter	Transliteration	Pronunciation
ض	<u>dh</u>	Like the d in *dead* yet heavy in pronunciation
ط	T	Like the t in *table* yet heavy in pronunciation
ظ	Z	Like the z in *Zorro* yet heavy in pronunciation
ع	<u>3</u>	Has no real equivalent sometimes they replace its sound with the A sound like, for example, the name *Ali* / 3ali /
غ	<u>gh</u>	Like the Gh in *Ghandi*
ف	f	Like the f in *fool*
ق	q	Like the q in *queen* yet heavy velar sound in pronunciation
ك	k	Like the K in *Kate*
ل	l	Like the l in *love*
م	m	Like the m in *moon*
ن	n	Like the n in *noon*
ھ ـھ	h	Like the h in *he*
و	W(aw, au, uu)	Like the W in the expression: Wow!
ي	Y (ay, ai, īi)	Like the y in *you*
ء	*hamza*	As in beginning to clear one's throat
أَ	*fatHa*	Like a in *apple*
إِ	*kasra*	Like i in *bit*
أُ	*dhamma*	Like u in German *punkt*

Adapted from http://www.arabic-keyboard.org/arabic/arabic-transliteration.php.

A New Introduction: Textual Rhetoric—The Missing Dimension

While the literature on translation theory, contrastive linguistics or **discourse**[1] analysis has certainly grown enormously in the last fifty years or so, very few books have attempted to fuse the three perspectives together. This book seeks to establish such links and to explore areas of common interest in the theory and practice of intercultural communication. Tackling the problem from this angle, this work will essentially be following a trend captured succinctly in these words by Reinhard Hartmann as far back as the early 1980s: Doing discourse analysis without a contrastive base is as incomplete as doing contrastive analysis without a discourse base. Using translation as the go-between provides us with an appropriate framework within which the entire enterprise of languages in contact may usefully be dealt with.

A specific aim of this book is thus to argue that, in any act of linguistic mediation, a careful consideration of the changes which a given **text** invariably undergoes when transferred across linguistic and cultural boundaries is a sure way of finding out what actually goes on inside and around texts, not only with reference to the language pair in question, but generally in the broader context of textuality. To appreciate how entire systems of source language rhetorical and linguistic conventions are brought to bear on the act of textual transfer, and how norms and conventions of a given language are reconciled with their counterparts in another language and culture, the analysis of a process such as translation is illuminative because it is precisely in that process that we see what happens in moving from one text world to another. This is particularly the case when we are occupied not only with the mechanical, lower-level vagaries of the

---

1 Terms in bold are defined in the Glossary at the end of this book.

linguistic system but also, and to a greater extent, with higher-order considerations of language in use and text in context.

In the course of the unfolding argument, authentic data from written and spoken English (or Arabic, mostly in back-translation) is used to add clarity to theoretical insights gained from a variety of disciplines,[2] including cognitive linguistics, translation studies, contrastive rhetoric and critical discourse analysis. A model of text processing will be outlined, and each aspect of the model proposed will be related separately to a problem of language processing, in domains as varied as translator and interpreter training, cultural studies, literary criticism and language teaching. The training of future linguists, and the sensitization of language users in general to the realities of discourse, are some of the overall objectives which this book seeks to pursue.

The book starts with a model-building chapter, which outlines the text-processing approach proposed and sees this in terms of three basic categories: **context, text structure** and **texture**. Context is defined in terms of three main strands: **communicative (register**-based), **pragmatic (speech act**-based) and **semiotic (sign**-based). Structure and texture, in turn, are seen from the vantage point of **text type** shown to be at the centre of contextual analysis. Schematically, strands of text in context may be represented as in Figure 1.

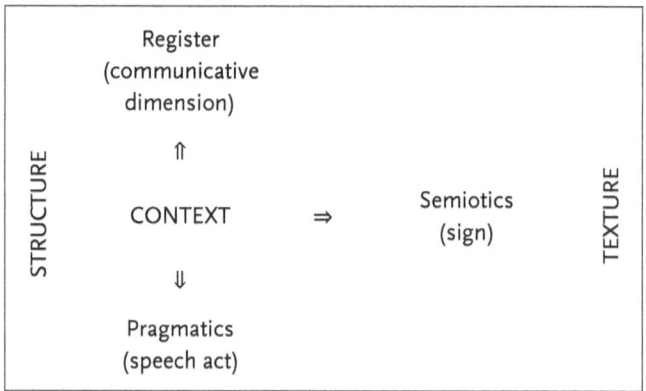

Figure 1 Strands of text in context

Thus, following the initial chapter on translator decision-making informed by **textual competence** (Ch. 1), several chapters are devoted to register theory and

---

2   Throughout in this book, all translations from Arabic are my own, unless otherwise indicated.

text typology, seen from the perspective of modern text linguistics and classical rhetoric (Chs. 2, 3, 4 and 5). Three new chapters written specifically for this edition follow, one on globalization and translation, another on culture and commodification, and the third on the notion of purpose in translating and interpreting (Chs. 6, 7 and 8). Text structure occupies us next and two further chapters deal specifically with the compositional planning of texts (Chs. 9, 10 and 11). Texture, or the various devices which lend texts the quality of being **cohesive** and **coherent**, is the concern of the following chapters (Chs. 12, 13 and 14), which build on the analysis of compositional **formats** such as the paragraph.

Once the various components of the model have been covered, we cast the net wider in the five chapters that follow (Chs. 15–19). Here, the general aim is to test out both theoretical and practical insights in various domains of language in social life. Text type and **politeness**, cultures in contact, the analysis and translation of **ideology** in literature, the analysis and translation of irony in non-fiction, and the oral mode of interpreting seen as a socio-textual act, are some of the issues tackled from the perspective of discourse contrastive linguistics adopted in this book. Finally, the volume is concluded with a chapter reviewing the more salient features of the model proposed, testing the basic hypotheses on new territories, notably oral interpreting (Ch. 20).

Now, a word on the choice of English and Arabic as the main language pair used throughout may be in order. Working with a language such as Arabic, which is culturally and conceptually different from, say, English, is extremely valuable and will, we believe, illuminate some of the more intricate contrastive discourse issues that concern the contrastive linguist in general, and translators and interpreters in particular. Like all viable linguistic systems of communication, Arabic is particularly rich in **rhetorical conventions** and norms of language use. However, unlike quite a number of other world languages, and certainly unlike many of the European languages with which we are familiar, Arabic is a highly **explicative** language (as opposed to a language such as English which tends to be more **implicative**). While losing none of the subtlety, Arabic often explicitly marks the finest fluctuations in context, be these related to **socio-cultural factors**, to intentions, or to general communicative matters such as the **formality** of a given text. This occurs not only at the lexical/semantic level (rich, flowery lexis to cater for every minute social nuance), but also, and perhaps much more significantly, at the grammatical/syntactic level, and beyond. Word-order manipulation in Arabic, to take but one example, is a highly **motivated** and context-dependent process that, over and above having significant effects on the basic lexico-grammatical meaning, helps to communicate a wide range of added rhetorical effects. Almost all of such meaning modalities are no doubt available in any language one cares to name. Nonetheless, particularly when translating into a language like English, Arabic word-order implications, to stay with this example, often prove to be an insurmountable hurdle.

On the question of the need to cater for cultural **distance** and related issues, a pertinent point once made by N.E. Enkvist readily comes to mind. In a review of a book on discourse and translation, Enkvist (1992: 127–28) concludes with a plea:

> The laudable emphasis on the importance of cultural differences might perhaps have been concretely exemplified with a few translation problems involving culturally and structurally distant or 'exotic' languages.

It is to reminders such as these that this book responds, and proposals are offered in the hope that some useful insights are gleaned into the way texts are put together in particular and into the communicative process at large. To pursue these aims, a number of questions obviously confront us and must be urgently answered: What is 'text' and what is 'context' in the first place? What are the relevant contextual factors that almost causally determine that which is eventually realized explicatively or **implicatively** in different languages? What is it that determines implicitness in a language such as English, and that a language such as Arabic finds particularly challenging in every respect? What is it that motivates Arabic explicitness? When is this implicitness or explicitness a case of **flouting** (and not breaking) communicative **cooperativeness** (i.e. what is the rhetorical **motivation**, if any)? Finally, is there any point in impressing these differences on users of languages that do not usually opt for any degree of explicitness worth noting? These and other questions will inform several debates that will form the basis of a number of the arguments marshalled forth in what follows.

The chapters in this volume have all been written with one unifying theme in mind: the applicability of a theoretical model of discourse processing to practical pursuits such as translation, interpreting and language teaching. Nevertheless, despite professional demarcation lines, these activities pursue goals that in reality show more unity than division. It is these common areas of interest that constitute the primary concerns of this book. The various chapters were written at different times during a period spanning several decades, a period in which, while initially based at Heriot-Watt University, Edinburgh (1980–1999), I had the good fortune of teaching on a wide range of courses at universities within the UK (Salford, Durham), Europe (Barcelona, Tampere, Athens), North Africa and the Middle East (Ecole Supérieure Roi Fahd de Traduction in Tangiers, the Jordanian

University for Women in Amman, Effat University in Jeddah, KSA) and, finally, at the American University of Sharjah in the United Arab Emirates, where I am at present. I therefore first owe a tremendous debt of gratitude to colleagues and students from these institutions for the warmth and understanding that they have so graciously given me.

Indeed, I owe so much to so many that I seriously do not know where to begin. Therefore, allow me to single out a few, as without their support and stimulating influence, this book would simply not have seen the light of day. One is Reinhard Hartmann, my doctoral thesis advisor at Exeter; the other, the late Chris Candlin, who was my thesis examiner. Then there is my long-standing colleague and collaborator on a number of projects, Ian Mason. There are also my two other colleagues, one from the old days, Gavin Watterson (now a freelance translator), the other, Ron Buckley (at present at the University of Manchester). Last and certainly not least, a special word of thanks goes to Ernst Wendland (Stellenbosch University, South Africa) for all his help and guidance in the final and most crucial stage of completing this revised edition. So to all of these mentors and colleagues, I am truly indebted for their unstinting encouragement and support and for sparing no time or effort in making more comprehensible what I have had to say over the years.

1 Translator Decision-Making Informed by Textual Competence

One useful way of seeing contrastive text linguistics at work is through translation, and an interesting way of looking at the translation process is by examining the kind of decision-making process, which, when dealing with texts, translators go through, consciously or by default. Examining this area of working with texts will enhance our understanding not only of what actually happens when text confronts text, but also of what it means to be textually competent in this area of cross-cultural communication. Our ultimate goal is to shed some light on the way forward in our endeavour to explain, teach and learn more about textual competence. This is a valid objective, whether our concern lies in human translation, machine translation, the wider field of artificial intelligence, applied linguistics and foreign language teaching or indeed contrastive linguistics.

To preview some of the issues likely to arise any time contrastive models of text processing are discussed, we will now set ourselves the task of analysing an assortment of texts and, at the risk of sounding too prescriptive, set about recording the various decisions which any textually competent language user would be called upon to make prior to, during and after engaging in an activity such as translation. Nevertheless, a caveat may be helpful before we proceed. Based on the experience of working with generations of translator trainees on the kind of texts being scrutinized, it would not be overstating the case to say that the options described or recommended here have largely been ignored by a sizeable number of the trainees tested, and that, on those rare occasions when these options *appear* to be followed, the process is often hit-or-miss and unsystematic. Coming from students and professionals whose bilingual competence is by and large beyond reproach, this is regrettable. Yet it highlights the value, indeed the indispensability, of discourse awareness and practical text analysis with a prominent contrastive-textual-linguistic slant. This is a worthwhile goal to pursue, whatever the activity being pursued—translating, teaching translation, assessing translations or translators. In the sections to follow, we will consider the notion of 'text' from several different perspectives.

Text from the Top Down

Consider this text sample:

Sample 1

Amnesty Appeal

The reason you join Amnesty is not words, but pain.
   It's the pain of children like 16-year-old Sevki Akinci, literally barbecued alive by Turkish soldiers who came to his village looking for guns which they didn't find.
   It's the tears of 17 year old Ravi Sundaralingam, tortured by Indian troops in Sri Lanka—tied upside down with a fire lit beneath his head and electrodes sparking at his genitals.
   It's the anguish of Angelica Mandoza de Ascarza, whose teenaged son was taken from home by the security forces in Peru, never to be heard from again. He joined the hundreds who have simply 'disappeared'.
   It's the terror of a 23 year old Tibetan nun, raped by Chinese soldiers with an electric cattle prod.
   It's the agony of children like Walter Villatoro and Salvadore Sandoval, street children in Guatemala City, whose eyes were burned out by police cigars, their tongues ripped from their heads with pliers.
   Maybe you simply don't realize that such vile things do go on.
   But for two years now, we have been running appeals in this newspaper. With one exception, all of these cases were mentioned in previous appeals.
                                         Amnesty International Fundraiser

Before embarking on the reading or translation of this or any other text, there is a crucial preparatory process to go through. This is the stage of gathering first impressions and forming initial hypotheses, to be confirmed or disconfirmed once the text begins to unfold gradually and reading proper gets under way. In tackling a text such as the one we have here, for example, the reader or translator exploits a variety of clues ranging from such rudimentary aspects of text in context as titles and subtitles (*Amnesty International, Appeal*), to more substantive issues such as the general level of formality at which the text is pitched or the particular ideology of the text producer, the publication, etc.

Then reading proper commences, and the first sentence of a text of this kind would usually present the reader with linguistic **elements**, which, among other things, tend to characterize the relationship between text producer and receiver. Consider, for example, the inviting tone in

The reason you join Amnesty is not words but ...

Note also how expectations are set up: When *not words but ...* is uttered, 'deeds' is anticipated, but this anticipation is immediately defied (*... but pain*), producing a powerful rhetorical effect we shall in due course examine under the label **informativity**. This is a standard of textuality that generally deals with linguistic norms and with rhetorically motivated departures from such norms.

Next, there is the topic or subject matter (what the text is about, 'human rights' in this case). Again at a glance, the reader's attention is most likely to be drawn to

It's the pain of children ...

This sentence continues with the identification of a young victim by age and name (*like 16-year-old Sevki Akinci*). The rhetorical effect of giving such personal details of the victim is stylistically powerful and highly persuasive.

This roughly **field** (**agency**) issue is closely bound up with the level of language formality, or what we shall refer to as **tenor** (**power** or **solidarity**). Note the sense of involvement established by how the second sentence picks up on the issue of pain in the first (*... not words, but* pain >>> *It's the* pain). This engagement, which the reader is invited to show towards the subject, is particularly worth noting in producing the overall rhetorical effect and persuasive appeal of the text. Equally, if not more, important is the reiteration of *pain* and the use of the anaphoric *It's the pain of ...* (repeated no less than four times). We are here well and truly into the domain of discourse **mode**, which together with field and tenor form a triad we shall deal with shortly in greater deal under the notion of register.

'Textualization' is a function of mode, and one aspect of this is **cohesion**, a standard of textuality that pertains to the way surface **text elements** 'stick together' and formal continuity is maintained. Cohesion is usually at the service of a higher-order rhetorical aim that seeks to identify underlying relationships of conceptual **coherence**. Together with field (level of technicality/agency) and tenor (level of formality and power or solidarity), mode thus becomes home to 'textuality', i.e. part of the strategy to produce a text with a focus of some kind that, in the present context of Sample 1:

- conveys the emotiveness and commitment with which the entire text is imbued (primarily a function of field),
- yields such readings as 'It is this very pain which should make you join Amnesty' (to be dealt with under tenor), and
- has a spoken-like quality about it, and not a text written to be read reflectively (issues to be referred to collectively as **mode of discourse**).

Thus, even a cursory glance at Sample 1 above would register various lexico-grammatical elements as communicative clues to the text's identity. These three factors (subject matter, tone, and the way the message is shaped) were used specifically by early formal register analysis, and may be schematically represented as in Figure 1.1.

REGISTER		
Field ⇒ Agency	Tenor ⇒ Power/Solidarity	Mode ⇒ Textualization

Figure 1.1 Register membership

Returning to the standards of textuality, we can now see how, within a given register specification, text elements tend to acquire cohesion (formal continuity), coherence (conceptual connectivity) and informativity (which, as we explained, introduces an element of creative shock and surprise). In the text being examined, these factors would, in addition, be serving the twin standards of **intentionality** and **acceptability**—these are 'pragmatic' parameters which ensure that everything we have depicted so far regarding the present text is being done to achieve a persuasive appeal (i.e. is intended and accepted as such). In fact, we know from our prior experience of 'fundraising appeals' what such texts should look like, and we would be disconcerted if this were not the case. This particular kind of allusive relationship is informed by a crucial standard which all texts must meet, namely **intertextuality**. Finally, there is the primary, all-encompassing standard to do with **situationality** that was met the moment we encountered and dealt with the examples of children like *Sevki Akinci, literally barbecued alive by Turkish soldiers*, or *17-year-old Ravi Sundaralingam, tortured by Indian troops*. All in all, then, there are seven standards of textuality to ensure that texts are effective, efficient and appropriate, obviously with varying degrees of success (Beaugrande and Dressler 1981; Beaugrande 1980, 1984, 1997). The standards may now be laid out in the order we have presented them here:

- INFORMATIVITY (surprise, creativity, shock value)
- COHESION (formal continuity)
- COHERENCE (conceptual connectivity)
- INTENTIONALITY (intended as ...)
- ACCEPTABILITY (accepted as ...)
- INTERTEXTUALITY (allusion)
- SITUATIONALITY (circumstances enveloping a text)

It has to be noted that in the mental processing of this or similar texts, only part of this overall picture is completed so far, and that the little that has been gleaned up to now is all part of first impressions, hardly anything solid to go by. Ephemeral and vague as they are, however, these impressions, even hunches, if confirmed, would go hand in hand with slightly more profound understanding of issues to be picked up and assessed as we go along. These will mostly have to do with such factors as the kind of text (e.g. persuasive), discourse (committed), **genre** (the fundraiser), alongside the political leanings of the publication (left, right, centre), the ideology of the text producer (activism), and so on. To achieve that level of awareness, we need to go deeper into the **structure** and texture of the discourse.

Text from the Inside Out

On closer scrutiny, what emerges as particularly salient in Sample 1 would be deeper resources of meaning intended to involve the reader more intimately. For example, consider the use of the inclusive 'you' to enhance the inviting tone of the text (tenor), the passive voice (e.g. *barbecued alive by Turkish soldiers*) (field), and the repetition of *pain* in *It's the pain*, as well as how this is further developed to convey a high degree of personal commitment through the use of rhetorical **anaphora** (*It is ..., It is ..., It is ...*) (mode). These are all pragmatic effects that must be heeded in any attentive reading, and must somehow be preserved in translation, particularly when working into languages where, to pick just one example, the use of the passive is discouraged, and is approved only if rhetorically motivated (e.g. Arabic).

The elements introduced above under tenor, field and mode may therefore be regrouped under three main headings, respectively: **interpersonal**, **ideational** and **textual** components of meaning potential. Schematically, these may be represented as in Figure 1.2.

REGISTER		
Field ⇒ Ideational	Tenor ⇒ Interpersonal	Mode ⇒ Textual

Figure 1.2 Register and beyond

The interpersonal component is thus essentially related to the appropriate level of formality or tenor. In the above text, we note the skilful manipulation of **mood**, that is, whether the utterance is a statement or a performative (e.g. imperative, interrogative). **Modality** (or adjusting the text's degree of certainty) is also fully tapped. These two aspects of **interpersonal meaning** convey power or solidarity, as the following examples from the sample text show:

The reason you join Amnesty is not words, but pain (This is a 'statement' in form, but an 'imperative' in implied function: 'sign up, it is a worthwhile cause!').

Maybe you simply don't realize that such vile things go on (but, think hard, for these tragedies do happen, and far more often than you thought was possible).

No less significant than this interpersonal dimension is the ideational component. This level of meaning which, as we have demonstrated above, has a great deal to do with **agency**, conveys the text-author's asserted knowledge of what is happening in the world outside, by whom, to whom, and how we feel about such happenings—a contextual domain that is no longer restricted to field but goes well beyond. Most likely to have attracted the attention of the reader is how the passive voice is exploited to convey a diverse range of rhetorical effects:

literally barbecued alive by Turkish soldiers
tortured by Indian troops in Sri Lanka
tied upside down
with a fire lit beneath his head
and electrodes sparking at his genitals
teenaged son was taken from home by the security forces in Peru
never to be heard from again
who have simply 'disappeared'
raped by Chinese soldiers with an electric cattle prod

whose eyes were burned out by police cigars
their tongues ripped from their heads with pliers

Saturated with passives, the text takes on a layer of **ideational meaning** that can only relay morbid 'agency', keeping the reader wondering: Who on earth would commit such atrocities? Agents are conspicuous by their absence (*tied upside down, a fire lit beneath his head*) and, if present, are highlighted as by-agents (*by Turkish soldiers, by Indian troops in Sri Lanka*). There is also the proliferation of inanimate agency to convey a Gothic horror effect (*electrodes sparking at his genitals, burned out by police cigars*). To conclude this list of features most poignantly, there is the use of verbs in scare quotes such as *'disappeared'* in *who have simply 'disappeared'* to relay the subtle meaning 'they were made to vanish, liquidated').

Finally, the whole process of reducing interpersonal distance to make room for solidarity (as opposed to power), while at the same time negotiating ideational agency to convey morbidity (and not the cheerful tone of, say, a travel guide book), is ultimately crowned by a process best termed textualization. This is where the interpersonal and ideational values are moulded (i.e. textualized) in particular ways within a given textual mode that visibly exhibits the formal qualities of cohesion, in the service of conceptual coherence. Examples from the textual dimension at a glance include:

not words, but pain
It's the pain of children
It's the tears of
It's the anguish of
It's the terror of
It's the agony of
Maybe you simply don't … But

An example which clearly shows how the interpersonal, ideational and textual are fused to generate powerful meanings is the 'irony' in

With one exception, all of these cases were mentioned in previous appeals.

The element *With one exception*, combined with the preceding *But for two years now*, may be read pragmatically as: 'And the irony of it all is that everything we have been saying after all this time seems to have fallen on deaf ears, but we hope not this time, with you acting on your convictions.'

We can now see how the traditional surface categories of field, tenor and mode are now conceived at deeper levels as the more pragmatically oriented ideational, interpersonal and textual resources of meaning. These are all factors that inevitably have a bearing on the way a text is interpreted by writer and reader alike. Values yielded by these and similar parameters (which essentially belong to the **context of situation**) are all subsumed under what might be described as radical register analysis, an orientation covered in some detail in Chapter 3. To wrap up this discussion, it is worth quoting Thompson (1996/2014: 28–29) at some length:

There is more to register's field than subject matter technicality:

> We use language to talk about our experience of the world, including the worlds in our own minds.

Similarly, there is more to register tenor than formality or informality:

> We also use language to interact with other people, to establish and maintain relations with them, to influence their behaviour, to express our own viewpoint on things in the world, and to elicit or change theirs.

Finally, there is more to register mode than spoken vs. written:

> In that using language, we organise our messages in ways which indicate how they fit in with the other messages around them and with the wider context in which we are talking or writing.

Text from Below

In a sense, text processing proper has already started, and tentative first impressions have now acquired form and substance. In fact, text processing begins the moment we go beyond generalities into how the various elements of text are put together. We deal with the initial so-called topic sentences (and elements within) as encapsulating the overall textual design, and the struggle to discover such a design would here begin in earnest.

As texts unfold, readers or translators assess incoming signals (the various text elements) in terms of their assumed **relevance** to the grand design of the text. By relevance we mean the contribution that a sentence element or a sequence of elements makes to the ideal goal of all communication, namely expending 'minimal processing effort' to gain 'maximal communicative reward', or **minimax** (Levý 1969). Staying with the persuasive attitude a little longer, we now want to try a different tack and deal with a different textual macro-structure from the above fundraiser—the editorial). The specific **rhetorical purpose** served this time is also slightly different from the fundraiser's **through-argument** above. Sample 2 is a persuasive **counter-argument** drawn from a longer editorial. Note in particular the crucial 'function words' in this short excerpt:

Sample 2 (The case of formally)

> Tomorrow's meeting of OPEC is a different affair. Certainly, it is formally about prices .... Certainly, it will also have immediate implications for the price of petrol ....
>
> But this meeting ... is not primarily about selling arrangements .... It is primarily about the future cohesion of the organization itself.
>
> From a *Times* editorial

To begin with, consider:

Tomorrow's meeting of OPEC is a different affair.

This initial sentence is intended to be an interest-arousing **tone-setter** and, as such, it really stands outside the main argumentative macro-structure. The counter-argument starts with:

Certainly, it is formally about prices ...

This puts forward a **claim** that is somewhat contentious and describes a situation as a 'given' with problems, a proposition that is entertained fairly widely, yet suffering from certain inaccuracies or shortcomings (from the present arguer's perspective, of course.)

Among a number of important assumptions that the astute reader makes at this stage, the one that stands out relates to the opening statement (and to the adverb *certainly* specifically) being a subtle 'send-up', 'tongue-in-cheek' in tone (essentially saying 'that's what they say, but it is not strictly speaking true or, at best, it is not the point'). Textually competent users of English use this counter-argumentative device as a **'straw-man gambit'**, or a **thesis cited to be opposed**, which is usually followed by a 'rebuttal'.

No **opposition** is forthcoming, however, and the expectation is slightly revised: the text may not be ready yet for a rebuttal. The text producer may have felt that the first attempt at citing a thesis to oppose is still too weak, or not comprehensive enough, to be questioned and attacked. Perhaps another *certainly* structure might do the trick:

> Certainly, it will also have immediate implications for the price of petrol ...

With this citation of another aspect of the given assumption to be opposed, the text is now ready to move on to the next step, namely presenting the 'new', or actual reality as the present arguer sees it, ushered in by the adversative *but*.

> But this meeting ... is not ...

This is an obvious rebuttal, and comes in the form of an opposition signalled by such adversatives as *however, but, nonetheless*.

These intuitions about the way texts are put together, which have serious implications for the efficiency and effectiveness of text production and reception in general and of translating in particular, are all part of dealing with 'text' or elements of text as 'signs' best dealt with under the general heading of semiotics. In fact as we proceed, this very same text will be revisited on a number of occasions, each attending to a different aspect of the text's constitution (see especially Chapters 4 and 5).

To Conclude

It might be helpful at this stage to summarize the story so far. Contextual categories like tenor, field and mode are enriched by further textual and contextual input to yield deeper interpersonal, ideational and textual shades of meaning. These macro-functions, in turn, collaborate to produce familiar discourse attitudes (human rights activism, pro-cohesion lobby within OPEC), genre structures (the fundraiser, the editorial) and text types such as the counter-argument. Schematically, we can now update Figure 1.1 to further define the central notion of 'register' and to include a semiotic triad of signs among signs.

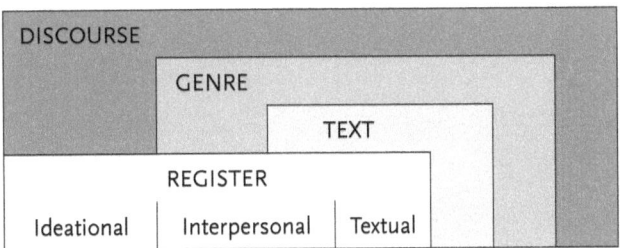

Figure 1.3 The semiotic triad

This semiotic triad—discourse–genre–text—will now occupy us in the next chapter. Discourse constitutes the mainstay of attitude and perspective and is thus an ideal vehicle for the expression of ideology (e.g. racism, sexism). Genre is a similar macro-structure, but what is attended to here is not so much attitude as communicative event or social occasion, one that is conventionally associated with set participants and set communicative goals (e.g. the fundraiser, cowboy films). Finally, these discoursal and generic values materialize only through what we shall from now on refer technically to as the unit 'text' (e.g. Through-argument, counter-argument). Thus, the linchpin of texts in communication is the notion of 'rhetorical purpose'.

2 Deeper Text Processing

In the previous chapter, we surveyed the textual terrain from the top down, from the inside out and from below, but very much in a bird's eye view fashion. We identified register as a central notion in the process of text production and reception, and we defined 'text' as the minimum unit of communication. However, we have also discovered that beyond text and, more specifically, beyond register, there is an entire universe of discourse to explore. To start with, beyond register's field, more than subject matter is involved; there is ideology and ideational meanings that regulate agency (e.g. **passivization**, **nominalization**). Similarly, solidarity can emanate from register's tenor that goes beyond mere formality to present text users with various layers of interpersonal meaning (e.g. mood, modality). Finally, register's mode is no longer restricted to spoken vs written communication, but transcends these distinctions to enjoy a wider remit—textualization (through meeting such standards of textuality as cohesion and coherence).

In this chapter, we maintain this snapshot focus but recognize how a multi-layered notion of register can account for a more intense expression of attitude or perspective, or what we shall now technically refer to as discourse. A more radical conception of register will also be behind the evolution of genre that can lend discourse its sense of communicative event or occasion. Moreover, a more dynamic approach to cohesion and coherence would give rise to rhetorical purpose as the pivot of an organizational unit we shall call text and treat as the minimum unit of communication.

As text processing becomes more focused on this level of text-in-context inter-relationships, the question that is always uppermost in the mind of the text user is how to make the transition **bottom-up** from the **micro**-level of words and grammatical structures to the **macro**-level of discourse, genre and text. Before addressing such questions, it might be helpful to take stock and schematically represent the story so far, as in Figure 2.1.

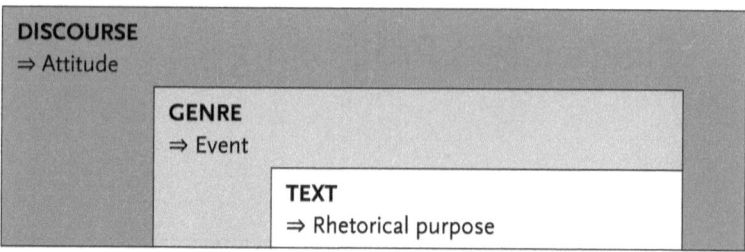

Figure 2.1 Register macro-structure

Relevance

In the transition to a macro-structure such as discourse, from a micro-structural element such as the passive voice or, to put it more concretely, in the journey from the passive micro-structure *literally barbecued alive by Turkish soldiers* ... via the macro-structure genre (the fundraiser) and the twin macro-structure discourse (the 'hortatory' variety) to Amnesty's sense of decency and commitment to human rights, the micro-element in question has to be assessed and reassessed in terms of what we shall now work with as the principle of 'relevance'. By relevance, we understand the contribution that a given micro-structural element makes to enhancing the integrity of a macro-structural sign and thus sustaining its internal and external cohesion and coherence. Viewed in more operational processing terms, the establishment of relevance (the potential of an utterance to yield maximal communicative reward for minimal processing effort) is essentially a **heuristic** or an exploratory hypothesis-testing procedure: why like this, why here, and what if ...? Nevertheless, this 'feeling one's way' into an array of alternatives, admitting what contributes to 'sense constancy' (Wienold 1990) and eliminating what does not, is a process that is not entirely unconstrained. To return to our OPEC example, reproduced here for convenience as Sample 1, there are all kinds of factors, both textual-linguistic and contextual which, in English, can regulate the process of reading, writing or translating this kind of text or part of a text.

Sample 1 (the issue of formally again)

> Tomorrow's meeting of OPEC is a different affair. Certainly, it is formally about prices .... Certainly, it will also have immediate implications for the price of petrol ....
> But this meeting ... is not primarily about selling arrangements .... It is primarily about the future cohesion of the organization itself.
>
> From a *Times* editorial

For example, we recall that in dealing with the utterance

Certainly, it is formally about prices ...

text users would normally be aware of certain 'gaps' as communicative clues strategically planted in initial argumentative statements. These 'seeds' alert the reader to *how* a claim is to be construed (and not only to *what* is cited). Among many other things, there will be

- a tongue-in-cheek tone, or what we have termed 'straw-man gambit',
- an air of nebulousness surrounding the claim,
- an impending opposition about to emerge.

Noteworthy in this sentence is how *formally* is exploited to convey that there is a gap deliberately left in the claim which needs to be plugged. On paper ('formally'), the OPEC meeting is about prices. This is what they say, but we know differently: the meeting is not strictly about prices, it is about something else—the cohesion of the organization, which is in tatters.

The Case of *Slightly Better*

To further illustrate this strategic planting of 'gaps' in the citation of an opponent's thesis as part of the counter-argumentative strategy, read through Sample 2 and pay special attention to:

- how opponents to the 'hope' scenario are represented (underlined),
- what the pragmatic meaning of the adverbial *slightly better* is (in bold),
- how this anti-hope campaign is opposed (italics), and
- how this 'opposition' interacts with and retrospectively sheds light on how the anti-hope stance is represented initially.

Sample 2

Lebanon
For the tenth time give us a chance

<u>The latest peace plan for Lebanon, signed in Damascus on December 28th, has a **slightly better** chance of success</u> than the nine previous plans hopefully pressed upon that sad country since the civil war began more than a decade ago. One of the signatories has already just survived an assassination attempt by disgruntled people within his own following.
 But there are reasons for hope. First ...
The Economist (highlights added)

For the moment, let us focus on the phrase *slightly better*, occurring as part of citing a commonly held view. This particular instance of language use shows most clearly how textural patterns ultimately link up with the structure of texts and with the requirements of context. Without this kind of analysis, the reader or translator would not be able to determine which of two rival readings of *slightly better* should hold sway:

(a) The peace plan is 'only slightly' better (and is therefore not worth even considering). The pragmatic focus would be on *slightly* and the speech act would be an 'assertion'.
(b) The peace plan is 'appreciably' better (and is therefore well worth considering as it is the best we have had for some time). The pragmatic focus would be on *better*, with the speech act remaining an 'assertion'.

To distinguish between the two readings properly and to adopt the more appropriate becomes necessary in certain languages, where there is no 'one size fits all' (as is often the case with English), but different forms would have to be selected to cater for one reading and not the other. Arabic is a language where such subtle pragmatic distinctions are reflected in the actual wording. Pragmatic reading (a) would best be served by the use of a so-called restrictive structure (*qasr*), thus:

laa tatamata'u illaa bi qadrin Da'il min furuSi al najaaH

Lit. 'does not enjoy but a minimal measure of success'

Pragmatic reading (b), on the other hand, invites a non-restrictive syntactic structure:

tatamata'u bi furaSi najaaHi la ba'sa bihaa (kabira)
Lit. 'enjoys a reasonable degree of success'

At work is a text structure best described as a teeter-totter (a 'balance' of some kind) in which the first part of a text cites someone's claim, only to rebut it in the subsequent discourse, with the second part providing the rebuttal. The segment in question occurs in the top 'claim-cited' part. Within this socio-textual strategy, conventions stipulate that what is used as a point of departure cannot be that which one would wholeheartedly endorse; this should come last.

In other words, the segment *slightly better* is now part of the so-called 'straw man', soon to be discredited. However, we are not yet out of the woods: Who or what is the straw man in this case? Is it the optimistic scenario of the peace plan (to be attacked shortly and the argument would ultimately be for 'hopelessness') or is it the pessimistic scenario of the plan (to be attacked shortly and the argument would ultimately be for 'hopefulness')? That is to say:

- in focusing on *slightly*, we would only be paying lip service to how great the thinking of the pessimists is (but the argument would eventually be won by the optimists),
- or, in focusing on *better*, we would only be paying lip service to how great the thinking of the optimists is (but the argument would eventually be won by the pessimists).

The day will be won by the optimists who are served better by the first scenario: Let the pessimists feel good but only for a short while. Forthcoming textual evidence supports this and the way the argument eventually develops move us towards:

But there are reasons for hope ...

In this sample, text-organizational constraints, together with other discoursal and generic values, are heeded as reliable clues to the arguer's real intent. However, as we shall argue at length in this monograph (Chs. 4 and 5), this common English counter-argumentative format is an alien rhetorical structure in a number of languages (e.g. Arabic). The linguistic means to implement such a strategy are certainly available almost universally, and Western-educated speakers of Arabic, for example, no doubt command this verbal routine as competently as any literate English-speaking text user. It is, however, not something that comes naturally to an average Arab arguer. In Arabic, it would be more conventional to present initially what one wants ultimately to prove and then proceed to defend this extensively.

The Unit 'Text'

Text, the technical term we shall use to refer to the set of mutually relevant intentions that collectively serve an overall rhetorical purpose (e.g. to counter-argue), is the ultimate linguistic unit in any activity to do with communicating in language. In all such activities (reading, writing, translating), there is hardly a decision taken regarding any element of language in use without constant reference being made to the text as the macro-structural frame of reference. Translation equivalence, for example, can be adequately established only in terms of criteria related to text-type membership, and in light of how these criteria govern the kind of compositional **plan** of the text opted for (structure). Nevertheless, as we shall see in due course, text structure (which is home to text coherence) must be seen in procedural terms, and this is where texture, or how a text is made internally cohesive, enters the equation. Texture effectively becomes structure in detail.

Specifically at the level of texture, the base level of text's global patterning, translators, in addition to text, must also refer to two other basic socio-textual units, mentioned briefly in our discussion so far: genre (e.g. the fundraiser, the editorial) and discourse (e.g. human rights activism, fundamentalist Islam). The three units (discourse, genre, text) tend to work in tandem and are invariably signalled by crucial signposts through a mechanism we have referred to as 'intertextuality' (Ch. 1). Intertextual allusions link given utterances to other prior texts and contexts, and are invoked to guide the interpretation process and steer the interpreter in the direction of previously stored knowledge. Behind these structures lurk some rhetorical purpose (a textual structure such as a 'claim cited to be opposed'), some communicative event conventionally enshrined in language (a genre structure such as the fundraiser), or some attitudinal statement (a discoursal structure such as the hortatory tone of activists).

A Socio-Textual Set of Dos and Don'ts

As presented here, this picture of what goes on inside and around texts is obviously much too simplified. In reality, interaction is far more complex and usually takes place

- between text producer and text receiver,
- between text producer or receiver and the text being processed, and
- between text and text (horizontally as in a reference to Shakespeare's *to be or not to be*, or vertically to Shakespearian style).

In other words, the interaction is far more open-ended than that which traditional register analysis would advocate. It is essentially about confronting language users with an enormous array of options to discern, take up, modify or exclude in the light of a diverse range of contextual factors. Let us together study Figure 2.2

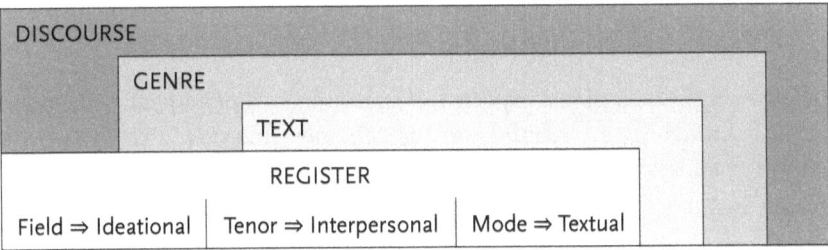

Figure 2.2 Layers of interaction

In examining these categories, it is of paramount importance to look at the kind of constraints within which these templates may be utilized, and which singly or collectively regulate effective language use. Consider, for example, Sample 3 and Sample 4, drawn respectively from an address given by a university dean announcing a new initiative linking two UK universities, and from a university bulletin press release reporting the event. In this communicative situation, the dean comments on the prospects for the joint venture by saying, to quote verbatim:

Sample 3

The University of X and Y University have a proven track record ... which this collaborative venture can only enhance.

This segment from the dean's address is certainly worth noting if only because, in the press release covering the event the following day, the 'active emphatic restrictive voice' (*this collaborative venture can only enhance*) magically disappeared and was replaced by an interesting passive structure. This is how it appeared in the university bulletin's report of the Centre's inauguration event (in indirect speech):

Sample 4

> Then the Dean went on to say that the University of X and Y University had a proven track record ... *which this collaborative venture was intended to enhance.*
>
> (Italics added)

The seemingly slight alteration is fascinating, and the reporter must be commended for remarkable journalistic skills and certainly for being discourse-, genre- and text-conscious. Operating within the constraints of

- hortatory evaluativeness (discourse),
- address at a reception (genre), and
- through-argument (text),

the dean is entitled, in fact expected, to make the kind of emphatic statement carried through by a structure such as *can only*. However, a reporter for a university bulletin would only be speaking out of turn if he or she were to operate within anything other than

- unbiased, detached discourse,
- the news report as a genre, and
- exposition as a text.

These reporting requirements are adequately met by the use of structures such as the impersonal passive and the kind of commitment-free lexis in Sample 4 (see also Ch. 16 on text politeness).

From Global to Local Patterns

As the focus of text processing gradually narrows and the attention becomes more concentrated on given elements (word, phrase, clause), one at a time, readers or translators tend to work closely with more localized patterns, while still functioning within the parameters set by the kind of global organization illustrated above. However, 'local' patterning and 'global' organization are two sides of the same coin. There is constant interaction between the two levels, and bottom-up local semantic, syntactic and textual decisions are constantly informed by all kinds of **top-down** broader contextual considerations. In fact, the scheme of textual activity identified so far at a macro-level of text organization is 'translated' into various register, discourse, genre and text features as these elements thread their way through the text, and pattern locally. The prime mover of this realization process is the by-now familiar mechanism of intertextuality, not only of micro-allusions to **actual** texts (e.g. a word referring horizontally to the *Crusades*), but also of our experience with prior **virtual** texts in their entirety (e.g. we expect a 'but' coming when we perceive a counter-argument coming—this illustrates vertical intertextuality).

Text Structure: Hierarchic Organization

In terms of register membership, mode (written- vs spoken-like) acquires particular prominence at this juncture in text processing. Alongside field (level of technicality) and tenor (level of formality), and together with the ideational and interpersonal resources deployed in these domains respectively (to do with agency, power/solidarity), mode avails the text user of a variety of textualization procedures. These regulate the choice of the most **effective** type of text, genre and discourse. And, to uphold **appropriateness**, they also determine optimally **efficient** compositional plans or 'structures'.

At this stage in the process, a 'structure' format of some kind usually begins to emerge. This stage marks 'reading for coherence' and negotiating deeper underlying conceptual relations. Pragmatic factors regulating aspects of text in context, such as intentionality or the purposes for which utterances are used, are crucial here, and these will feature most prominently in the analysis of the way texts are put together (Ch. 9 and Ch. 10), and are made operational (Ch. 11 and Ch. 12). Elements of structure (and the various patterns of cohesion to be discussed shortly) are all there for a purpose. In effect, they are 'speech acts' performing various explicit and implicit functions within the **text act**.

Text structure awareness (which includes the textual plan and the intentionality behind it as we saw in Sample 2 with *slightly better*) enhances anticipation and thus acts as an effective signposting system that guides the reader (or the translator, interpreter) in navigating the textual terrain. We recall how, in the OPEC text (Sample 1 above), for example, building on the status of the initial 'claim cited to be opposed' led us to expect a **counter-claim** (opposition) followed by a **substantiation** and some form of conclusion. Schematically, the counter-argumentative structure with which we have been working regularly so far may now be represented schematically as in Figure 2.3.

⇓ Claim cited to be opposed
⇓ Opposition (counter-claim)
⇓ Substantiation
⇓ Conclusion

Figure 2.3 The structure of the counter-argument

Context (in the sense of register, **pragmatics**, semiotics) may thus be seen to underlie our awareness of genre, discourse and text type that, in turn, almost causally determines the compositional plan (structure and texture) deemed most appropriate. Internalized as part of the language user's textual competence are a set of structural configurations (and attendant textural patterns) corresponding to a set of text-typological foci and a range of genre- and discourse-related considerations. These serve a number of rhetorical purposes that is by no means infinite. Work on such **schemata-**, **script-** or **scenario**-like conceptual structures carried out within artificial intelligence, discourse sociolinguistics, etc. is highly relevant.

Texture: Structure in Detail

The analysis of structure can become more relevant but only when we involve texture analysis which properly marks the final phase in the process of comprehending a text (in tandem with the transfer and reformulation in the target language, if translation is involved). By texture we mean negotiating cohesion and coherence, or the various devices that ensure continuity of text surface forms and consistency of deeper underlying conceptual relations. These devices (semantic, syntactic and textual) collectively lend texts their basic quality of 'sticking together' (cohesion) and 'hanging together' (coherence) and, of course, of being goal-directed. It is in this area that readers or translators entertain the further assumption that texture realizes given structure formats which, as we have just seen in the sample analysed in this chapter, are more or less causally determined by higher-level contextual factors (notably, text type). It is also in this area that, at the realization end of the context–text chain of interaction, languages differ and decisions have to be taken as to how cross-cultural as well as translinguistic differences are best reconciled.

To Conclude

The primary aim of this chapter has been to pave the way further for some of the themes that will form the basis of our argumentation in this book. The areas covered have had mostly to do with the notion of **socio-textual practices** (specifically the triad discourse–genre–text). We then branched out to deal with text structure, a discussion that naturally concluded with texture. This has all been part of the decision-making involved in the reading or translation process. In opting for this angle of vision, the intention was to demonstrate that, for the discipline of contrastive linguistics to be viable, it must first and foremost get to grips with linguistic structures of a syntactic and a semantic nature (i.e. the lexico-grammar), and to see these not within units such as the sentence and below, but as beyond-the-sentence phenomena. It must also encompass not only surface features yielded by intra- or inter-lingual comparison and contrast (e.g. negation in English and Arabic), but also the underlying strategies that regulate the entire interaction (e.g. negation as part of the discourse of alienation in Orwell's *1984*). The choice of translation as the basic skill from which to draw illustrations and examples is justified because here we can most comprehensively observe the various contrastive discoursal processes at work.

3 The Myth of the Single Register: A Discourse Perspective on Linguistic Variation

This chapter reviews a number of attempts to expand the notion of register variation. One way of approaching the concept of 'register' is to see it in terms of the user–use variables that make up what is here referred to as the 'communicative' dimension of context. This alone has proved too rudimentary to account for a communicative act as complex as text processing. Thus, this dimension has to be seen in terms of two other domains of contextual activity: 'pragmatic', catering for 'intentionality', and 'semiotic', catering for 'intertextuality'. In this radical, multifaceted way, register can have sufficient explanatory power to handle entire texts, discourses and genres, enriching, and in turn becoming enriched by, text structure and texture.

It is interesting to note, however, that, in the whole gamut of contextual activity depicted here, 'text' is a particularly privileged category. Simply put, it is the prime mover of the communicative process: through it, we are able to realize not only a variety of rhetorical purposes, but also a range of discursive attitudes and generic structures. To determine text type, two basic contextual orientations may be recognized: **monitoring** and **managing**. A given communicative situation may either consist of observations made at a distance, in a fairly detached manner, or be used as an arena for all kinds of persuasive purposes to be pursued with vigour and commitment. Once the entity 'text' emerges, texture and text structure account for the underlying principles of ensuring that the various elements of a text literally 'stick together' and conceptually 'hang together'. Texture is the mainstay of formal 'cohesion', while structure is in a real sense the foundation for conceptual 'coherence'.

However, it is through a finite set of text-typological foci (**exposition**, **argumentation** and **instruction**) that text users operate and institutions begin to find a mouthpiece. For this to be effective, efficient and appropriate, what is required is discourse that tends to cater for attitude, and genre that deals with communicative events. Thus, context seems almost causally to determine the way texts, discourses and genres are hierarchically organized (compositional plan or structure), and the way these macro-structures become interwoven together (texture). Whether one approaches these textual variables bottom-up (with textual manifestations as a point of departure) or top-down (starting with the context that has given rise to a particular text in the first place), an inevitable conclusion to be reached would simply be that text is the ultimate unit of effective communication.

Situational or Contextual?

One of the primary aims of the project promoted in this book is to show how a comprehensive view of register can counter the prevalent **myth** that one situation 'equals' one register, essentially treating register as a situational category (e.g. physics register). We shall argue that register is not situational, it is contextual. True, one situation may indeed be catered for by a single register (e.g. weather bulletins). But one situation may also be dealt with through the deployment of multiple registers (the war on terrorism served by a range of what we may for now call 'languages'—analytical-explanatory reports, hortatory-condemnatory editorials, etc.). By the same token, one register may indeed cater for multiple situations. Analytical-explanatory reports, for example, can indeed be used by both terrorists and law enforcement agencies.

Along similar lines, the following text samples all relate to the Maastricht Treaty initially signed by the representatives of the then twelve nations of the European Community. It is important to note that, in the heyday of register analysis way back in the early 1960s, the first three text samples (Samples 1, 2, 3) would have all been glossed as 'legalese', leaving us with 'journalese' as the register label of the last two (Samples 4, 5). Nevertheless, as will become abundantly clear from the arguments advanced throughout this book, these texts differ from each other in a number of fundamental ways. To deal with what is essentially 'one' situation, what is involved in these texts may certainly cater for one 'subject matter', and even one 'level of formality', but other systems of language variation are also clearly at work and should be heeded in the analysis of such texts, especially if they are to be communicated in another language and cultural setting. For one thing, mode will fluctuate from one text to the other, bringing in its wake some very interesting variations in the way context is approached, text structure dealt with and texture moulded. It is this process of 'textualization' that will occupy us substantially throughout.

Sample 1

Part Two
Citizenship of the Union
Article 8

Citizenship of the Union is hereby established. Every person holding the nationality of a Member State shall be a citizen of the Union.

From *The Treaty of Maastricht*

Sample 2

The treaty creates citizenship of the European Union. Everybody holding the nationality of a member state will be a citizen of the Union, with rights and duties conferred by the treaty. (See note 10)

Abridged by *The Independent* (11 October 1992)

Sample 3

Note 10

This was designed to give the idea of the union some meaning. But it has proved to be one of the most controversial elements in some countries, since it means that 'foreigners' get the vote.

Annotated by *The Independent* (11 October 1992)

Sample 4

European Community
Decommissioned

From our Brussels Correspondent

The mood inside the European Commission has not been so glum for almost a decade. Since 1985, when Jacques Delors became its president, the Commission has enjoyed seven years of growing power and influence. Its proposals, including those that created the single-market programme, made it the motor driving the European Community. But the recent wave of hostility to interference from 'Brussels' has badly dented the Commission's self-confidence. It is reluctant to make any proposal that could upset entrenched national interests, lest EC governments seek to trim its powers. The motor has all but stalled.

The Economist (10 October 1992)

Sample 5

Sir Leon Brittan and Martin Bengemann, whose responsibilities are respectively competition and the single market, argue that the Commission should risk courting unpopularity and push on with its legislative programmes. Other commissioners think that would be folly. Christine Scrivener, the taxation commissioner, has called for a legislative pause. Mr Delors, the president, now stresses the need for caution.

The Economist (10 October 1992)

As already noted, this kind of textual material would in the early days of register analysis have all too readily been assigned single, generic labels (Samples 1, 2, 3 above are in legalese; Samples 4, 5 in journalese). But anything beyond a superficial view of the way language varies would immediately reveal that such a categorization barely scratches the surface of what is actually going on inside and around these texts.

For the moment, however, a brief description of what is actually happening in each of these texts is in order. Sample 1 reflects the powers assumed by the text producer to form the future behaviour of the text receiver in a binding way (the language of law, of 'do this', 'don't do that'). Sample 2, on the other hand, displays the total relinquishing of such powers since the summarizer's sole responsibility is, ideally, to the facts as he or she sees them (i.e. as presumably intended by the original formulators). Finally, in Sample 3 and Sample 4, one is, curiously enough, in a domain not dissimilar to that of Sample 1 (i.e. forming future behaviour) but with one basic difference: the option available for the receivers of Sample 3 and Sample 4 of not heeding the argument (they may take it or leave it), no matter how persuasive it turns out to be, and the absence of such an option in the reception of Sample 1 (rules are to be obeyed). But here we may observe that, while the producer of Sample 3 would not take exception to being ignored, as the argument is, after all, not his or her own but somebody else's, the producer of Sample 4 has put forward an argument that is very much his or her own, and it is credibility as arguer that is at stake. Yet, arguing is not our Brussels correspondent's only card: he or she could play a different hand

and achieve the overall persuasive objective through different means (e.g. in the capacity as a 'reporter' in Sample 5).

Cast in more practical terms, these issues give rise to a number of relevant questions. What are the criteria for judging one kind of language as appropriate or inappropriate for a given situation? What is it that lends texts efficiency when used in their appropriate contexts? What is it that lends texts effectiveness even when not used in their expected contexts? In what way does our reaction to text-in-context appropriateness, efficiency or effectiveness in instances like these form part of our textual competence? Are these critical skills teachable and learnable? What are the ground rules for register variation, if such a contextual option exists at all?

The Communicative Dimension: Use and User

Within the model of text processing adopted in this book, context is taken both as a point of departure and a destination for text users in their attempt to communicate or appreciate meaning. In this domain of sense making, there are the usual contextual dimensions: who is speaking to whom, where, when, etc. (the communicative dimension). But there is also the social 'goal' or communicative 'purpose' (pragmatics) and, finally, there is the kind of socio-cultural (verbal or non-verbal) signs deployed (semiotics). The communicative dimension subsumes the various aspects of the communicative **'transaction'** between text producer and text receiver primarily as 'users' of a particular dialect, idiolect, etc. (e.g., the colloquialism of *foreigners will get the vote* (Sample 3)).

However, user-related variables are not sufficient in and by themselves, hence the need for a different set of communicative factors. Producers and receivers of texts operate within constraints imposed by the particular 'use' to which language is put. This provides us with the second basic aspect of variation, which includes 'field' (e.g. the legal jargon of Sample 1), 'tenor' or level of formality (Sample 1 being by far the most formal of our samples), and the 'mode' of interaction (Sample 1 as written to be read reflectively).

It is tenor, however, that is perhaps the more crucial factor in regulating the complex relationships between addresser and addressee. In its simplest form, this is the formal–informal stance that co-communicants adopt towards one another and which can range from 'casual' to 'deferential', or from most 'intimate' to most 'impersonal'. Different terms have been used by different writers for this level of variation: 'style', 'status', 'attitude', 'relative social status' and so on.

The various terms, however, all converge on the central point that, as Young (1985: 284) points out, tenor has essentially to do with 'the level of formality of the relation between the participants in the linguistic event'.

Functional Tenor

There is more to tenor than the simple relationship between addressor and addressee. The level of formality is in fact an 'inter-level' in that it overlaps in a number of important ways with 'field of discourse', on the one hand, and with 'mode of interaction', on the other. Diagrammatically, this interrelationship may be represented as in Figure 3.1.

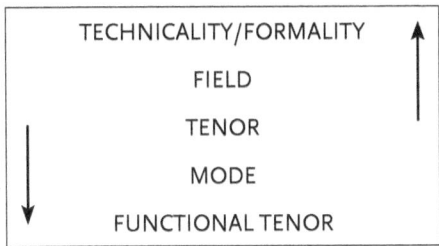

Figure 3.1 Tenor vs field and mode

The cross-fertilization taking place between tenor and field results in the familiar categories 'formality' and 'technicality' emerging as two aspects of tenor. This is collectively viewed in terms of stabilized patterns of 'role' relationships which Halliday (1978: 222) explains in the following terms:

> The language we use varies according to the level of formality, of technicality, and so on. What is the variable underlying this type of distinction? Essentially, it is the role relationships in the situation in question: who the participants in the communication group are, and in what relationship they stand to each other.

The overlap between tenor and mode, on the other hand, gives rise to what Gregory and Carroll (1978: 53) call **'functional tenor'** defined in the following terms:

> the category used to describe what language is being used for in the situation. Is the speaker trying to persuade? To exhort?

Alternatively, is he or she trying to 'instruct' (as in Sample 1) or trying merely to 'inform' (as in Sample 2)?

Functional tenor regulating the activity of such text producers as the persuader, the instructor, the informer, tends thus to build into the analysis a set of 'role relationships' that are fairly stable and well established, such as politician and electorate, doctor and patient, lawmaker and the public, reporter and a particular readership. The participants and their utterances are now defined not only in terms of single-scale categories such as formal or informal, but also in terms of other aspects of message construction, such as the precise level of technicality, the degree of formality and, more fundamentally, the implications of all this for the use of language in social life. That is, in addition to the semi-formality of the 'persuader' in Sample 4, the slightly more formal tenor of the 'informer' in Sample 5, and the ultra-formality of the lawmaker in Sample 1, these text producers may also engage in different role relationships with their receivers which entail particular shifts in functional tenor (e.g. the arguer-reporter role-switching in Samples 4 and 5). Communicative transactions thus acquire an interactive, dynamic character which is the domain of the other level of context—that of semiotics.

Semiotic Interaction: The Meta-Functions

So far, our investigation of both personal tenor and functional tenor, with technicality and role relationships forming the two basic aspects of functional tenor, has highlighted the ways in which communication materializes institutionally in terms of use and user of language. However, for rhetorical goals such as 'persuading', 'informing' and so on to be properly pursued, and for role relationships to stabilize, language users tend to 'negotiate' meanings in texts and thus deal with context more interactively. As Hatim and Mason (1990: 64–65) point out from the perspective of discourse and the translator:

> Seeing the meaning of texts as something which is negotiated between producer and receiver and not as a static entity, independent of human processing activity once it has been encoded, is, we believe, the key to an understanding of translating, teaching translating and judging translations.

This process of negotiation between speaker and hearer or writer and reader forms the basis of an important level of what we shall here refer to as 'semiotic interaction'. In its most basic form, semiotic interaction involves the exchange of meanings as 'signs'. However, co-communicants do not merely exchange meanings that display a certain level of technicality, exhibit a certain degree of formality, or bear the features of a certain mode of interaction (spoken vs written). Rather, they perceive a range of **ideational** meanings within a given field, **interpersonal** meanings within a given tenor, and **textual** meanings within a given mode. Field would here begin to cater for social processes and social institutions (e.g. racism), tenor would subsume aspects of power and solidarity (e.g. the ambivalent status of the middle manager in Sample 6 below), and mode would take care of moulding and re-moulding texts (e.g. the proximity of the footballer to the ball when actually playing on the field, the commentator in the BBC box above giving us a running commentary on the match, or indeed the journalist reporting the match the following day). To illustrate the ideational, interpersonal and textual **meta-functions**, let us briefly consider the following exchange between an interviewer and a middle manager:

Sample 6

> Interviewer: If I asked you to draw a line in this factory between managers and below managers, where would you draw the line?
> Middle manager: Oh, I think that would be difficult ... because, really, if you look at the management of our division, it consists, really, of several people with a figurehead.
> I: What do you mean by a figurehead?
> MM: Well, literally, he,—he's the face that is nailed at the front of the ship. But [this ship] is officered, if you like, by people who form the management team.
>
> From Jones and Kress (1981)

Here, the middle manager is being deliberately ambiguous about his occupational status and role that he intends to defend relentlessly. True, features of language use or user are crucial contextualization cues without which no proper processing of any text is conceivable. However, as we listen to such an exchange, we are not solely tuning in to, say, business administration as the **field of discourse**, but also, and perhaps far more significantly, to a range of ideational/institutional processes such as the motivated **suppression of 'agency'** in:

(a) nominalizing 'someone manages' and opting for 'management', and
(b) passivizing 'X officers the ship' and ending up with 'it is officered'.

This is, of course, not to forget how 'someone who manages' becomes a 'figurehead'! The aim in all of these linguistic processes is without doubt to maintain the ambiguity and, in the words of Jones and Kress (1981: 70), they tell us 'nothing about actual management, who does what'. By the same token, features of the spoken mode or the generally informal tenor (*because, really, if you look*) must surely be seen not merely as normal features of a given register, but as a reflection of the textual 'masking' going on (an aspect of mode), and the need to maintain a semblance of 'interpersonal solidarity' (tenor).

The aim of this play with signs (or 'semiotic' activity), then, is to transform institutional-communicative transactions into more meaningful cultural encounters. The way in which levels of basic communicativeness (field, mode and tenor) acquire a semiotic specification may be represented diagrammatically as in Figure 3.2

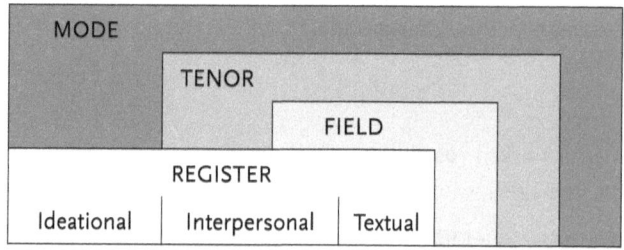

Figure 3.2 The semiotics of field, mode and tenor

A given text or part of text is the product of all three semiotic categories. The ideational component captures cultural experience and expresses what goes on in the environment, exploiting the linguistic resources of 'agency' (e.g. *the ship is officered* vs *X officers the ship* in the middle manager's answer above). The textual component utilizes the various devices of texture and thus renders ideational expression both cohesive and coherent within a given textual environment (the use by the middle manager of *really*, repetition, etc.). Finally, the interpersonal component helps co-communicants to express attitudes and assess what is happening around them and through them (e.g. the middle manager's use of *you* to secure the endorsement of his interlocutor). On these and related notions, see Halliday (e.g. 2014) and Thompson (2004). For more extensive treatments, see Martin (1992), Matthiessen (1993) and Halliday and Matthiessen (1999).

It is in the domain of interpersonal activity, however, that interaction moves to a slightly higher level than that of merely speaker–hearer exchange. Interaction now becomes an arena in which the speaker interacts not only with the hearer, but also with the utterance he or she is producing. The hearer would similarly interact, not only with the speaker, but also with the utterance he or she is receiving. In this way, utterances become 'signs' or semiotic constructs that embody the assumptions, presuppositions and conventions that reflect the ways a given culture constructs and partitions reality.

Let us now cast our minds back to Samples 3 and 4 in Chapter 2, and recall how, by using an emphatic assertion, the dean manages to enhance the basic interaction between him and his audience, whom he presumably takes to be 'sceptical', 'eager', 'bored' or whatever. We also recall how the reporter suppressed such emphasis, once again evidence of some form of interaction taking place not merely between him and his readers (who are there to be informed and not persuaded or entertained) but also between him and his utterance. This is all undertaken within a 'universe of discourse' that seems neatly divided into 'monitors' and 'managers', 'persuaders' and 'informers'. It is as if by some divine linguistic convention that an element of territoriality emerges from this kind of division of labour that is both well charted and securely guarded. Encroachments, transgressions or excesses are immediately spotted and shunned as 'going over the top' (a label which our reporter would have earned had he dared to write *this venture can only enhance*) or as 'being coy' (how the dean would have been described had he opted for the passive *this venture is intended to enhance*).

Intertextuality

For an optimally effective, efficient and appropriate expression of meanings, utterances themselves interact with each other as signs within and across texts. That is, in tandem with the interaction between a speaker (and utterances produced) and a hearer (and utterances received), another, far more important, level of semiotic activity involves how signs actually interact with other signs. The principle that regulates this activity is 'intertextuality', a process through which textual occurrences are recognized in terms of their dependence on other relevant, prior texts. The language of the exhorter, for example, belongs to a universal code we associate with 'exhortation'. Within this kind of linguistic 'managing', devices such as emotive repetition and other forms of emphasis would be tokens of a type of communicative occurrence easily recognized as such. Our ability to recognize and catalogue these types of context-dependent meanings is a prerequisite for successful communication.

Genre, Discourse and Text Revisited

As we have pointed out on a number of occasions so far, a number of semiotic macro-structures are recognized in order to impose order on seemingly open-ended types of interaction of signs among signs. These structures are genre, discourse and text, introduced briefly in Chapter 2. Signs occurring within parameters and under constraints set by these categories constantly move about by means of the semiotic mechanism of what we have called 'vertical' intertextuality (to be distinguished from 'horizontal' intertextuality as in alluding to a phrase from the Bible or an expression from a Shakespearean play, for example). Genres are conventionalized forms of language in use, each with its own goals and functions adopted by a given community of text users or socio-cultural grouping to cater for a particular social occasion or communicative event. The ineffective orator opting for 'coy' impersonal constructions (such as the passive structure) or the over-the-top reporter waxing lyrical with emphatic constructions (such as repetition) are all instances of mishandling genres (see Ch. 16 on text politeness).

The textual component, on the other hand, reflects fluctuations in rhetorical purpose from, say, 'arguing' (e.g. Sample 4 and, to a lesser extent, Sample 3) to 'narrating' (e.g. Sample 2 and, to a lesser extent, Sample 5). These rhetorical purposes impose their own constraints on how a sequence of sentences becomes a text. Texts are units of interaction, both intended and accepted as coherent and cohesive wholes realizing a set of mutually relevant communicative intentions appropriate to a given rhetorical purpose.

But, in the same way as the pursuit of a given rhetorical goal in a text requires that this be conducted within a particular generic framework, it must also strike an ideological note of some kind. That is, in their attempts to serve a given rhetorical purpose, within the dos and don'ts of a particular genre, text producers and receivers necessarily engage in the composition or analysis of 'attitudinal meanings' (e.g. the Eurosceptic in Sample 3). This attitudinal, interpersonal component is what we have been referring to as 'discourse'.

Genres and texts, then, ultimately involve attitudinally determined expression or 'discourse'. The polemic as the genre of Sample 4 above, utilizing argumentation as a **text-type focus**, has entailed a particular attitudinal stance (the manipulative discourse of situation managing). On the other hand, the report as the genre of Sample 2, utilizing **narration** as a text format, has engaged its producers and receivers in a different set of attitudinal meanings (the **non-evaluative** discourse of monitoring). Discourse values relay power relations and help define an ideology. This aspect of meaning is properly the domain of what

Halliday (1978: 112) used to refer to as the 'participatory function of language, language as doing something'.

Pragmatics and Intentionality

As we have already shown, the two basic levels of semiotic interaction—that of the text producer with a text receiver and that of utterance with utterance—necessarily involve another level of interaction, namely that of speaker or hearer interacting with utterances produced or received. For its success, this latter kind of interaction primarily relies on intentionality—the ability to 'do things with words', the capacity to deploy one's utterance for a 'purpose'. Here, semiotics or signification through signs acquires a pragmatic dimension which Stalnaker (1972: 380) defines as:

> The study of the purposes for which sentences are used, of the real-world conditions under which a sentence may be appropriately used as an utterance.

Utterance signs within Sample 1 above are thus pragmatically different from those of the other texts in our data. Apart from the **locutionary acts** involved, or lexical and grammatical well-formedness, distinct communicative functional forces (**illocutionary acts**) are always in evidence (e.g. 'directing' and 'representing'). Directive speech acts are intended to form future behaviour. Representative speech acts, on the other hand, seek simply to depict a state of affairs for the benefit of the text receiver. Such illocutionary forces inevitably lead to what has been termed a **perlocutionary** effect, or the ultimate communicative objective sought (e.g. persuading, informing). Texts such as Samples 2 and 4 above may now be seen to involve two distinct kinds of audience: those to be informed and those to be persuaded.

Managing Participants and Monitoring Spectators

From the slightly different perspective of creative writing and literary discourse, Britton (1963: 37) puts forward an interesting audience dichotomy akin to the two kinds of audience reaction envisaged for texts such as the summary and the counter-argument. Britton explains these in the following terms:

> If I describe what has happened to me in order to get my hearer to do something for me, or even to change his opinion about me, then I remain a

participant in my own affairs and invite him to become one. If, on the other hand, I merely want to interest him, so that he ... appreciates with me the intricate patterns of events, then not only do I invite him to be a spectator, but I am myself a spectator of my own experience ... As a participant, I should be planning ... As a spectator, I should be daydreaming.

The distinction between participant and spectator (see also Britton 1982) is almost identical to another distinction from artificial intelligence made popular and more accessible by pioneering work in text pragmatics (e.g. Beaugrande and Dressler 1981). This is the difference between 'managing' or 'monitoring' a given situation, a distinction that we have been using in a fairly rudimentary fashion so far and to which we shall return in more detail in the coming chapters. The goal of the producer of Sample 4 is clear enough: to manage by arguing for the need for firmness in government. The goal of the producer of Sample 5, on the other hand, is far less personalized though not totally void of ulterior motives: it is primarily to monitor by reporting a sequence of events. It should not be overlooked, however, that what is involved in Sample 5 is not merely introducing a speaker, but introducing someone whose ideas are going to be examined rather critically.

To Conclude

In this chapter, the notion of register was presented in terms of both the original framework proposed in the early 1960s and the modifications to the original model that were made some twenty or thirty years later. The latter developments are seen here within a model of discourse processing that owes a great deal to the view of language as social semiotic put forward by Halliday and his colleagues as well as to contributions made to the science of texts by text linguists such as de Beaugrande and Dressler.

4 Argumentation: A Contrastive Text-Type Perspective

Given the crucial role established for 'text type' so far in our discussion, we now present a model of argumentation that supplements the model of contextual analysis presented in this book. In this chapter, we focus on argumentation both to reflect the importance of this particular type of 'managing' activity as a vehicle of persuasive discourse and to highlight our interest in cross-cultural differences in utilizing such a discourse strategy. Cross-cultural differences exist not only between different languages but also within one and the same language, and at times point to deeper divisions among the various subcultures within a society.

Texts can thus be seen as carriers of ideological meaning, a factor that makes them particularly vulnerable to changing socio-textual norms. A case in point is the dormancy and recent revival of a particular form of argumentation in Arabic (the 'counter-argument'). This chapter will demonstrate how the mode of arguing by 'citing an opponent's thesis' (claim) then countering it (counter-claim), a format which is common in languages such as English, also exists in Arabic, but has had mixed fortunes in the rhetorical history of the Arabs. The form was well known centuries ago but experienced a demise in subsequent eras. Now, due to a diverse range of socio-cultural reasons, it has recently been resurrected. In other words, a communicative deficit was recognized when the counter-argumentative form in question became particularly rare, the situation has had to be reversed, and the deficit is now all but remedied. This fall and rise of a text form has serious implications for a pragmatics of language in social life, notably when intercultural communication is involved.

A Model of Text Types

It is remarkable that, in the last fifty years or so, so many attempts have been made to set up a text typology. However, primarily because of the absence of coherent descriptions of context, almost all attempts have suffered from serious shortcomings. Classifying texts according to situational criteria such as 'field' amounts to little more than a statement of subject matter, with unhelpful labels such as 'journalistic' or 'scientific' text types. Similarly, categorizing texts in terms of an over-general notion of 'domain' is very much akin to well-known and often spurious professional demarcation lines (e.g. literary translation), with unhelpful text types such as 'literary', 'technological'—categories that are simply too broad to yield a useful classification to work with. Both field and domain constituted the mainstay of early register analysis in the 1960s (for a criticism of this kind of register analysis and the text typologies advocated within this trend, see classic critiques such as Crystal and Davy (1969) and more recent accounts by Lukin et al. (2011)).

In the text-type model adopted in this book, a view of context is taken which is sufficiently broad to accommodate register use–user specifications, pragmatic considerations to do with intentionality, and semiotic values relating to cultural expression and to such **macro-signs** as genre and discourse. Yet the notion of context advocated is also sufficiently narrow to ensure that, through intertextuality, the various domains of contextual activity (use–user, intentionality and cultural expression) are in constant interaction, ultimately leading to the emergence of the unit 'text' as a distinct communicative occurrence. In the process, a text-type focus slowly emerges which, at a fairly general level of abstraction, may be identified with an orientation towards either 'monitoring' or 'managing' a given situation. Beaugrande and Dressler (1981: 162) define these cognitive tendencies in the following way:

> If the dominant function of a text is to provide a reasonably unmediated account of the situation model, SITUATION MONITORING is being performed. If the dominant function is to guide the situation in a manner favourable to the text producer's goals, SITUATION MANAGEMENT is being carried out.

Recognizing a broad distinction between texts that set out to monitor a situation and texts which manage a situation, we may here invoke the notion of 'predominant contextual focus' introduced by Werlich (1976) as the basis of a typology of texts along lines to be explained shortly.

Expository Texts

Exposition focuses on analysis and synthesis in dealing with given concepts. Conceptual exposition of this kind can be illustrated by Sample 1 below, which combines synthesis (paragraph 1) with analysis (paragraph 2):

Sample 1

> The chief causes of this pollution are alleged to be the non-enforcement of the law for the prevention of smoke from factories, the imposition of inadequate penalties, the neglect to limit works which produce noxious vapours to special areas where they can be closely supervised and so do the least possible amount of harm; and lastly, the absence of any provision in the law compelling the occupants of dwellings to produce the least possible quantity of smoke.
>
> On the point of prosecutions, it was stated that there are people in Manchester who systematically pollute the air and pay the fine, finding it much cheaper to do so than to put up new plant. The trial of such cases before benches of magistrates composed of manufacturers or their friends creates an atmosphere of sympathy for the accused, and it was alleged that magistrates who had sought to give effect to the law encountered the indifference and sometimes the positive opposition of their colleagues. It was explained that ...
>
> *Pollution of Atmosphere*, from the Report of the Inter-Departmental Committee (Van der Eyken 1973)

Alongside the focus on concepts, two other variant forms of exposition may be identified: *descriptive* texts which deal with objects or situations, and *narrative* texts which deal with actions and events. These text forms may be illustrated respectively by Samples 2 and 3 below:

Sample 2

> The hours will be long, fifty-five per week, and the atmosphere he breathes very confined, perchance also dusty. Employment of this character rarely fosters growth or development; the stunted child elongates slightly in time, but remains very thin, loses colour, the muscles remain small, especially those of the upper limbs, the legs are inclined to become bowed, the arch of the foot flattens and the teeth decay rapidly.

The girls exhibit the same shortness of stature, the same miserable development, and they possess the same shallow cheeks and carious teeth.

Conditions of Employment, from the Report of the Inter-Departmental Committee, 1904 (Van der Eyken 1973)

Sample 3

There were fifteen of us boarders. We paid £150 a year, and we never had enough to eat. We rose at 7 a.m. and had breakfast at 8.30, consisting of weak tea, a thick bit of bread with a thin smear of butter. Butterine was substituted for butter until complaints were made, and then we had salt butter. Once a month a boiled egg was given at breakfast. Dinner, which came at one o'clock, consisted of two courses, soup and meat, or meat and pudding.

From *Parsimony in Nutrition* (Van der Eyken 1973)

Upon closer scrutiny, these samples reveal a hybrid focus: while a primary text-type focus is always discernible in the case of conceptual exposition, description or narration, these forms tend to intermesh and shade into one another in a variety of ways. Furthermore, the cognitive processing patterns globally utilized by all three types of exposition are the **frames** (knowledge stating which things belong together in principle) and the **schemata** (knowledge establishing a sequential order for the occurrence of events).

Argumentative Texts

Argumentation focuses on the evaluation of relations between concepts. In the words of Beaugrande and Dressler, argumentative texts are 'those utilized to promote the acceptance, rejection or evaluation of certain beliefs or ideas as true vs. false, or positive vs. negative. Conceptual relations such as reason, significance, volition, value and opposition should be frequent' (1981: 184). Within the text typology proposed here, two variant forms of argumentation may be distinguished: through-argumentation, where a thesis is put forward to be supported, and counter-argumentation, which presents a thesis that will subsequently be opposed (see the following section for more detail). The cognitive processing pattern globally exploited by this type of texts is the **plan** (how events and states lead to the attainment of a goal).

To appreciate how **evaluativeness** is conveyed within the argumentative text plan, let us consider the following example:

Sample 4

> The first step in finding a cure for those defects is to recognize the fact that the real root of the evil does not lie in the condition of what is called military education, but in a general deficiency in the mental training of the English youth at large.
> It is, however, not with our universities, or with popular conceptions of education, that we are now more immediately concerned, but with those great institutions known by the name of public schools, to whom the education of our ruling classes is committed. It is these which must be held responsible for the initial stages of our military as well as of our general education.
>
> From C.C. Perry's *Our Undisciplined Brains* (Van der Eyken 1973)

Instructional Texts

It is perhaps worth noting, if only briefly, that a striking similarity exists between argumentative texts such as Sample 4 and texts belonging to another 'operative' type, namely the instructional (e.g. the article from the Maastricht Treaty [Sample 1, Ch. 3]). However, the similarity may be seen in terms of the 'goal' aimed at and not the 'means' adopted in attaining such a goal. That is, while the argumentative and instructional text types, each in their own ways, set out to 'manage' a situation and thus focus on the 'formation of future behaviour', the means of achieving such an aim are different: instructional texts attempt to 'regulate' through instruction, **without option** (as in contracts, treaties); argumentative texts tend to 'evaluate' through persuasion, **with option** (as in advertising, propaganda).

The three basic text types and sub-types discussed so far may be represented schematically as in Figure 4.1.

Exposition	– Conceptual exposition – Narration – Description
Argumentation	– Through-argumentation (thesis cited to be argued through) – Counter-argumentation (thesis cited to be opposed)
Instruction	– Without option, e.g. contracts, treaties, etc. – With option, e.g. advertising

Figure 4.1 Basic text types

Argumentation: A Typology

As already mentioned, within the text typology proposed here, two variant forms of argumentation may be distinguished: through-argumentation and counter-argumentation.

Through-argumentation

This is initiated by making an 'assertion' and immediately following this up with 'support'. In this form of arguing a point through, there is no explicit reference to an adversary:

- ⇓ Assertion
- ⇓ Support
- ⇓ Conclusion

Sample 5 is a classic example of through-argumentation:

Sample 5

> The decentralizing approach has not one fundamental defect, but two. Either of them by itself would have crippled the reforms. Together, they interact powerfully and guarantee failure. First, as Karl Marx might have put it, is the question of property relations; second, the related issue of the enterprise's financial environment. In short, who owns the firm, and can it go bust?
>
> *The Economist* 28 April 1990

Counter-argumentation

This is initiated by the citation of a particular view endorsed by an adversary (a claim), followed immediately by the 'opposition' to such a view (a counter-claim), then a substantiation which presents the grounds for the opposition, and finally some form of conclusion:

- ⇓ Thesis cited to be opposed
- ⇓ Opposition
- ⇓ Substantiation of counter-claim
- ⇓ Conclusion

Sample 6 is an example of counter-argumentation:

ARGUMENTATION: A CONTRASTIVE TEXT-TYPE PERSPECTIVE

Sample 6

In the decentralized, self-managed model, workers and managers control the enterprise and have a direct personal interest in the income it produces. But they do not own the enterprise. That may seem an academic distinction, but it turns out to be crucial. Because of it, the self-managed enterprise suffers from catastrophic short-termism.

Owners are free to sell their assets. They are therefore interested not just in the income their assets generate, but also in their market value ...

The Economist 28 April 1990

Within counter-argumentation, two sub-types may further be distinguished:

(1) The Balance. Here, there will be two '**chunks**', one presenting one side of an issue (e.g. a 'claim'), the other another side of the issue (i.e. a 'counter-claim'). Each position is put forward in some detail, with the text producer enjoying the option of signalling the contrastive shift between the claim section and the counter-claim section, either explicitly (as in Sample 6 above) or implicitly as in Sample 7 below (cf. Nash 1980):

Sample 7

Mismanaged Algeria

The country's troubles are so glaring that it is easy to forget Algeria's strengths. At three o'clock in the afternoon in the poor, over-crowded Casbah of Algiers, children leave school not to beg but to do their homework. Investment of some two-fifths of GDP a year during much of the 1960s and 1970s gave Algeria the strongest industrial base in Africa north of the Limpopo. The Northern coastal bit of the country, where 96% of its 23m people live, is rich and fertile. It used to feed the Romans. It could feed Algerians if it were better farmed.

These strengths are being wasted. ...

The Economist 10 December 1988

(2) The Explicit **Concessive**. In this sub-type, the counter-claim is anticipated by an explicit concessive (e.g. *while, although, despite* etc.). Sample 8 illustrates this counter-argumentative pattern:

Sample 8

FEARLESS FIXX

Sir: While it was, as the Weasel implies (Up & Down the City Road, 17 February), ironic that Jim Fixx (author of The Complete Book of Running) had his heart attack while out running, it could have occurred at any time or place. His family had a history of heart disease, and his father died of a heart attack ...
The Independent Magazine 24 February 1990

In dealing with the various text forms identified as variants of the argumentative type, one cannot help but notice an intriguing phenomenon to do with how the various argumentative formats may not be equally available for all language users to choose from all the time, and with how the preference for one or the other strategy varies within, as well as across, languages and cultures. In other words, the choice of this or that form is not unconstrained, and the preference for one or the other form is certainly not unmotivated. These constraints and motivations range from politeness, to ideology, to power, and may sometimes even impinge on aspects of language in social life, such as the political system in place or the nature and role of the family. It is therefore important for future research to describe and explain this sociolinguistic phenomenon which pervades texts and infuses them with crucial discourse meanings (Martin and Rose 2008; Halliday and Matthiessen 2014; Lemke 1994).

Text-Type Hybridization

So far, we have deliberately glossed over the phenomenon of '**text hybridization**' and the essentially 'fuzzy' nature of all text types. In the typology adopted here, an important admission was made at the outset: texts are essentially multifunctional, normally displaying features of more than one type, and constantly shifting from one text-typological focus to another. To account for this hybrid nature of texts, and on the basis of the analysis of argumentation and exposition presented so far as idealized text types, the following discussion focuses on how a given predominant text-type focus could be shifted to admit other subsidiary typological foci.

The distinction between 'predominant' and 'subsidiary' text-type focus is fundamental. Our experience with texts has certainly shown that, while rarely if ever will there be a text that serves a single focus, no text can equally effectively and to the same extent serve two predominant functions, at one and the same time. By the same token, while the co-existence of two foci is very much the norm, no text can be sustained by two subsidiary functions without one of these somehow becoming the predominant one. Thus, for texts to function efficiently, more than one focus must be in evidence, and one of these must predominate. According to Beaugrande and Dressler (1981: 186), text type is after all only:

> A set of heuristics for producing, predicting and processing textual occurrences, and hence acts as a prominent determiner of efficiency, effectiveness and appropriateness.

But, for this heuristic to serve as an adequate determiner of the viability of texts, a number of organizing principles must be recognized, and one of these is inevitably the notion of the 'predominance' of a given text function.

Text-type hybridization takes many forms. One particularly complex arrangement is that which we will refer to here as 'embedded' hybridization. This is when, in very subtle ways, the 'official' function of a text is shifted to serve another function. The two functions vie for recognition, but this will ultimately be settled in favour of one function predominating. As Sample 9 demonstrates, a common occurrence of this kind of hybridization is when the expected text-type focus (which is to monitor or review within the type 'conceptual exposition') admits a measure of evaluativeness, obviously for ideological reasons:

Sample 9

> Jean Jacques Rousseau was the revolutionary, the impertinent, who, for the first time, directly and effectively challenged the accepted rationalist view held by the enlightened century in which he lived. He made a real breach in that long tradition of reasonableness which, building up in North Italy before 1600, dominated the French and English academies in the seventeenth century and was carried on actively by Voltaire and the Encyclopaedists in the eighteenth century. Partly under Rousseau's pounding, the formal structure of French salon life gave way to a more equalitarian society, and its belief in science and satire yielded to a view which seemed to glorify instinctive, irrational and emotional behaviour.
>
> Bronowski and Mazlish (1974)

In processing this text sample, a text-type focus as neutral as **expository** monitoring is generally opted for in response to generic, discoursal and textual norms endorsed in this kind of writing by the community of competent language users almost by default (factual narration of **events**). This requirement, however, is gradually relaxed to admit values that relate to a slightly different text-type focus, responding to different textual, discourse and generic factors (evaluation of events). Fluctuation between 'informing' and 'evaluation' is now in evidence, replacing what could have been described as straightforward exposition. But we must stress that the other, intruder, function (evaluation, in this case) is allowed to manifest itself only up to and not much beyond a certain point. That is, the two functions cannot be seen to enjoy equal prominence, and the original function (exposition, in this case) would thus always remain supreme. The success of this particular text sample may therefore be ascribed to the subtlety of introducing an 'axe to grind' and allowing an alien function to creep in almost unnoticed.

True, discourse interaction makes its own rules, depending on the context. However, relegating phenomena such as hybridization to the rubbish bin of 'performance fuzziness' is an unhelpful attitude to take. The process is certainly elusive, but it is not haphazard. Stubbs (1983: 15) fleshes out this argument by calling for the need to recognize higher-level patterns in discourse:

> It has sometimes been maintained that there is no linguistic organization above the sentence level. However, I suspect that some people believe this because they have never looked for such organization.

Text-type hybridization may be little understood at this stage in the development of text typologies, and certainly further research into its causes and manifestations is urgently needed. However, the mere fact that impurity exists lends credence to the psychological reality of text types. In the midst of fuzziness, we seem to operate with a foolproof system of expectations upheld or defied. To do this, we constantly refer to some 'norm' against the backdrop of which **deviations** are assessed as motivated departures.

Argumentation across Cultures

Pending further quantitative and qualitative research, initial investigations into the argumentative text type in English and Arabic from the perspective of translation seem to point to a remarkable tendency in English towards counter-argumentation (claim cited—opposition—substantiation—conclusion). Furthermore, of the two counter-argumentative formats, English seems to prefer the balance (Chunk A vs Chunk B) to the more explicit concessive (e.g. *although* ...). Modern Standard Arabic, in contrast, veers more towards through-argumentation (assertion—substantiation—conclusion). No doubt, counter-argumentation is also in evidence in Arabic, but when this occurs, it is usually the explicit concessive which seems to be the more preferred option stylistically. The distribution of preferences may be displayed diagrammatically as in Figure 4.2.

	ENGLISH	ARABIC
A	The counter-argument	Through-argumentation
B	The balance argument	The explicit **concessive argument**
C	The explicit concessive argument	The balance argument
D	Through-argumentation	The counter-argument

NB. Alphabetical order is order of preference, from most to least preferred. This is based on the analysis of a sizeable number of text samples but does not purport to be a conclusive appraisal of the trends involved.

Figure 4.2 Order of preference of argumentation type, English and Arabic compared

To demonstrate how the textual resources of Arabic are particularly stretched when handling counter-argumentation in general, let us consider Sample 10 below. It was presented as Sample 7 above. Here, it is reproduced with the deleted segment of the argument restored (underlined). Thus, Sample 10 may now be taken as an example of complex counter-argumentation in English where a micro-balance is embedded within another macro-balance:

Sample 10

Mismanaged Algeria

The country's troubles are so glaring that it is easy to forget Algeria's strengths. At three o'clock in the afternoon in the poor, over-crowded Casbah of Algiers, children leave school not to beg but to do their homework. Investment of some two-fifths of GDP a year during much of the 1960s and 1970s gave Algeria the strongest industrial base in Africa north of the Limpopo. The Northern coastal bit of the country, where 96% of its 23m people live, is rich and fertile. It used to feed the Romans. It could feed Algerians if it were better farmed.

> These strengths are being wasted. <u>Some 180,000 well-schooled Algerians enter the job market every year. Yet a hobbled economy adds only 100,000 new jobs a year, and some 45% of these involve working for the government.</u> Algeria lacks the foreign currency it needs to import raw materials and spare parts to keep its factories running. The collective farms have routinely fallen short of their targets, leaving Algeria ever more reliant on imported food.
>
> *The Economist* 10 December 1988

For various reasons to do with text structure, the macro-counter-argument (the entire sample) in English is a form already difficult enough to process and to translate into languages such as Arabic. Far more difficult to deal with, however, is the embedded micro-counter-argument above (the sequence underlined). The difficulties encountered in dealing with this textual strategy relate both to source-text comprehension and to target-text production. To handle this case of multi-level argumentation, the micro-text would have to be transformed into an explicit concessive in Arabic. Sample 11 is a back-translation of the Arabic rendering of Sample 10 above:

Sample 11

Mismanaged Algeria

> These strengths are being wasted. <u>For although some 180,000 well-schooled Algerians enter the job market every year, a hobbled economy adds only 100,000 new jobs a year, and some 45% of these involve working for the government.</u>

On this particular point, and to avoid giving a distorted view of what actually happens in Arabic, we must hasten to add that, regrettably, a yawning gap exists between the rich rhetorical tradition of the Arabs and the way the language is being currently used or abused. Nowadays, counter-argumentative texts are almost exclusively found in the discourse of Western-educated literate Arabs and probably only those familiar with their classical Arabic rhetoric. But there are reasons for hope. The negligence witnessed in this area of language use is not a permanent condition. What we now have is a situation in which a particular set of textual resources are lying somewhat dormant. Nevertheless, there is a rich legacy to counter and dispel this temporary state of malaise. The classical Arab rhetoricians have advanced what could unreservedly be described as one of the most elegant theories of text in context, a set of valuable insights that would have to be somehow resurrected for positive change to materialize. In fact, this is being resurrected and brought back to life with the broadening of education to encompass the heritage of the nation, with the general spread of literacy to combat endemic orality, and with such universal phenomena as globalization positively pervading everyday life. In short, the Arabs seem ready to experiment with and excel at new text forms, new discourses and new genres.

To Conclude

In this chapter, a model of text types has been presented which recognizes two basic kinds of texts: exposition and argumentation. Within the latter, two further forms are identified: through-argumentation and counter-argumentation. Further, counter-argumentation is divided into the balance counter-argument and the explicit concessive. The basic aim of this chapter has been to demonstrate that, while Arabic shows a particular preference for through-argumentation, with the explicit concessive preferred if counter-argumentation is at all involved, counter-argumentative texts are not unknown in classical Arabic rhetoric. What is in evidence in the rhetorical practices of present-day Arabic as a 'text-type deficit' is therefore only a by-product of social and political (i.e. pragmatic and discoursal) conditions that have contributed to a temporary stifling of a certain text type. However, a semiotics of culture capable of smothering certain forms of expression is also capable of breathing new life and vigour into them, once the problem has been discerned.

5 A Model of Argumentation from Arabic Rhetoric

Within the text-type model adopted in this book, two basic forms of argumentation are distinguished: through-argumentation and counter-argumentation. A through-argumentative text is characterized by extensive substantiation of an initial thesis or assertion. A counter-argumentative text, on the other hand, involves the rebuttal of a cited thesis or claim, followed by a substantiation of the counter-claim and a conclusion. These two forms are discussed extensively in Chapter 4, and it is suggested that the use of one or the other strategy is closely bound up with such socio-textual norms as dictated by politeness, orality vs literacy or preferred persuasive strategy. It is also suggested that other factors of a socio-political nature such as attitude to truth and freedom of speech may similarly be involved.

We will return to some of these issues in greater detail in the following chapters. The point to emphasize here is simply that relations such as that between language and truth claims can be used to explain the tendency in certain languages and cultures to adopt a more direct argumentative style (i.e. through-argumentation). A language such as Arabic, for example, appears to be averse to using a counter-argumentative strategy. One plausible reason for this is that, in Arabic, the *Of course ... However* kind of style would be seen as disingenuous, with a 'thesis emphatically cited only to be opposed out of sight' considered as compromising the truth.

Thus, in contrast with English, Arabic displays a distinct preference for through-argumentation, a text form that either advocates or condemns a given stance, riding roughshod over beliefs and assumptions entertained by an adversary. However, as stressed in Chapter 4, it would be wrong to assume that counter-argumentation is altogether alien to the rhetorical system of Arabic.

Instead, it is best to see communicative tendencies like these as temporary deficits, as certain text forms lying dormant to be revived once societal conditions become more conducive.

The main aim of this chapter, then, is to substantiate this note of hope by describing a model of argumentation from classical Arabic rhetoric, outlined most comprehensively in the work of an Arab rhetorician of the eighth century AH, Abdul Qaahir Al-Jurjaani, in his two best-known books, *Asraar al-balaagha* ('The Secrets of Rhetoric') and *Dalaa'il al-i3jaaz* ('Proofs of [Qur'anic] Inimitability'). In the course of our discussion, a comparative account of argumentation is presented in terms of what was recommended at a certain stage in the development of Arabic rhetoric nearly a thousand years ago, and what is actually encountered day in, day out, in the rather sad state of neglect in which Arabic finds itself today, hopefully not for too long.

The Text Receiver in Classical Arabic Rhetoric

Keenly aware of the intimate relationship between text and context, Arab rhetoricians (e.g. al-Jurjaani, d. 471 or 474 AH (AD 1079 or 1085); al-'Askarii, d. 395 AH (1005); al-Sakkakii, d. 626 AH (1229)) analysed with a remarkable degree of rigour how what we might these days call 'text evaluativeness' ultimately relates to the context of reception. This has to do with the 'state of the receiver', or how prepared he or she is to accept or reject the propositions put forward. Three particular types of text production/reception contexts are identified, each with its own typical linguistic realization:

(1) The context of the 'denier'. Utterances addressed to a denier (*munkir*) (someone who is not prepared to accept a given proposition as valid) must be made maximally evaluative (through emphasis, repetition, etc.). The degree of evaluativeness will depend on the degree of the denial displayed or perceived.
(2) The context of the 'uncertain'. Utterances addressed to the uncertain (*mutaraddid*) (the sceptic) must exhibit some uncertainty. The degree of uncertainty with which an utterance is imbued will depend on the degree of uncertainty or doubt displayed.
(3) The context of the 'open-minded'. Utterances addressed to the open-minded (*khaali al dhihn*) (someone who is effectively a tabula rasa, with no predispositions) must be minimally evaluative, since no denial or uncertainty is detected in the first place.

The degree of denial, uncertainty or open-mindedness may best be seen on a continuum, with maximal utterance evaluativeness catering for a greater degree of denial at one end, minimal evaluativeness catering for the absence of such a denial at the other, and with the category 'uncertain' occupying a place somewhere in between. Put in terms of our own linguistic model of text types, deniers and those who are somewhat uncertain are likely to be confronted with texts displaying varying degrees of 'argumentativeness'. This manifests itself in the use of various forms of emphasis, repetition, parallelism, and other linguistic devices of intensification. In the case of the open-minded text receiver, on the other hand, minimal use of such evaluative devices will be resorted to, since the aim of the text would invariably be to describe, narrate or deal with a set of concepts objectively through various forms of 'exposition'.

An Arab Rhetorical Model of Argumentation

Later rhetoricians built on these insightful analyses of the text receiver and developed what may even by today's standards strike us as some of the most elegant typologies of texts. Among the works inspired in this way is a classic slim volume entitled *Naqd al-Nathr*, on 'prose criticism', by Qudama b. Ja'far, an Arab rhetorician of the eighth century AH. It is surmised that the rhetoric of Aristotle was perhaps one of the foreign sources influencing the thinking of the author. Nevertheless, Qudama must have fully understood the Greek rhetorical tradition, to remould it in terms familiar to the Arab mind and in harmony with Arab rhetorical thinking. The end product is without doubt a pioneering attempt in the history of rhetoric to relate text to what we nowadays refer to as the **'context of situation'** and **'context of culture'**. To Qudama (whose exact terminology I translate here and put in single quotes), rhetoric is the art of producing utterances that convey intended meanings effectively ('purposefully'), efficiently ('transparently ordered') and appropriately ('linguistically eloquent'),

In his work on argumentation, the author of *Naqd al-Nathr* seems to have relied on earlier proposals put forward by Muslim orators and theologians, drawing heavily on the Qur'an, the traditions of the Prophet (*Hadiith*) and the works of numerous philosophers and men of letters. A new rhetoric was in the making aimed at the description of those text qualities which we associate with the true orator, writer or poet: the skill and the ability to express what goes on in the heart and mind with elegance and economy. Also discussed were the most effective means of expression and delivery.

In connection with this wealth of rhetorical insights, it may be worth noting that most of these proposals went unheeded at the time and subsequently, with Arab writers persisting in writing the way they had always done. In *Naqd al-Nathr*, from which we shall quote extensively in this section, argumentation is defined as:[1]

> a type of discourse essentially intended to present proof for resolving differences of belief between arguers. It is thus heavily used in promoting or questioning certain ideologies, engaging in religious debate, and pursuing legal proceedings as a crucial part of disputes and defenses.
>
> Argumentation may be found in both prose and poetry, and is divided into commendable (*maHmuud*) and condemnable (*madhmuum*). The first kind is truthful, upholding what is right. The second type is more akin to prevarication in which the end justifies the means and through which renown is sought for its own sake.
>
> This is not the case with exposition [Qudama's term is *baHth*, literally 'research']. Correct exposition builds its premises on what is more immediately accessible to the mind, because what is sought is the truth and what is aimed at is both clarity and clarification, in disregard of any opponent's approval or disapproval.

It would perhaps be helpful at this stage to consider some of the claims concerning argumentation and exposition in terms of our own model of text types. Expository texts build on a so-called 'topic sentence' whose function is simply to **set the scene**. Various aspects of the scene, or frame of reference, are then presented non-evaluatively, and an informative conclusion of some kind is finally reached. Ideally, the aim of such texts is to engage in conceptual analysis or synthesis, to narrate, to describe, or perhaps to serve a combination of these communicative goals, in as detached a manner as possible. As for argumentation (*al-jadal*), on the other hand, this text type relies for its validity on an evaluative thesis (a claim, an assertion) whose function is to **set the tone**, or agenda, for the unfolding argument. In modern text-linguistic terminology, we would say that, while exposition is intended simply to 'monitor' a situation, argumentation

---

1   As noted earlier, throughout this book, all translations from Arabic are my own, unless otherwise noted.

involves text users in situation 'managing', guiding the receiver in a manner favourable to the text producer's goals.

The Rhetoric of Rebuttal

At the heart of this rhetorical model of argumentation is the 'rebuttal', or what we have termed counter-argumentation. Sample 1 (so far discussed in some detail from two different angles in Chs 1 and 2) provides an illustration of this text format from English:

Sample 1 (The case of certainly)

The Cohesion of OPEC

Tomorrow's meeting of OPEC is a different affair. *Certainly, it is formally about prices and about Saudi Arabia's determination to keep them down. Certainly, it will also have immediate implications for the price of petrol, especially for Britain that recently lowered its price of North Sea oil and may now have to raise it again.* But this meeting, called at short notice, and confirmed only after the most intensive round of preliminary discussions between the parties concerned, is not primarily about selling arrangements between producer and consumer. It is primarily about the future cohesion of the organization itself.

The Times

The citation of one's real or projected opponent (in italics) and the opposition which follows (underlined) constitute a counter-argumentative structure favoured by arguers within both classical and modern Western rhetoric (where it even has a name—the **straw-man gambit**). Nevertheless, for many users of English as a foreign or second language (e.g. Arab learners), this text format seems to be particularly problematic. To illustrate the kind of difficulties encountered in dealing with this text form in English, let us consider how the adversary's claim can often be misperceived by language users or translators alike. What usually goes unappreciated is the function of text-initial adverbials such as *certainly*, that they are anything but emphatic devices that express conviction. With this function misperceived, the end result of whatever one wants to do with this text (e.g. translating) would often be based on a seriously flawed reading in which the crucial point, namely that 'OPEC is in disarray', gets completely lost (for a fuller discussion of this and related issues, see Chs 1 and 2 in this volume; Hatim and Mason 1990).

As stressed on more than one occasion so far, the irony in all of this is that this kind of counter-argumentation (which now constitutes a blind spot for many an Arab learner of English) was not unknown to the classical Arabic rhetorician. As documented above, sources like *Naqd al-Nathr* are among the earliest attempts at recognizing, describing and actually using such argumentative strategies. In this book, Qudama characterizes counter-argumentation in the following terms:

> Proper argumentation is that which anchors initial premises in what the opponent agrees with. Argumentation is most effective in confronting the opponent with evidence by initially citing the opponent's very own words.

That is, since the intention of the arguer is to steer an opponent into accepting a particular line of thinking, the initial presentation of the evidence with which the opponent agrees must surely be the most effective means of establishing credibility and ultimately achieving the argument's goals. To illustrate the use of this device, Qudama cites Qur'anic examples in which the counter-argument builds on the initial citation of theses drawn from the very Book which the Israelites endorse. In other words, to achieve optimal effectiveness, the Qur'an cites an Israelite thesis which includes the very strictures being argued for.

However, the citation of one's opponent is never altogether without ulterior motives. According to Qudama, the text producer cites an opponent in a way that does not display so much conviction as to render the subsequent rebuttal of the opponent's thesis ineffective. The content of the citation is therefore normally presented with an air of subtle dismissiveness, even irony, showing up serious conceptual gaps. This most valuable insight into the necessarily opaque nature of 'citing one's opponent without giving too much away', which classical Arab rhetoricians have obviously known and analysed, is the hallmark of counter-argumentation in languages such as English, and, as Sample 1 above shows, a potential pitfall especially for ESL users of English in this context.

Argumentation and Language Use

In response to a hypothetical claim that 'in country X (a particular country), there is no freedom', a committed supporter of country X's regime might very well argue along the following lines:

Sample 2

> X is not in the hands of Y (the leader). It is in the hands of the people, because it was the people who handed the country over to the person who is their servant, and who seeks only what is good for them.

Following Johnstone-Koch (1983) who analyses a similar text, the argument in Sample 2 reaches the conclusion 'X is not in the hands of Y' through the juxtaposition of a minor premise ('the people handed the country over to Y') and a major premise ('if people put themselves under someone else's control, they have shown that they are free'). Johnstone-Koch remarks that the claim (conclusion) and the datum (the minor premise)

> are related through a concept of freedom with which we [in the West] are not so familiar ... Our difficulty with this notion is what makes it so odd to hear East Bloc officials claiming that their countries are free, and it is at the heart of the debate about religious cults and 'de-programming' (p 91).

So far so good. But Johnstone-Koch and a few others writing on contrastive rhetoric seem always to imply that this kind of 'lopsided' reasoning is a cognitive characteristic of the 'users' of certain languages and is ultimately explainable in terms of those languages being characterized by 'ideational vagueness and formalistic rigidity', where persuasion 'works aesthetically' (i.e. 'by presentation and not by proof'). In pronouncements of this kind, rarely if ever do we come across blame being attached where it legitimately belongs, namely, to an incompetent language 'user'. The kinds of communication breakdowns illustrated by the above text samples are precisely what a careful reading of books such as *Naqd al-Nathr* would help us avoid. In this book, the anatomy of counter-argumentation is lucidly displayed, and the theory of logical sustainability (what Arab grammarians called *'illa*) is advanced perhaps as one of the more sophisticated analyses ever attempted in the history of Arabic grammar.

To Conclude

Building on the model of text types presented earlier, this chapter sought to demonstrate how Arabic (particularly the modern standard variety) shows a particular preference for the kind of argumentation in which the arguer either advocates or condemns a given stance without making any direct or indirect concession to a belief or an assumption entertained by an adversary.

Among other things, this form of through-argumentation generally lacks credibility when translated wholesale into languages (e.g. English) where a variant form of argumentation holds sway. Nevertheless, it had to be said that, while through-argumentation remains the preferred option in the case of Arabic, this is generally bound up with a host of socio-cultural and political factors and circumstances, and not with Arabic per se. It is therefore speakers and not languages which must be held accountable if the use of a particular form of argumentations happens to be appropriate or inappropriate, especially where translation is concerned.

6 Globalization, Academic Writing, Translation: A New Perspective on Culture

Here we will deal with language use in such domains as academic, or rather **pop-academic**, writing, and we will specifically assess the implications of the information explosion witnessed recently all over the globe for how we view communication in general. More particularly, we will look into how we actually communicate as academicians, both in English and, through translation, across cultural and linguistic divides. Thus, globalization, and the role of translation, are considered crucial themes to mull over: In a world of ever-changing socio-cultural values and textual-linguistic norms, can we not benefit from the arrival of newly imported registers, text types, discourses and genres? Should we not nurture a positive attitude towards these 'new arrivals', as opposed to constantly decrying their arrival as linguistic imperialism or, worse, foreign cultural onslaughts? These and a host of similar hotly contested issues shall now occupy us, taking us smoothly from bygone days and classical rhetoric into the modern era of language use in social life.

To encompass these new developments, the notion of socio-textual practices is put forward as a framework for the analysis of culture, indeed of language as a social semiotic. The focus here is on the analysis of texts as vehicles of successful communication, but only if and when seen within discourses which grant them perspective, and within genres which lend them a sense of communicative occasion. To demonstrate the value of such an approach for practical purposes such as translating, translator training, language teaching and curriculum development, we shall stick to the methodology systematically adopted so far in this book, namely, the use of mostly published translations of authentic texts into and out of English, with back-translation in English if the target language happens to be one from a range of world languages, including Arabic. These texts will this time be drawn from *Scientific American* (and its Arabic version *Al-3uluum*), together with a series of parallel texts published by the Egyptian Arabic daily *Al-Ahram*, and its twin publication, the English-medium *Al-Ahram Weekly*.

Overview

In this chapter on pop-academic English and Arabic, and on how linguistic performance in this domain interacts dynamically with such socio-economic developments as globalization, the focus will be on the notion of **culture**, along with the idea of the 'verbal sign', and on the practitioner (translator, interpreter, language teacher) trying to make sense of how linguistic expression can intermesh with belief, even with dogma. This particular language–ideology nexus will be dealt with in terms of a distinction established between two competing senses of culture as:

(1) entities best referred to as socio-cultural 'objects'—artefacts or products of socio-economic, geopolitical or scientific and technological forces and institutions,
(2) 'textual practices'—socio-facts, menti-facts or the linguistic means of representing products, legitimating them or in whatever manner concretizing them in actual texts.

Within the latter domain of textual practices, a scheme will be proposed whereby entities identified within given **cultural codes** ('objects') and the means to codify them in language ('practices') are all treated as part of culture, in turn taken to be part of language as a social semiotic.

The two areas of identifying cultural artefacts (objects, products) and codifying them (i.e. textualizing them as practices) tend to work together and as such constitute an important aspect of the way we communicate within one and the same language and culture, or across linguistic and cultural boundaries. But, as will be argued shortly, the tendency in certain languages and cultures (English not excluded) has been systematically to overlook, or at best treat as secondary, the macro-structural side of the equation (e.g. entire genres such as the academic abstract) and to focus instead on linguistic minutiae to do with rudiments of subject matter or level of formality (e.g. in restricted registers such as 'weather bulletins'). It will be further argued that it is those neglected textual practices (discourse, genre and actual texts) that typify a given mode of communication such as academic or pop-academic writing, and that ultimately set the scene for the act of communication both within and across cultural and linguistic boundaries. In fact, the obsession with the 'word' as an isolated verbal sign can be rectified only when the minimal unit of communication (or translation) becomes the 'text', a framework within which the word is seen as an element within the broader perspective of the sentence, and the sentence within the wider remit of such macro-structures as text, discourse and genre.

To preview the basic arguments presented in this chapter, we will start with a discussion of the semiotic dimension of context and how this interacts, on the one hand, with other contextual domains such as pragmatics and register membership and, on the other, with how texts exhibit cohesive and coherent texture and structure. As we have maintained throughout this book, this mutually enriching symbiotic relationship between text and context is crucial and must not be glossed over if we are to make headway with understanding the essence of true communication. This text-in-context set of relationships may be schematically represented as in Figure 6.1 (adapted from Hatim and Mason 1990).

Register membership	⇔	Pragmatic intentionality	⇔	Semiotic interaction
User (dialects etc.)	⇔	Speech acts	⇔	Socio-culture
Use (field, tenor, mode)		Presupposition		Socio-textual practices
		Inference		Text
		Implicature		Genre
				Discourse

INTERTEXTUALITY
text, genre and discourse typologies

STRUCTURE

TEXTURE

Figure 6.1 Text in context

To reiterate the core belief we entertain, text production and reception in general and the process of translation in particular may be envisioned within a model of text processing which captures the various contextual relationships in terms of the following interactive dimensions:

(a) the semiotics of culture or the way language use relies on a system of signs which, singly or collectively, signify knowledge and beliefs essential for members of a social community to operate in an acceptable manner,
(b) the pragmatics of the communicative act or the way language is used, whether directly or indirectly, to relay diverse **intentions**,
(c) the register membership of the text or how language is used in a manner that is appropriate to a given **field** (subject matter), tenor (level of formality), and **mode** or the spoken- or written-like nature of message construction.

These domains of context are systematically related to the way texts actually shape up, exhibiting a variety of:

- structure formats (compositional plans), and
- texture patterns (cohesion and coherence).

Finally, it has to be noted that the relationship between text and context is not unidirectional but cyclic and highly interactive. We as text users (producers and receivers) constantly shuttle between the two domains—the textual and the contextual—allowing context to inform wording and determine strategy (monitoring vs managing), and, if need be, allowing wording to modify context as we go along.

Pop-Academic Writing: An Example

To illustrate the interaction in which text users engage when analysing or constructing texts, let us conveniently take text reception as our chosen point of departure, and let us try out a bottom-up strategy first, looking at how a particular sequence of utterances may be handled by a model reader.

Sample 1

> Since the Enlightenment, science has stirred hearts and minds with its promise of a neutral and privileged viewpoint, above and beyond the rough and tumble of political life. With respect to women, however, science is not a neutral culture. Gender—both the real relations between the sexes and cultural renderings of those relations—shaped European natural history and, in particular, botany.
>
> *Scientific American* (February 1996, p. 98)

The variable cohesion caters for the way the various linguistic elements (words, phrases, etc.) concatenate to form a sequence which exhibits 'formal' continuity (Halliday and Hasan 1976). Here, a variety of conjunctive and reference relations, thematic patterns, kinds of information, lexical repetition and other lexico-grammatical choices, all become part of the fabric out of which texts are made. These features can all be found in Sample 1 above, ensuring that the various surface components are mutually connected (i.e. 'stick together').

In ploughing through the various grammatical, lexical and logical/conceptual relationships, text users constantly refer to a number of 'schemes' within which to fit the emerging structure. These scenarios, frames, schemata etc. help in the construction of a **text world**. Here, we would be in the area of coherence. Discovered compositional plans point us in the direction of 'events' in a story sequence, 'concepts' in an explanation, 'aspects' of a description or 'steps' in an argument. Sample 1, for example, is a counter-argument where a position is first stated to become the backdrop against which the counter-position of the text producer is then presented. The 'neutrality of science' is posited only to pave the way for the subsequent position taken vis-à-vis the 'prevalent bias of science', a view which is intended to hold sway in this text.

As we explained in Chapter 2, the translator, like any competent reader, goes into this armed with an important stylistic principle with which to assess 'what one is given' (e.g. a fronted adverbial *Since the Enlightenment, science has*) in terms of 'what one might have been given but was not' (e.g. an embedded adverbial, as in 'Science has since the Enlightenment ...'). The latter option, if available, would be deemed **marked** (i.e. deviating from ideal norms for a reason) and, to retrieve coherence, questions would be asked regarding the motivation behind its use. Such rhetorical effects (or absence of such effects) are meaningful in the work of the translator, who would ideally aim to render the letter and the spirit of the source text.

The Semiotics of Culture

The retrieval of coherence relations and accompanying macro-structures such as a 'narrative' or an 'argument' is conducted against the background of text semiotics or the way cultural codes develop and evolve. Here, the notion of the 'sign' is absolutely crucial. But, for the signifier–signified unity which underpins all signs to be fully appreciated, the 'sign' as a semiotic construct must be seen at local as well as global levels of analysis. Locally, text users utilize what we have referred to as 'objects', a collection of 'socio-cultural' entities captured in language by the use of, say, specialized terminology. This is to be distinguished from the more dynamic level of global utilization in which these same concepts take part in the evolution of macro-structures to do with:

(a) expressing attitudinal meanings and promoting particular worldviews or ideological positions (e.g. racial hegemony as discourse),
(b) operating within highly conventionalized forms of language use and upholding the communicative requirements involved (e.g. the compositional format of a cooking recipe as genre),
(c) fulfilling particular rhetorical purposes and achieving a variety of rhetorical aims (e.g. arguing, narrating, explaining, as texts).

Socio-Textual Practices Exemplified

The relationship between socio-cultural objects and textual practices is rather intricate and can only be captured in relative terms, depending on a number of factors, including the level of formality and technicality which typify the interaction. Fowler (1985: 61) succinctly portrays this relationship in the following terms:

> There is a dialectal interrelationship between language and social structure: the varieties of linguistic usage are both *products* of socio-economic forces and institutions—reflexes of such factors as power relations, occupational roles, social stratification's, etc.—and *practices* which are instrumental in forming and legitimating those same social forces and institutions.

To focus our attention on 'socio-textual practice' for the moment, we see this as essentially subsuming how language use can become a vehicle for the expression of attitudinal (i.e. ideological) meanings (when we convey racist or feminist sentiments, or indeed adopt an 'analytical' as opposed to a more 'committed' and 'involved' attitude). An example showing discourse at work is the following text from *Scientific American*:

Sample 2

> Then, too, botany among all the sciences was considered least offensive to the delicate spirit. As Rousseau pointed out, the student of anatomy was faced with oozing blood and stinking cadavers, entomologists with vile insects,

geologists with dirt and filth. After Linnaeus, the study of plants seemed to call for more attention to sexuality than might seem suitable for ladies. Still, botany continued to be advocated for women, especially in England, as the science leading to the greatest appreciation of God and His Universe.

Scientific American (February 1995, p. 98)

What is interesting about this sample is not only the feminist discourse and the attitude resenting male-dominated 'sexist' institutions in doing science, but the portrayal of the way sexism and religion have discursively conspired in blocking the advancement of women.

Alongside such discoursal attitudes there is that part of textual practices which relates to how language use is made appropriate to conventionalized formats involving certain communicative 'events' and the participants in them (the 'vignette' as a genre, with its characteristic use of language). For another example of genre at work, consider Sample 3 from *Scientific American*:

Sample 3

It was an overcast July morning as we hopped on board the motorboat that would take us away from open spaces, dry land and summer breezes for a week and a half. We were about to begin an underwater mission in the *Acquarius* habitat, a six-person research station 6.5 kilometers off Key Lagos.

Scientific American (October 1996, p. 66)

Notice how the 'popular fiction' genre is appropriately signalled, and the flow of events typical of the social occasion or communicative event in question upheld.

Finally, text users pursue a variety of 'rhetorical purposes' when they engage in, say, argumentation or detached exposition. The more involved mode of Sample 1 is a case in point. For another example from *Scientific American*, let us have a look at Sample 4, which clarifies the unit 'text' and how it is used as an element of socio-textual practice:

Sample 4

But how does the olfactory cortex, which receives signals from the olfactory bulb, decode the map provided by the olfactory bulb? The question is one of the central and most elusive problems in neurobiology. It seems likely that some form of spatial segregation, similar to that seen in the olfactory bulb but undoubtedly far more complex, will be maintained as the signals project into the cortex. This arrangement, however, merely places the problem of interpreting spatial information one level beyond the olfactory bulb, in the cortex. How does the cortex prompt the range of emotional or behavioural responses that smells often provoke?

Scientific American (October 1995, p. 137)

Here, the pattern of counter-argumentation threads its way in a highly elaborate fashion throughout this multi-layered text. But the fulcrum of the rebuttal is the sentence which contains the adversative signal *however*. These render the part preceding this utterance as a claim cited to be rebutted or at least questioned, and the subsequent rhetorical question as part of the 'substantiation'. Explicit signals have to be used to guide the processing, and these signals may have to be rendered explicitly when translated into more explicative languages such as Arabic, as we will see shortly.

To refresh your memory, see Figure 6.2 (reproduced here from earlier chapters).

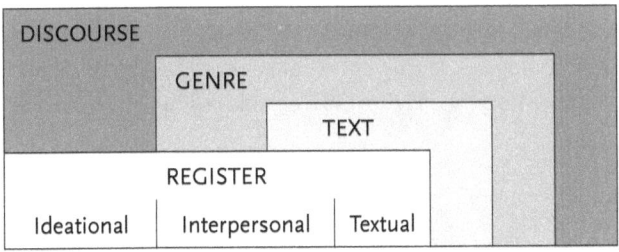

Figure 6.2 The semiotic triad

A Dynamic View of Register Membership

Socio-textual practices, then, are 'signs' that interact with texture and structure as texts unfold. Practices are part of what Ernst Wendland calls 'contexture'— 'that is, the influence of the conceptual world, including world view, on communication events, oral and written' (personal communication). They may also be viewed within the wider scope of David Katan's incisive proposals in his *Translating Cultures* (2004). Once established, these essentially semiotic constructs tend to enrich and be enriched by such pragmatic factors as intentionality and acceptability. They also, and equally meaningfully, cross-fertilize and cater to social institutions and social processes. This latter tendency (the evolution of registers) is by far the most important, and is achieved through the deployment of the lexico-grammar in particular ways to serve:

- agency and technicality requirements (fields of discourse),
- power or solidarity as part of tenor,
- cohesion and coherence, propping up mode, finding expression in the structure and texture.

Consider, for example, how the view of 'botany' and the role of women and religion depicted in Sample 2 turn into ideational resources of meaning, serving attitudes that essentially resist the status quo. Is this not reminiscent of what we have envisioned as discourse? This, together with solidarity (as opposed to power) as a function of tenor or what we can now label the 'interpersonal' dimension, gives texts their distinctive level of (in)formality. Is this not primarily a genre issue? Finally, to mobilize such diverse resources of meaning-making and ultimately develop texts that are both cohesive and coherent, the textual dimension of register would inevitably be involved. This 'enabling' function covers the mode within which linguistic expression accruing so far is typically cast, from spoken to written, and from, say, analytical to emotive or reflective dialogues or monologues. Is this not what we have been calling text all along? To refresh your memory, see Figure 6.3 (reproduced here from earlier chapters).

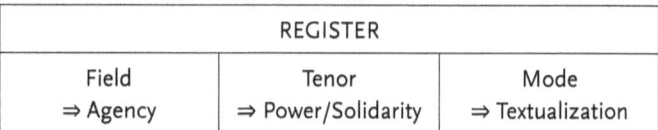

Figure 6.3 Register membership

Culture in the Process of Translation

Now that the full cycle from text to context and back is covered, we are in a better position to deal with the notion of culture. This is part of semiotics which, as we have argued above, is particularly privileged in the way we conduct our textual business. The minimal unit of semiotic analysis is the 'sign' which, according to Peirce (1934: vol. V, para. 228) is 'something which stands to somebody for something in some respect or capacity'. Such a conception has made signs ideally suited for dealing with cultures. In fact, it is this notion of signification (or semiosis) that has proved fundamental in the study of intercultural communication (Scollon and Scollon 1995) and as such has also appealed to the more context-sensitive theories of discourse and translation (Hatim and Mason 1997).

In translation studies, however, 'culture' as a domain of enquiry has had mixed fortunes over the years. The so-called 'cultural model' of translation emerged as a reaction to earlier conceptions of translation geared primarily to account for 'equivalence' in terms of grammatical and lexical categories as elements of the linguistic system. This was a time when, disillusioned, both linguists and translators felt that the attitudes and values, along with the experience and tradition of a people, inevitably become bound up with the freight of meaning carried by language. In effect, the argument ran, one does not translate languages, one translates cultures. (On these developments, see Chau 1984.)

These ideas were not totally new to translators who had already been operating with ethnographical-semantic methods. Here, meaning was defined in terms of 'cultural fields' reflecting the world views of given communities of language users. To study the ensuing 'culture-boundness', formal methods such as chain analysis, hierarchical analysis and componential analysis were heavily used (e.g. Nida 1969). For example, it was important to point out blind spots (cultural gaps) such as whether certain languages and cultures needed to lexicalize the difference between 'maternal' and 'paternal' uncle. Within this paradigm, theoreticians and practitioners came to be equally preoccupied with the 'civilization' aspects of culture that enveloped the source text.

The culture-bound view of meaning relations, however, was soon to be found wanting and more dynamic views of translation equivalence were promoted: anything that can be said in one language can be said in another, unless the form is an essential element of the message (Nida and Taber 1969). Issues such as 'reader response' came to the fore, and the focus shifted to aspects of the process such as the purpose of translation (*Skopos*) in the Formalist School and the requirements of the immediate situation. Translation strategy had to be adjusted as a result and, instead of excessively indulging in comparative ethnography, cultural adaptation to meet different needs was encouraged as a translation procedure.

All of these developments, welcome as no doubt they were at the time, were a far cry from a full-blown theory of translation committed to the dictum 'a word is a world'. But, although insights into what constitutes cultural meaning within this paradigm were rather static, the views which emanated proved to be too influential to go away quietly. They lingered and are still with us today in some of the more recent studies of the translation process. To a large extent, this is still justified in terms of the need to get to grips with the elusive notion of 'equivalence' across languages which invariably and, as Baker (1992/2011: 16) observes, 'understandably tend to make only those distinctions in meaning which are relevant to their particular environment, be it physical, historical, political, religious, cultural, economic, legal, technological, social, or otherwise'.

Various theorists have thus attempted to categorize cases of such cultural non-equivalence. Newmark (1988), for example, adapts Nida's breakdown of the various aspects of culture and presents his own scheme along the following lines:

(1) ecology: animals, plants, local winds, mountains, etc. (*qaat* [a plant with a tranquilizing effect chewed in Yemen] and the numerous Arabic words for camel),
(2) material culture: food, clothes, housing, transport and communications (*kuufiyya* [Arab headgear]),
(3) social culture: work and leisure (*hammaam* [Arabic for bathroom, shower room, toilet]),
(4) organizations, customs, ideas: political, social, legal, religious, artistic (*al-Azhar* [an Islamic, educational establishment in Egypt], *awqaaf* [religious property owned by the state]),
(5) gestures and habits (a shake of the head means 'no' in English but 'yes' for an Indian).

Recent Developments in the Study of Culture

The aim of citing catalogues of features such as these is merely to illustrate the basic thesis that, while terms denoting, say, organizational culture in a domain like science and technology are indeed important in the work of the translator, these must be considered finite for any language and therefore manageable in any communicative task. A good glossary of such terms should suffice in most cases (cf. Geeraerts 2010). However, elements of such a categorization can and often do acquire varying degrees of dynamism, and culture becomes less a nomenclature and more a way of thinking. Unless and until such dynamism is accounted for, these items remain dormant and should not therefore exact so much attention. Within this dynamic conception, culture would be a 'totality of knowledge, proficiency and perception', with language becoming 'not an isolated phenomenon suspended in a vacuum' but 'an integral part of culture' (Snell-Hornby 1988: 40). The American ethnologist Ward H. Goodenough captures this broad sense of 'culture' in the following terms:

As I see it, a society's culture consists of whatever it is one has to know or believe in order to operate in a manner acceptable to its members, and do so in any role that they accept for any one of themselves. Culture, being what people have to learn as distinct from their biological heritage, must consist of the end product of learning: knowledge, in a most general, if relative, sense of the term. By this definition, we should note that culture is not a material phenomenon; it does not consist of things, people, behaviour or emotions. It is rather an organization of these things. It is the forms of things that people have in mind, their models for perceiving, relating, and otherwise interpreting them (1964: 36).

Agar (1994: 211) echoes this, thus:

> Culture is not something people *have*; it is something that fills the spaces *between* them. And culture is not an exhaustive description of anything; it focuses on differences, differences that can vary from task to task and group to group.

It is in this sense that Agar (1991: 168) speaks of 'rich points'—'from lexical items through speech acts up to fundamental notions of how the world works'—which are differences that can cause culture conflicts or communication breakdowns.

Socio-Textual Practices in Translation

These mainly socio-cultural elements of linguistic expression and the way they are organized ultimately realize what we have been referring to as 'discourse', 'genre' and 'text', embedded in the context of culture (not only a 'context of situation'), and structured in specific ways as part of 'doing things with words'. This is all subsumed under the cover term 'socio-textual practices', as distinct from 'socio-cultural objects'. We recall that, after Fowler (1986/1996: 21), socio-culture involves

> varieties of linguistic usage seen as *products* of socio-economic forces and institutions, [as] reflexes of such factors as power relations, occupational roles, social stratifications, etc.

As the above catalogue shows, this includes categories such as organizational culture or ecology, as well as elements of linguistic expression mostly to do with the way texts are put together (i.e. with the process of textualization, including such aspects of usage as idiom, metaphor, cliché, collocation). Socio-textual practices, on the other hand, are varieties of linguistic use seen as *'practices which are instrumental in forming and legitimating those same social forces and institutions'* (Fowler, *ibid.*).

In this final section, the aim is to analyse a parallel English/Arabic sample of political writing. But first a word on the sample. The Arabic and English texts are written independently, by the same writer, in response to the same or similar situation. In other words, they are not translations. What is remarkable in this form of writing is that, while bilingualism, even bi-culturalism, are very much in evidence at the socio-cultural level (the level of objects or products), the same cannot be said of the socio-textual level (the level of practices or genre–discourse–text), which leaves a great deal to be desired. Consider the following example from the English version:

Sample 5

> *From the very start, the Middle East peace process did not proceed along a well-defined and clearly marked course. But never before has it been as shrouded in uncertainty as it is now.* At this stage, the only thing that can be regarded as certain is that Israel will withdraw from southern Lebanon by no later than, and possibly even before, 7 July.
>
> (Italics added)

On the surface, this is a well-formed text, a well-structured counter-argument comprising a 'claim', with *but* ushering in the 'opposition'. That is, it is cohesive, but is it coherent? Closer scrutiny immediately reveals that it is not, or not entirely:

- The 'claim' cited is too solid to be opposed, that is, it has no gaps to pave the way for the opposition; *did not proceed along a well-defined and clearly marked course* is simply too fortified to qualify as a 'straw-man gambit' and to be subsequently opposed.
- The opposition is too faint-hearted to be an effective force, that is, the opposition is really opposing nothing: The process was mysterious before > the process is mysterious now!

True, there is a subtle semantic difference between *did not proceed along a well-defined and clearly marked course* and *shrouded in uncertainty*. But the difference is so slight that it does not amount to anything with a contrastive potential to justify an adversative.

But what is even more intriguing is how, true to Arabic preferences, the text lapses into through-argumentation (assertion–substantiation) in content if not in form.

No guesses for how the Arabic version proceeded. Quite in keeping with the spirit of Arabic through-argumentation, the author finds it more convenient to start the Arabic version at the point where the so-called 'claim' and 'counter-claim' are dispensed with, and where substantiation of the counter-claim begins (i.e. *At this stage* ...). In other words, all in a day's work, the entire initial thesis cited and incoherently opposed (in italics above) was left out.

Sample 6 (back translated from Arabic)

> At this stage, the only thing that can be regarded as certain is that Israel will withdraw from southern Lebanon by no later than, and possibly even before, 7 July.
> [Assertion stated, then extensively argued through]

But, before we rush into any conclusions and assert that 'counter-argumentation' is all but absent in writings of this kind in Arabic, it might be helpful to see how both the English and the Arabic versions continue:

Sample 7 (English version)

> There is no doubt that the withdrawal represents a victory for the Lebanese resistance movement, particularly for Hizbollah, which led the armed resistance against Israeli occupation and forced Barak to invoke UN Security Council Resolution 425 to justify an unconditional Israeli withdrawal from Lebanon. However, it would be wrong to explain the Israeli decision only as an admission of defeat in the face of Hizbollah's systematic harassment of the Israeli occupation forces. Rather ...

The Arabic version continues in the same way counter-arguing the issue:

Sample 8 (back translated from Arabic)

> There is no doubt that the withdrawal represents a victory for the Lebanese resistance movement, particularly for Hizbollah, which led the armed resistance against Israeli occupation and forced Barak to invoke UN Security Council Resolution 425 to justify an unconditional Israeli withdrawal from Lebanon. However, it would be wrong to explain the Israeli decision only as

an admission of defeat in the face of Hizbollah's systematic harassment of the Israeli occupation forces. Rather ...

Nevertheless, neutralizing the counter-argument and systematically lapsing into through-argumentation ('assertion' defended, in content if not in form, as we saw in Sample 6 above) seems to be a tendency that Arabic encourages; indeed it is almost a stylistic predilection in this language (see Hatim 1991). As a text form, a through-argument is more compatible with the 'hortatory attitude' that the discourse of the Arabic 'commentary' is usually expected to convey. It is also more compatible with the genre 'position paper/polemic' which Arabic generally favours. This is in contrast to counter-argumentation favoured in English writing of a similar description. It is also in contrast to the analytical discourse that the genre pop-academic commentary favours in English.

Hortatory vs Analyticalness: Preliminaries

We certainly seem to know more about the rhetorical norms and conventions governing modern English socio-textual practices than those operative in modern Standard Arabic. However, the few examples cited above should be sufficient to reveal that tendencies along the lines suggested point to deeper differences in how English and Arabic texts are shaped and made to function.

To pinpoint these differences further, this time with a focus on texture, it might be helpful to cast a glance at the level of general hortatoriness (a socio-textual practice) which appears to dominate in Arabic. If preserved intact, this hortatoriness will be too excessive to be acceptable in English, where analyticalness is the predominant mode. To demonstrate this, let us consider how certain highly emotive use of language in Arabic gets toned down, if not thoroughly domesticated, in English. Read on and keep an eye on elements in bold:

Sample 9

> The 1999 report presented for discussion at this year's seminar **provoked a heated controversy** among Egyptian intellectuals, many of whom, myself included, described it as reflecting a **complete turnabout** in political and strategic thinking ... The report devoted the first chapter to the Kosovo crisis, which was portrayed as **a typical example** of what it called the dangers of misreading the global situation, whether **intentionally or unintentionally** [*sic*. out of ignorance or as a result of deliberate distortion]. Proceeding from

this premise, the report goes on to **criticize** those who condemned NATO's military intervention in Kosovo, accusing them of **downplaying the facts** which prove that it was a legitimate response to aggression, specifically, to the campaigns of genocide and ethnic cleansing which Serbs began launching against Muslims in Kosovo since the end of the seventies.

Let us now get an inkling of what the Arabic sounded like, to get a sense of the hortatotariness saturating texts in this language before they get down-toned drastically in the manner shown above.

English rendering	Arabic rendering	Back-translation
provoked a heated controversy	موضع زوبعة mawDi3a zawba3a	'in the eye of the storm' 'In the midst of a hurricane'
complete turnabout	انقلاب في الفكر السياسي 'inqilaab fil fikr al siyaasi'	A coup in political thinking
a typical example	بوصفها نموذجا صارخا Biwasfiha numuthajan SaariKHan	A glaringly flagrant example
intentionally or unintentionally	عن جهل أو تزييف 3an jahlin aw tazyeef	Whether out of ignorance or the desire to distort (fake)
criticize	ندد بأولئك الذين Naddada bi ...	Condemned/denounced those who ...
downplaying the facts	'طمس الحقائق Tamas al Haqaa'iq	obliterating facts (suppressing them out of existence)

Now that we have shown the down-toning process that the English parallel text exhibits, the argument we wish to pursue is two-fold:

- What would happen if, in translation from Arabic into English, we uncritically preserved the Arabic hortatoriness?
- What would happen if, in translation from English into Arabic, we boldly preserved the English analyticalness?

To preserve Arabic hortatoriness uncritically, we would no doubt end up with an English rendering that is flawed on the grounds that:

- The argument would be heavily slanted towards a through-argumentative mode, with words by the 'opposition' either opaquely rendered or not rendered at all.
- The discourse would be heavily slanted towards a hortatory mode, with the element of 'analyticalness' either heavily compromised or not retained at all.
- The genre would be heavily slanted towards 'emotive commentary', with the element of 'analyticalness' once again either heavily compromised or not rendered at all.

Inappropriateness would thus set in, with the target text beginning to infringe all rules of 'text politeness' (see Chapter 16; Hatim 1998).

Let us now entertain the alternative scenario, namely that of translating from a subdued English commentary into a form of Arabic likely to be highly hortatory for a commentary to be effective at all. Of course, one should ideally be able to exploit latent tendencies in the target language, and capture in the Arabic target text dormant patterns of socio-textual practice, thus producing a version that is highly through-argumentative (in content if not in form), emotive, hortatory, etc. But do we know enough about these stylistic preferences in Arabic in order for us to be able to engage in a realistic re-creation? And, even if we had some idea of what is involved, are these practices really what we would like to encourage in a language that is already suffering from a heavy dose of residual orality. True, the Arabic language had a glorious rhetorical history before it was damaged by incompetent modern users (Hatim 2010), but, let us admit, Arabic has not had the benefit of modern linguistic scholarship until very recently and at the hands of very few. In other words, should we not seize this opportunity to introduce a new genre and a new discourse to Arabic to enable this language to handle not only what it is good at (i.e. hortatoriness, etc.) but also what it desperately requires to cope with the needs of a global thinking, namely more effective analyticalness?

These and similar questions raise the issue of whether globalization is something we wish to resist across the board, welcome wholeheartedly or welcome selectively? The latter course of action (i.e. eclecticism), I suggest, is by far the more prudent, and one way of effecting this would be through adopting a unique form of translation strategy that simply revolves around:

- 'domesticating' socio-cultural objects (products, artefacts),
- 'foreignizing' socio-textual practices (text, genre, discourse).

In other words, while English *skyscrapers, peak hour* or *brain-storming*, for example, are tolerated in Arabic as calques for *naaTiHat SaHaab, saa3at dhurwa, 3aSf dhihni*, and while *head scarf, head gear* or *robe* are tolerated in English as calques for Arabic *Hijaab, 3iqaal, 3abaaya*, what Arabic must also learn to tolerate is more counter-argumentation, more balanced commentaries and more analytical discourse. In no sense would this mean obliterating alternative forms; we simply cannot do that because language does not work in this binary way. But we could certainly adopt a strategy of less of this and more of that (as *Readers' Digest* has admirably succeeded in doing for its Arabic version *Al MuKHtaar*, or as the BBC has also done for its Arabic output): less through-argumentation (as text), less unbalanced commentary (genre), less hortatoriness (discourse). But this is a topic for another occasion and further research into what can be done in this area of the eclectic re-creation of alternative forms of discourse.

Academic Writing Example: Revisited

The kind of translation we are calling for will in the fullness of time act as a shaping force, introducing new styles and in the process new ways of thinking. The purists would at first resist the new developments. Ultimately, however, it is the sound, healthy and analytical mode of thought that will win the day and remain as one of the positive results of globalization.

These are areas of text in context which are neglected in the training of our future linguists, translators or interpreters. To show how this has not been without adverse effects on the translations we encounter on a daily basis, it might be helpful in the remainder of this chapter to assess the published translation of the sample texts cited above from *Scientific American*. It is noteworthy that the translations which appear in the Arabic version *Al-3uluum* is of the highest order in terms of socio-cultural objects, products, terminology, etc. In fact, the Kuwaiti institution sponsoring the Arabic version of *Scientific American* is to be commended on the high-calibre translators commissioned, who are normally Arab holders of higher degrees in the subject matter areas in question and thus possessing first-class knowledge of the fields covered. The problem is that these top-notch translators are rarely 'text-trained', with prerequisite sensitivity to text, discourse or genre as we have defined the triad here and as we believe that translators should be. The translations into Arabic of the selected texts in this chapter are singularly flawed, not in catering for the socio-cultural but for the socio-textual, where, regrettably, they are simply unsuccessful. This is revealing since, to reiterate, these translators did not lack the training in the field of discourse (science, technology) or the terminology sanctioned by the discipline. Yet, they did not possess sufficient 'cultural' knowledge of what is essentially socio-textual in approaching the language and culture with which they have been working (in this case English).

We recall that the problem encountered in the translation of Sample 1 had to do with the structure of the argument presented. Admittedly, the difficulty began with a mishandling of what is essentially a socio-cultural element (the idiom *with respect to*), which is taken literally and is rendered as 'with all due respect to women'. But what is really at stake is the structure of the source-text argument. What is not appreciated properly is the entire counter-argumentative format, leaving us with a flawed rendering. Note the relevant section which I have italicized:

Sample 1a (Back translation from Arabic)

> Since the Enlightenment, science has stirred hearts and minds with its promise of a neutral and privileged viewpoint, above and beyond the rough and tumble of political life. *And with all due respect to women*, science is not a neutral culture. This is because gender—both the real relations between the sexes and cultural renderings of those relations—shaped European natural history and, in particular, botany.

The translator achieved a remarkable degree of success in producing an extremely fluent text in terms of both cultural and technical terminology. This transparency, however, tells only part of the story (when the various expressions, terms etc. are seen as isolated entities). But when the entire structure is scrutinized, the translation is hardly comprehensible. Cohesion may be intact, but coherence has suffered badly. The translator has drastically failed to negotiate text strategy, and this has had some serious repercussions on the discoursal thrust (the feminist leanings) and perhaps indirectly also on the genre structure.

To Conclude

In this chapter, we distinguished between socio-cultural knowledge (subsuming such aspects of texts as 'terminology' as well as nomenclature of societal objects and products), on the one hand, and socio-textual knowledge which goes beyond words and focuses on aspects of the texts such as the compositional plan of texts and patterns of cohesion, on the other. The basic argument put forward is that while terminology, for example, constitutes an important part in the work of both scientists and translators of science, the training of translators and other language users should also cater for and deal more adequately with the fundamental role played by macro-plans such as discourse, genre and text. The various strategies involved in these areas of the production as well as reception of texts are referred to as socio-textual practices. These constitute a crucial part of message construction in the use of language in general and in communicating science and technology in particular.

This is not unrelated to globalization, and translation should be exploited as a way of importing and particularly welcoming new text formats, new discourses and new genres. The examples tackled show how practices such as 'academic writing' in Arabic are predominated by text forms leaning too heavily towards through-argumentation, a discourse that is too emotive, and a genre heavily slanted towards unbalanced commentary. In translating into Arabic, a foreignizing strategy could impose new patterns and thus restore to academic writing an element of analyticalness as a rhetorical purpose, as an attitude and as a fashion of speaking and writing in this domain.

7 Cultures within Cultures: Commodification Discourse

The principal aim of this text-type-themed chapter is to further argue for the need to see linguistic expression as a realization of some higher-level semiotic (Halliday 2014). The various lexico-grammatical choices we make are essentially determined by a number of contextual factors, mainly to do with the register membership of texts (subject matter, level of formality, etc.), the intentionality of text users (pragmatics) and the fact that texts are part of the socio-cultural practices sanctioned by given communities of language users (semiotics).

An Alternative View of Rhetorical Purpose in Texts

Consider the current environmental debate, for example. Linguistically, this area of discursive practice may usefully be seen in terms of predominant modes of speaking or writing that collectively operate within the dos and don'ts of some cultural code (what can or cannot be said, by whom, where, when, etc.). Here, we can identify particular contextual configurations reflecting the mores of various subcultures (e.g. the multinational companies with vested interests regarding a given ecological issue). Within such contextual specification, there will be particular modes of reasoning which reveal certain attitudes. To convey such attitudes, text users find certain types of texts (e.g. analytical exposition) more suitable than others (all part of the semiotic process and the cultural code sanctioned). In the case of analytical exposition, the overall intention would be to persuade people *that* something, say, the status quo, is OK (a pragmatic concern). This would obviously involve text users in particular ways of perceiving, approaching and dealing with reality (a register matter) (Martin 1985, 2002).

Analytical exposition just cited may usefully be compared and contrasted with another text form—hortatory exposition.[1] Here, a considerably higher degree of involvement and personal commitment would be the order of the day, not only in the way the arguer (e.g. a consumer) reasons the whole thing out, but also in the kind of attitudes conveyed and the types of texts utilized to transmit this attitudinal meaning. These emanate from a drastically different set of intentions (namely, to persuade people *to do* something, say, to challenge the status quo), and from a perception of reality that is radically different from that of the status quo (i.e. one in which people matter).

Stirrers vs Resolvers

The basic distinction emerging from the above juxtaposition of those with vested interests and thus with power to lose (in the analytical domain), on the one hand, and those who basically have nothing to lose, in fact have power to gain (in the hortatory domain), on the other hand, is, then, one that is closely bound up with different 'fashions' of speaking or writing (Martin 1985). To introduce how such groupings emerge and evolve, we have selected ecological debates as a theme that at times attract opposites. Following in the steps of Australian Systemic Linguist J.R. Martin, the way we shall approach this conflict will be to presuppose that any debate essentially involves people of two kinds. Firstly, there are the 'resolvers' (from both the Right and the Left) whose job it is to make issues go away by working out all kinds of compromise (typical of the 'analytical' domain). Secondly, there are the 'stirrers', the so-called radicals of the Left and conservatives of the Right (note again, regardless of political leanings) who see their job as that of 'creating' issues (typical of the hortatory domain).

But to get to discourse proper and view this linguistic output from a plausible contrastive angle, we would do well to concentrate not on what stirrers or resolvers do with their language by dint of their political leanings (that is a political issue), but more productively on what, say, a stirrer or a resolver does with language, regardless of political leanings (this becomes a discourse-analytic issue). Stirrers (Left or Right) tend to exhibit similar textualizations of their 'extreme' intentions (to persuade someone *to do* something). Similarly, resolvers

---

1 Analytical exposition vs hortatory exposition is the terminology employed by J.R. Martin (1985). We have adopted the conceptual framework but, to be consistent with the text typology we have been using in this book, propose a slight modification: retain analytical exposition, but alter hortatory exposition to hortatory argumentation.

(Left or Right) tend to opt for similar textual strategies to persuade someone *that* something is good or bad. Thus, when a stirrer's text is compared with a resolver's text (virtually regardless of politics), we as analysts are more likely to benefit not only from the Left–Right distinction (which remains a variable to take into account but which may or may not be relevant), but also, and far more significantly, from the fact that different discourse strategies would most likely be utilized. These inevitably involve the entire gamut from mode of reasoning, to intentionality, and ultimately to the type of text, discourse and genre.

The basic hypothesis entertained in this study, then, is that stirrers and resolvers in something like the ecological debate tend to favour different modes of speaking or writing to present their case. Resolvers tend to favour what we shall call analytical exposition (as a type of discourse, regardless of the kind of genre). Their editorials, letters to the editor, speeches and articles try to persuade people *that* the status quo is OK—that nothing needs to be drastically changed and that, if anything, only a slight modification will do. That is, analytical exposition is seen as an effective way of arguing that minimal action is required. It presents what we already have as a *fait accompli*, a foregone conclusion, an inevitability that is fairly correct and hard to challenge or change.

Stirrers, on the other hand, tend to favour hortatory argumentation, often making use of editorials, etc. to persuade people *to do* something. Admittedly, this mode suits Left stirrers better than Right resolvers, but both groups could safely be assumed to entertain a doctrinaire kind of attitude to their subject matter, audience and texts. Taking stirrers as hortatory arguers *par excellence* is thus a useful way of seeing this kind of discourse at work and of looking into the types of texts and genres generated in the process.

Let us now sample what the language of analytical exposition, and that of hortatory argumentation, would sound like. Texts are presented segment by segment in Samples 1 and 2 (drawn from Martin 2002):

Sample 1 (Analytical Exposition)

International WILDLIFE: Dedicated to the wise use of the earth's resources
The Northwest Atlantic Sealing Controversy
Summary

Based on the facts, certain conclusions may be drawn in reference to the seal hunting issue.

The management regime established by the Canadian Government is achieving the objectives established for the program; this is to achieve a gradual but certain increase in the Harp Seal population that falls within the jurisdiction of the Government of Canada.

The regulations established to control the conduct and level of the seal harvest respond to the needs of the Harp Seal population and are being effectively applied.

The Harp Seal population is not endangered and is in fact expanding faster than originally estimated.

International WILDLIFE, March–April 1983

Sample 2 (Hortatory Argumentation)

ACFText
Habitat: a magazine of conservation and environment
Editorial: Kangaroos—Is Our National Conscience Extinct?

Let us try to define our conservation goals but on two levels.

First comes the level of species survival on which our rather smug government biologists prefer to operate. We seriously question what is happening under their approving eyes: The massive level of killing, the population distortions related to the favoured killing of bigger, heavier male kangaroos, the pathetic lack of supervisory staff. The programme is unsatisfactory and questionable on a number of counts.

Secondly, let us turn to a deeper level: that web of life embracing the human species as well as the easy, trusting targets in the night spotlights. We are talking here about 'deep ecology', about the ethics related to all wild creatures. We don't feel the need to apologise for looking beyond the figures on 'harvests', 'quotas' and 'management' to think for a moment about 3 million other living creatures whose lives will be obliterated, often painfully, this year. We are in good company, in November 1785, the great poet with the human touch, Robert Burns, wrote a famous poem 'To a Mouse' ... on turning up her nest with the plough.

Habitat, Vol. 11, June 1983

From Register to Genre, Discourse and Text

Fluctuating between stirrers and resolvers, and between Left and Right, the various modes of writing or speaking to which we as language users habitually resort, once register membership (field, etc.) has been established, tend to materialize in two different, yet overlapping, ways:

- One, through how field, tenor and mode evolve respectively into ideational, interpersonal and textual meaning resources (discussed in detail in Ch. 2 and schematically represented in Figures 7.1 and 7.2 below).
- Two, through how we tend to explore a range of genres, discourses and texts by independent socio-textual means (introduced in Ch. 2 and schematically represented in Figure 7.3).

On the meaning resource plane, it becomes clear that there is more to register's 'field' than mere subject matter or technicality. It might be useful to reiterate here that, alongside 'level of technicality', there is agency regulating how 'we use language to talk about *our experience of the world*, including *the worlds in our own minds*, to describe events and states and the entities involved in them' (Thompson 1996/2014: 28, italics added).

Similarly, there is more to register's 'tenor' than mere level of formality. There is power and solidarity, where 'we use language *to interact* with other people, to establish and maintain relations with them, to influence their behavior' (ibid.: 29).

Finally, at this macro-functional level, there is more to register's 'mode' than the simple spoken- vs written-like mode. There is the entire domain of textuality (cohesion and coherence) attending to how 'we *organise* our messages in ways which indicate *how they fit* in with the *other messages* around them and with the *wider context* in which we are talking or writing' (ibid.: 30). Schematically, this is represented as in Figure 7.3 below. But first to Figure 7.1 and 7.2 schematically capturing what is going on in the journey from register to meaning macro-functions:

REGISTER		
Field ⇒ Agency	Tenor ⇒ Power/Solidarity	Mode ⇒ Textualization

Figure 7.1 From register to macro-functions I

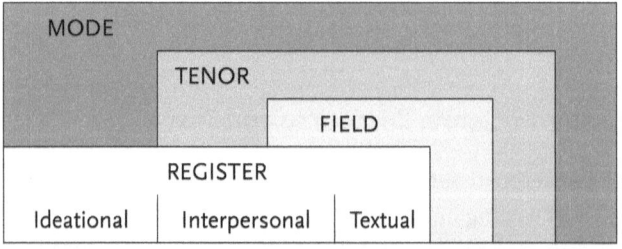

Figure 7.2 From register to macro-functions II

Alternatively, at the other socio-textual plane, a different classification of the way we do things with words emerges. Here, text processing begins to operate at a higher level of socio-textual practice, through routes taking us through texts, discourses and genres, as represented in Figure 7.3.

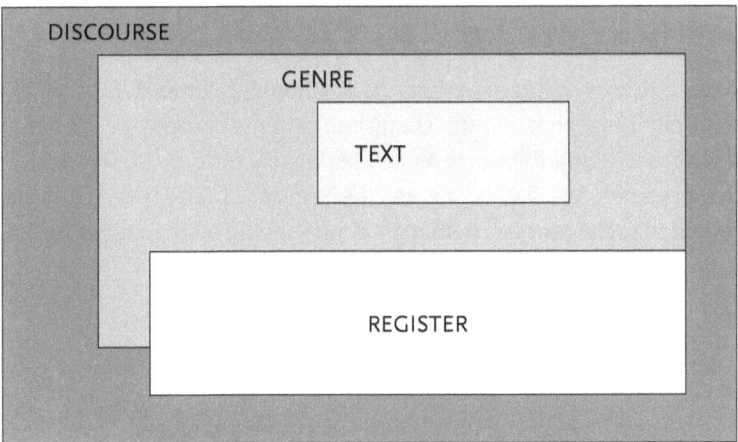

Figure 7.3 The discourse–genre–text triad

A Systemic-Functional Perspective on Meta-Functions

In a well-established Hallidayian tradition, J.R. Martin (1992, 2002) sees the relationship between text and context in essentially the following terms: An intimate relation is struck between linguistic organization and the organization of social reality, around the notion of discourse meta-functions, and in terms of register and genre as crucial intermediaries. To set the scene for the following discussion, a recap of what the basic meaning resources involve is in order. In this framework:

- Ideational meaning is related to the construction of institutional activity or field (including subject matter). Field, in turn, is concerned with such facets of an activity as descriptions of the participants, process and circumstances involved in these activities.
- Interpersonal meaning is more to do with social relations that reflect social distance or tenor. This is ultimately bound up with social semiotic and pragmatic constructs such as power and solidarity.
- Textual meaning is the prime mover of the unit 'text', regulating

information flow across the spoken-like or written-like divide. It is thus also to do with distance but of the semiotic proxemic type, and not of the social variety. Textual meaning is thus home to 'mode' that is concerned with channels of communication and with how these tend to mobilize in actual texts the range of ideational (field) and interpersonal (tenor) values.

Register, then, subsumes patterns of ideational, interpersonal and textual-linguistic choices. Genre, in turn, comprises patterns of register choices that, in harness with text and discourse as defined above, form an additional level of context, beyond tenor, field and mode (i.e. register). Genre is seen as a staged, goal-oriented social process, with most genres taking more than a single phase to unfold.

Into the Socio-Textual Dimension Proper

Following Kress (1985b), genres evolve as conventionalized forms of texts, reflecting the functions and goals of participants involved in particular social occasions or communicative events. The Letter to the Editor may be taken as an example of a popular genre across the languages and cultures of the world. Here, the social occasion conventionally involves participants in certain functions and goals that are specific to particular cultures inter- and intralingually. While in English, the purpose of writing to the editor has always been one of taking someone or something to task, for example, this has until very recently been largely light-hearted and congratulatory in Arabic.

Discourse, in the Foucauldian sense of institutionalized modes of speaking and writing, is the mouthpiece through which we communicate particular attitudes towards areas of socio-cultural activity (Fairclough 1992). Like genre, discoursal expression is conventional and culture-specific. Central to this proposition is the question of how any competent reader is able to 'read off' the discourse of a particular message, be this 'sexist', 'feminist', 'racist' or whatever. In a famous speech from the 1960s, British politician Enoch Powell (known for his racist views) is observed systematically to exclude actual reference to 'children' and instead talk of 'offspring' every time the context of 'immigrants and their children' arose. Here, hijacking 'legalistic' discourse provides the basis for another kind of discourse, arguably 'racist and dehumanizing' (Sykes 1985).

Finally, text is a semiotic construct (i.e. a socio-cultural sign) deployed in the service of a given rhetorical purpose (e.g. arguing, narrating). Here, we have a sequence of mutually relevant utterances concatenated to implement a given rhetorical plan conventionally recognized as such by a community of text users (Beaugrande and Dressler 1981). No doubt, actual texts are generally hybrid, mixing, for example, evaluativeness (typical of argumentation) with neutral exposition. However, one or the other of these functions must always ultimately predominate and it is this which is recognized as the overall rhetorical purpose of the text (Hatim and Mason 1990). Once again, the key element in text production and reception is the conventional nature and cultural specificity of all texts. Signals such as *Of course*, *Certainly*, *No doubt*, used as sentence-initial and text-initial will in English usher in what we have labelled 'a straw-man gambit' (claim cited) to be followed by some form of opposition (*Of course John Major is going through a bad patch. However* ...). As the previous chapters have made amply clear, in Arabic, such concessive signals as *of course* invariably relay conviction, and the statements they introduce are to be substantiated and not opposed, hence the difficulty of dealing with counter-argumentation of this kind by many a translator into or out of Arabic (Hatim 2005).

The Medical Novella: Oliver Sacks, a Pioneer

Neuro-surgeon-turned-writer Oliver Sacks's so-called 'medical novellas' are chosen as a prime example of how discourse may be de-commodified (i.e. become less impersonal, less mechanical, less analytical). With Sacks, the hortatoriness quality finds expression through registers that are impure, texts that are hybrid, genres that are blurred, and discourses that are jumbled. Sacks's mission is literally to reach the hearts and minds of a much wider audience through what are essentially technical texts, medical case histories to be exact. In short, the experiment embarked upon by Sacks has ushered in a radical rethinking of what it means to practise and write about medicine.

Through Sacks's writings, then, we have specifically experienced a genre shift from the forensic (e.g. science report) to the epideictic (a popularization of the report) (Fahnestock 1986). That is, we have witnessed a leap of some magnitude from a discourse whose main purpose is to validate its claims (analytical), to a discourse whose primary aim is to celebrate the uniqueness of its topic (hortatory). Text as a sign has had to follow suit, responding to an urgent need to be more and more interactive. As Sacks (the neuro-surgeon specializing in the affliction 'agnosia') so brilliantly put it:

Our cognitive sciences are themselves suffering from an agnosia essentially similar to Dr P.'s [a patient of his]. Dr P. may therefore serve as a warning and a parable—of what happens to a science which eschews the judgmental, the particular, the personal, and becomes entirely abstract and computational. (1985: 19)

In their groundbreaking study of Sacks's 'medical novella' as a genre, functional-systemic linguists Gill Francis and Anneliese Kramer-Dahl (1992) state that it is highly edifying to see how the lexico-grammatical patterns (or registers) of Sacks's discourse (best described as 'hortatory' in our terminology) compare with what may also be described as the more 'analytical' type of texts generated by your average diehard core scientist. In terms of the model of text processing we have been advocating so far, this means that different metafunctional resources are exploited, and different options taken up, to come up with unique ideational, interpersonal and textual profiles, typifying this or that discourse, genre and text. In other words, it is highly instructive to see how the various layers of meaning tend to mobilize in the implementation of options made available by the larger context of culture (and subculture), by a universe of discourse inhabited by 'stirrers', by the communicative events set, and by the rhetorical purposes pursued. Let us now sample how this focus on the 'human', not on the 'commodity', pans out in the work of visionaries like Sacks. This may then be compared with how core science deals with this particular semiotics, set of intentions and register configurations. Texts are presented sentence-by-sentence for easier readability:

Sample 3

Excerpt from medical-novelist Oliver Sacks

Dr P. was a musician of distinction, well-known for many years as a singer, and then, at the local school of Music, as a teacher.

It was here, in relation to his students, that certain strange problems were first observed.

Sometimes a student would present himself, and Dr P. would not recognize him; or, specifically, would not recognize his face.

The moment the student spoke, he would be recognized by his voice.

Such incidents multiplied, causing embarrassment, perplexity, fear—and, sometimes, comedy. For not only did Dr P. increasingly fail to see faces, but he saw faces when there were no faces to see.

At first these odd mistakes were laughed off as jokes, not least by Dr P. himself.

Had he not always had a quirky sense of humor, and been given to Zen-like paradoxes and jests?

Sample 4

Excerpt from core scientist Kertesz

The nature of frequent confabulatory responses often from confusions, also points to perceptual clues being misinterpreted.

This is in agreement with Geschwind's (1965) interpretation that confabulation may represent a response from the disconnected speech area to incomplete information.

Perception, in fact, seems to take place but it is disconnected (not passive) from visual memory by an associative defect.

This patient had a severe and persistent amnestic syndrome, an often observed phenomenon with visual agnosia (Benson et al. 1974, Lhermite and Beauvois 1973).

The Supremacy of Discourse

It has been found useful from an applied-linguistic perspective to distinguish between two basic kinds of 'discourse analysis', emanating from two different senses of the term 'discourse' itself (Candlin's preface to Coulthard 1985). The first of these is concerned with the way texts are 'put together' in terms of product and form, sequential relationships, intersentential structure and organization and mapping. The second sense of discourse is that which concerns the way texts 'hang together' in terms of negotiative procedures, interpretation of sequence and structure and the social relationships emanating from interaction. But for the dichotomy 'mapping' vs 'negotiation' to be usable, we have to be fairly flexible in adapting the distinction to our purposes. We may usefully opt for the latter, more negotiative, interpretive, procedural sense of 'discourse' in accounting for what we are calling 'discourse' proper (attitudinal expression), reserving the former organizational and mapping sense for the unit 'text' the way we have defined the term (home to rhetorical purpose), with 'genre' perhaps occupying a place in between these two macro-units (i.e. possessing an enabling textual function, and facilitating discourse to materialize).

It is, however, important to note that, within this three-way distinction (which we have already discussed under 'the semiotic triad discourse–genre–text'), discourse may be accorded supremacy. It may be seen as the institutional-communicative framework within which both genre and text exercise an 'enabling' function as vehicles of communication and carriers of meaning. For example, by employing the Letter to the Editor as a genre and the rebuttal as a counter-argumentative text strategy, one could conceivably engage in any of a number of discursive practices (e.g. express racism, camouflage real intentions whatever these happen to be). The general argument underlying this particular scheme of language use is that, while awareness of the conventions governing the appropriate use of this or that genre or text format is essential, it is awareness of what the discourse implies that ultimately constitutes optimal appreciation of text meaning, of how ideology is served and what kind of power relations are at work.

Analytical vs Hortatory: A Framework for Analysis

Analytical or hortatory values are thus discoursal values which various genres and texts take on and utilize in pursuing a variety of communicative aims and rhetorical purposes. Put differently, available to users of analytical or hortatory discourse is a range of text types and genres. Some of these would obviously be more suitable than others for this or that analytical or hortatory purpose. By the same token, certain discourses, texts and genres would be more commonly utilized by certain groups of text users and not others. However, the demarcation lines are often fuzzy and there are no hard and fast rules for resource sharing in this area of socio-textual practice, which in a sense accounts for the inherently seamless nature of discourse in general.

In this final part of the chapter, we shall propose a scheme for analysing hortatory-argumentative and analytical-expository texts, with the aim of arriving at a comprehensive list of features that can be used as assessment criteria in any future analysis. The various features of analyticalness and hortatoriness have already been highlighted in the discussion of the parallel samples from English cited above (Samples 1–4). Before we commence, let us remind ourselves of the working thesis regarding the hortatory discourses chosen above: Australia should stop killing kangaroos, or patients in Sacks's kind of world always enjoy an -*er* status (as opposed an -*ed* status). A working thesis of the analytical discourse presented, on the other hand, would be something like: Canada is harvesting seal pups in a responsible way, and what matters in science is the 'process' and not 'who does what to whom'.

Underpinning the following analysis is the hypothesis we have advanced several times so far, namely that those we are here calling 'resolvers' favour analytical exposition, whereas so-called 'stirrers' prefer hortatory argumentation. Resolvers wish to appear rational and, while seeking a compromise, the thrust of their argument seems constantly to point in the direction of the status quo, actual or virtual: the way power is shared is simply a fact of life, with some of us more equal than others. Stirrers, on the other hand, seek to stir people's emotions, persuading them to question the way things are.

Overall, we will see that producers of hortatory discourse are more involved and committed. The discourse is personal and is about people and their feelings and attitudes. Producers of analytical discourse, on the other hand, are more detached. The discourse is impersonal, dealing with facts and figures or the way the world is according to the experts.

To pin down these generalizations analytically, we will adopt a text analysis framework which owes its impetus to the discourse analysis conducted by Martin (e.g. 1985, 2002), and to the genre analysis conducted by Francis and Kramer-Dahl (1992). This is an eclectic attempt on our part to examine actual language use in the discourse on the environment, and within a genre developed by visionaries like Oliver Sacks. Martin's analytical vs hortatory (and resolvers vs stirrers), and Francis and Kramer-Dahl's revisiting ideational, interpersonal and textual meanings, are presented here in terms familiar to us by now, namely text, discourse and genre, and the attendant lexico-grammar.

Ideational Resource Analysis

Passivization

When 'agency' is manipulated, text users (receivers and producers alike) register how experience, both of the outside world and of the inner world of consciousness, is encoded. As indicated above, Dr P. (Oliver Sacks's patient) assumes an *-er* role in the majority of the processes in which he participates (e.g. *He took the initiative to consult ... He came to me ... He was a musician of distinction*). But in considering the performance of how patients are reported by a core scientist-physician, we will be struck by the *-ed* role which pervades the discourse (e.g. *she was institutionalized, she was discovered to have, she was considered bright by her family*).

Nominalization

In this area of the lexico-grammar, a phenomenon to note is how processes are encoded as 'nouns' rather than 'verbs'. The relations encoded are thus typically static (not 'dynamic' as they would be if expressed through verbs), timeless (not human and provisional as they would be through verbs). What is involved here is an emphasis not on processes, but on objects stripped of humanity (which shows an obsession with the scientific method, as in *her recall of digits ... Her memory for digits ...*). This may be compared with how Sacks goes about his textual business in this area of language use, how he tends to encode his patient's reactions more dynamically (e.g. *he could remember, he remembered*).

Interpersonal Resource Analysis

Mood

This level of macro-functional activity is concerned with the interaction between the writer of the text and the intended audience. So the sentence would be cast as a statement (constative) or as an originative (performative) utterance. Examples: an imperative (*Consider, for example*), an interrogative (*What precisely is happening here?*). This is, of course, all bound up with how opting for 'statements' promotes detachment, whereas originative utterances invariably signal involvement. Francis and Kramer-Dahl in their study of this particular text manifestation find that in core-scientist linguistic output, only two clauses happened to be 'non-declarative' and projected in 'direct speech' in any way. This kind of text sets itself the task of merely imparting information. It is at variance with the kind of text writers like Sacks would produce: of 662 clauses, 65 (10%) are non-declarative. Of these, 54 are 'interrogative' and the remainder 'imperative' and 'exclamative'.

Modality

Modality, another crucial aspect of interpersonal meaning, manifests itself through such expressions as evaluative epithets, intensifiers, connotative meanings, parallel arrangements. Francis and Kramer-Dahl once again report that core-scientist analyticalness would find as more conducive so-called 'usuality' expressions (e.g. *often, frequently, usually*). Sacks, on the other hand, uses language with a mission and a promise for a new perspective, hence the spareseness of modulation, and, where modality is selected, it is extreme (*always, never, precisely, of course*). In short, there is uncertainty everywhere in Sacks.

The Textual Meta-Function Analysis

This taps meaning resources from the other meta-functions and employs them as the backdrop against which the text is set and presented. The presentation may be ordered as **theme/rheme**, focused as given/new or identified as known/unknown. One variable that may be distinguished here is that related to the typical choice of theme: Will it be human or otherwise, for example. Core-scientist texts are likely to be dominated by 'patient' as theme (95, eleven of which are thematized as passive subject, fourteen in 'could not' processes, thirteen in negatively marked processes like 'forgetting'). Compare this with Sacks's typical preference: patient as theme numbers 153 (that is, as Francis and Kramer-Dahl succinctly put it, Dr P.—Sacks's patient—is never asked or observed but is always depicted in positive activities).

Themes other than the patient, on the other hand, display the following areas of comparison and contrast: In Sacks, *I, you, we* account for 85 (17%) of total themes. This is a remarkable finding which may be strikingly compared with one *we,* one *you,* in core-science writing. Sacks is about involvement and concern which he wishes to share with the reader, not rigorous objectivity that is detached and dispassionate.

Another area worth noting on the textual plane is to do with the use of nominalized and abstract themes. Francis and Kramer-Dahl identify a scale from more active *-ing,* through derived and underived verbal nouns, to abstractions. Core science has 65% of themes as nominalized abstractions (*the relative uniformity of success in the identification is ...*). Half of these (17% of the text) are problems, failures, difficulties and disturbances. Note that here Sacks has only 27% of these, only eight of which are deficits.

As for Argumentativeness of Theme, Sacks tends to use marked, persuasive thematic structures (*what had been funny was tragic ...*). Marked themes also serve as boundary markers to better orientate the reader (*And so, as a result of this referral, Dr P. came to me*). Interestingly, core science is characterized by total absence of such a level of markedness: Boundaries are never signalled by marked themes.

To Conclude

As this kind of analysis comes to a close, a number of questions not addressed in sufficient detail will now be raised for future analyses:

- Passivization is one way of avoiding reference to people, thus suppressing true agency. But the passive is also used to distract us from getting into the 'active' mode of some processes. The question to ask here is simply: How often is the passive used, and with what kind of function?
- As for so-called experiential metaphor and the issue of congruence, the question to ask is: are actions expressed by nouns or by verbs? What kind of incongruent nominalization is used in place of verbs to realize actions: Is it action put into modifier of a nominalized noun (e.g. *sealing operation*)? Is it a nominalized form of a verb (*statement*)? Or is it simply realizing the action as a noun (*the seal hunt*)?
- Congruent references focus on a process, say, 'killing'. Incongruent references superficially draw our attention to the 'facts'; in essence, however, they treat the process as a kind of thing, which has the effect of subduing the more unpalatable aspects of a problem process. In referring to an issue that is particularly salient in the text (say 'the killing of seals or kangaroos'), is the reference done congruently (i.e. directly as a process—*the level of killing*) or incongruently (i.e. indirectly—*killing techniques*)?
- As for verbs of perceiving, feeling, thinking and saying, this variable may be used to indicate whether the text is interested in processes that go on in the world or in people's heads. How often does the verbal element in the text refer to *perceiving, feeling, thinking* or *saying*? In using any of these verbal processes (and particularly in the case of 'saying'), who is the doer (who is doing the talking), is it an individual or a report, for example? Alternatively, is what is being described an individual or the way things are?
- Expressing attitudes. Is the text 'expressive', stirring the reader through the use of strongly attitudinal vocabulary, metaphors, etc.? Who is the target of such strong feelings? Is irony or sarcasm in evidence, and who is being ridiculed? Is emotive language used and who or what is the focus?
- Statement, suggestions, questions. The type of 'mood' used is indicative of whether the text is more people-oriented, active and interactive, talking and involving the reader, or simply informative, talking at the reader. That is, the type of mood helps establish the writer–reader relationship either as a more participatory one or a more impersonal, information-oriented one.

What is the ratio of 'statements' to either 'suggestions' or 'questions'? Do the pronouns 'we' and 'our' refer to the writer and editors or to these and readers as well? Regarding questions, what is the frequency of rhetorical questions, and are they of the reader-involving or the information-giving type?

- Modality: Are modal meanings such as 'necessity' used in a personal or an impersonal way (*it is necessary to recognize* vs *you must recognize*). The impersonal way is felt to be more objective, but it does not make explicit who must act, the writer or the reader.
- Intensification. What intensification devices (e.g. parallelism, repetition, typographical conventions such as scare quotes and bold face) are in use and how frequently?
- How often does the text refer to people or to individuals by name, not simply organizations or people as professional experts (observers, veterinary pathologists, etc.)?
- Is first person, second person or third person used, and what are the implications?
- First position in the clause is important in languages like English because it signals what a sentence is about, with the entity being referred to inevitably becoming more focal. How often is the theme used to refer to people? If this is not the case, what is the thematic reference to?
- Regarding the lexical density of theme, differences here generally reflect a text's degree of 'informativeness' or level of technicality. How high is the lexical density per clause? In particular, how high is the lexical density of the theme?
- There is another issue here, related to so-called grammatical metaphor. This involves the substitution of one grammatical class or structure for another, often resulting in a more compressed expression (Halliday 1985). For example, *the fifth day saw them at the summit*, compared with *on the fifth day they arrived at the summit*. How frequently is grammatical metaphor used and for what purposes?

8 On Purpose

Now that text type has been approached from a variety of perspectives, classical and modern, Arab and Western, the notion of 'purpose' seems to have acquired such a diversity of meanings that a pause to consider the term closely is certainly in order. In this chapter, the notion of purpose in translation is approached from three different vantage points: rhetorical, functional and translational. *Rhetorical purpose* is self-explanatory, and is the sense with which we have been working so far. Similarly, **functional** purpose is a *linguistic* notion that is by now familiar from the kind of communicative, pragmatic and semiotic analyses conducted throughout up to this point.

It is the translational angle, however, that may require a little explanation in this overview. *Translational purpose* is seen in terms of the purpose of *the translation* as determined by the 'commission' (i.e. the *skopos*, externally imposed), or the purpose of *translation* as a general strategy (i.e. usually self-imposed or culturally normative). This latter, 'strategy', sense is closely bound up with *the ideology of translation* (what one holds valid by conviction or what the culture has sanctioned as the norm, e.g. that a translator is a communicator). This is distinguished from *the translation of ideology* as discourse. The latter involves dealing with *discursive practices*, defined in textual terms as those that convey *attitude* or *perspective* and thus project a *stance* towards areas of socio-cultural reality such as race or gender. This is underpinned by the notion of Culture, taken here with a capital C to include not only *cultural artefacts* (kinship terms, modes of dress, etc.) but also, and perhaps more significantly, entire *textual practices* that regulate what we do with *texts*. To illustrate the notion of translation purpose and how it fits within this model of translation practice, examples will touch on a range of activities, such as written translation, interpreting and subtitling.

Purposefulness Contextually Dissected

The notion of 'purpose' in the study of translation will thus occupy us from several perspectives, all converging to underline the all-important status of 'text' in the process of translation. To start with, there is source-text (ST) *rhetorical purpose*, a notion closely bound up with register, text, genre, discourse, etc. In order to see this kind of purpose as a target text (TT) phenomenon, we need to invoke other senses of 'purpose'. We need to delve into:

- the purpose of *translation* in the abstract (i.e. translation strategy),
- the purpose of *the translation* to hand (i.e. the nature of the assignment as specified by the translation 'commission', etc.),
- the purpose of *the translator* (in terms of his or her own individual interest, bias, ideology, etc.).

These different notions of purpose are seen in the light of constraints emanating from at least three senses of 'context':

- context of situation (e.g. register),
- context of culture (e.g. text, genre, discourse),
- context of utilization (e.g. socio-cultural setting).

It is worth noting that context of utilization is becoming increasingly more important for the translation practitioner. It involves purposes entailed not so much by the ST or the TT or the translator as by:

- the 'professional setting' in which the act of translating takes place (e.g. court interpreting, doctor–patient interpreting), and
- the nature of the particular 'skill' involved in doing a translation (i.e. interpreting seen in contradistinction to translating).

Schematically, then, the typology of 'context' and 'purpose' may be set out as in Figure 8.1.

FOCUS ON:	
Source-text purpose	Target text function
Context of situation (e.g. Field)	Purpose of translation (e.g. documentary)
Context of culture (e.g. societal institutions)	Purpose of the translation (e.g. TV voice-over)
Context of utilization (e.g. subtitling)	Purpose of the translator (e.g. ideology)

Figure 8.1 A typology of context and purpose

Rhetorical Purpose

To appreciate fully the notion of 'rhetorical purpose', which we identify closely with the source text and the goals of the text producer, we need a comprehensive model of 'textuality'. This is the quality of 'texthood' which sequences of linguistic elements acquire as they become functional and turn into communicative occurrences, not a mere concatenation of words or sentences. The 'textual' turn in translation studies, heralded by pioneer text linguists and translation theorists such as Beaugrande (1978), has thus focused on the various ways in which texts or parts of a text relate to context in this way, and on the implications of these textual interrelationships for the work of the translator (Hatim and Mason 1990).

In this framework, it is established that the 'sentence' or elements below ('words', etc.) cannot be a legitimate unit of translation. This role can be fulfilled only by 'text in communication', with the text or elements within yielding not just one definite meaning but rather an array of possible meanings. To account for this multifaceted nature of all texts, several primarily relational standards have been identified which all actual texts must meet to acquire texthood (Beaugrande 1980).

In terms of the way texts evolve bottom-up, *cohesion* covers how units of language in use are related to each other on the surface of the text, with *coherence* catering for the conceptual relatedness of meanings at a deeper, underlying level of text organization. Top-down, on the other hand, *situationality* captures the relatedness of utterances to the situation in which they occur, while *intertextuality* attends to how whole texts (vertically) or elements within (horizontally) relate to other texts or elements within texts, in subtle and intricate ways. Within the pragmatics substratum of context, the *intentionality* of the text producer and the *acceptability* of the texts produced provide us with two basic factors regulating communicative purpose and pragmatic effect. Finally, context includes an interactive dimension, with *informativity* serving as the forum where text elements become part of overall text meaning. These elements would be presented as known vs unknown, expected vs unexpected, highlighted vs background, tedious vs interesting, etc. and always with the intention of taking the text receiver by surprise.

Text rhetorical purpose, then, is an amalgamation of different values yielded by this compliance (or contextually **motivated** non-compliance) with the various standards of textuality.

An Example

To illustrate the interaction in which language users become immersed while constructing texts as writers or speakers, or analysing texts as readers or listeners, let us conveniently take text reception as a point of departure, and let us try out a bottom-up strategy, looking at how a particular sequence of utterances may be handled by a model reader:

Sample 1

> Since the Enlightenment, science has stirred hearts and minds with its promise of a neutral and privileged viewpoint, above and beyond the rough and tumble of political life. With respect to women, however, science is not a neutral culture. Gender—both the real relations between the sexes and cultural renderings of those relations—shaped European natural history and, in particular, botany.
>
> *Scientific American* (February 1996, p. 98)

As we have noted above, the way the various linguistic elements concatenate to form a sequence that exhibits 'formal' continuity is subsumed under cohesion (Halliday and Hasan 1976). Here, a variety of conjunctive and reference relations, thematic patterns, kinds of information, lexical repetition and other lexico-grammatical choices all become part of the fabric out of which texts are made (e.g. *With respect to women, however, ...*). These features can all be found in Sample 1 above, ensuring that the various surface components are mutually connected (i.e. 'stick together') (Beaugrande and Dressler 1981).

In working through the various grammatical, lexical and logical/conceptual relationships, text users constantly refer to a number of cognitive 'schemes' or 'templates' within which to fit the emerging structure. These are scenarios, frames, schemata, etc. stored to facilitate the construction of 'text worlds' of various kinds. Here, we are well and truly in the area of coherence. The compositional plans discovered point us in the direction of 'events' in a story sequence, 'concepts' in an explanation, 'aspects' of a description or 'steps' in an argument. Sample 1, for example, is a counter-argument where a claim held by some adversary is first stated to become the backdrop against which a counter-claim by the text producer is then presented. The 'neutrality of science' is posited as a position, only to pave the way for the subsequent counter-position taken in the light of the 'prevalent bias of science', a view which is intended to hold sway in this text (e.g. ... *however, science is not a neutral culture*).

Coherence relations in turn shed light on the way various micro-intentions (conceding that science has been influential, has promised us neutrality, then countering this by arguing that women have been discriminated against, etc.), are woven together to serve a particular macro-intention (e.g. presenting a feminist perspective on how science has evolved through the centuries). Macro-intentions of this kind are recognized in terms of an 'intertextual' potential that, although on a smaller scale, is similarly exhibited at a micro-level (e.g. quoting from other texts). At a macro-level, however, we are face to face with how a text 'alludes' in the abstract to other texts, other stories, other descriptions, or indeed other counter-arguments, as is the case with Sample 1). And, of course, there will always be an element of unpredictability (i.e. informativity), which tends to be considerable in creative texts but perhaps slight, even negligible, in factual texts such as Sample 1. This is all seen within a 'situationality' that frames the interaction in terms of who is saying what to whom, where, when, how formally, how technically, etc.

Like any reader, the translator goes into this armed with an important stylistic principle with which to assess 'what one is actually given' (e.g. a fronted *Since the Enlightenment*, science has ...) in terms of 'what one might have been given but was not' (e.g. an embedded adverbial, as in 'Science has since the Enlightenment ...'). The latter option, if available, would have been deemed 'marked' in English and, to retrieve coherence, questions would be asked regarding the motivation behind its use. Such rhetorical effects (or absence of such effects) are meaningful in the work of the translator who would ideally wish to render the letter and the spirit of the source text.

The Function of the Translation

But is it reasonable to expect that all these values can or should be catered for in translation? Here, we need to bring in the target text reader (ideally represented by the translator who can visualize what it would be like to receive this text) and invoke target-language conventions (or contrastive rhetoric). To do this, we need to revisit the source text and the various standards it must meet to be a 'text' in the first place, but this time in the light of a different level of text-in-context analysis, namely 'dynamism'. From the reader's perspective, dynamism has to do with the extent to which an instance of language use happens to be expected or unexpected, interesting, engaging, creative, etc.). It is thus a textual variable (and consequently a translation phenomenon) which is not totally unconstrained. An approach to translation underpinned by such text-driven criteria as cohesion, intentionality, and so on, is bound to confront dynamic aspects of language in use such as 'defamiliarization' or 'foregrounding': the effect produced by opting for marked (i.e. expectation-defying) structures (e.g. repetition, parallelism) (Fowler 1986/1996).

In dealing with what is not familiar, it is accepted in the practice and theory of translation that, in the majority of cases, non-ordinary constructions in the source language (SL) (strange word order, emotive vocabulary, etc.) are translated by non-ordinary usage in the goal language. But is this necessarily always the case? Non-ordinariness of language use (like the process of translation itself) cannot be seen in such static terms: the 'unfamiliar' is not simply reconstructed in the TT with the forms of the ST transferred more or less intact. Rather, a process is set in motion in which some form of negotiation is undertaken to establish what precisely is intended by the ST, and then to ascertain how the target reader is to be made aware of the intricacies involved. The communicative resources of the target language (TL) may have to be stretched to accommodate an 'alien' ST feature, but this has to be always interpretable (i.e. any disturbance will be there for a reason). In other words, the target reader must always be in a position to assess and appreciate more or less fully how he or she is supposed to react to what is said in the translation (as opposed to what might have been said but was not). One way of enhancing this sense of interpretability is to exploit the target user's language and cultural experience.

To illustrate the issue of interventions on the part of the translator of the kind being called for here, and to assess whether or not they are justified (i.e. how far we can go), consider the following text sample that is a literal back-translation from Arabic. As you read, pay special attention to the elements in italics:

Sample 2a

> I was 24 years old and I was *enamoured of* gambling. The matter *like so many things in life started* with small easy things, such that one never dreams that one's whole life would change. At first we would *play for* walnuts, then we began to *play for* poultry, and then came the day when I *played for* the three calves I had. Finally, I *played for* the trees.
>
> Munif *The Trees* (1973); italics added

Here, a number of features contribute to a narrative characterized by what has come to be known as 'residual orality' (Ong 1982; Hatim 1997 'orate' text), where aspects of text constitution such as repetition become part and parcel of text meaning-making. But can this be assumed to produce a similar effect on the English target reader, or should aspects of the ST such as repetition be jettisoned or at least drastically modified, in the interest of readability, fluency, literary quality, etc. (as the published English translation did in Sample 2b below)?

Sample 2b

> I was 24 years old *and fond* of gambling. *Like so many things in* this world, *the whole thing started* in a very small way. *In such cases* you never dream that your whole life is going to change *as a result*. At first we *used to gamble with* walnuts, then we began to *play for* poultry; and then came the day when I *gambled with* the three calves I had. Finally, I *threw the trees in*.
>
> The Iraqi Cultural Centre *The Trees* (1980); elements in italics highlight what is modified by the translator)[1]

Ideology

An important factor in the kind of decision-making involved, say, in whether to preserve or to jettison repetition in Sample 2a is ideology. To avoid misconceptions surrounding the use of the term, we define ideology as a body of assumptions that reflect the beliefs and interests of an individual, a group of individuals

---

1 It is interesting to note a personal communication I have received from a professional translator colleague reading this book in manuscript form: 'I would have kept "played for". It functions as a sort of constant pivot as the stakes grow higher, as the threat of what he has to lose is ratcheted up. By keeping "played for" as a constant, it is the increase in the stakes which becomes emphasized—the author's original intent.'

or an institution (Simpson 1993). Two perspectives may be distinguished: the translation of ideology, and the ideology of translation.

The Ideology of Translation

From this perspective, to accept the decision made by the English translator who opts for jettisoning repetition in Sample 2a above is to entertain the assumption that the translator has harnessed mediation in the service of straightforward, fluent communication only and not much beyond. Source-text ideology has been neutralized, and the discursive edge taken off by a translator constrained not so much (or necessarily) by his or her own ideology, but also (and perhaps more to the point) by the requirements of an entire culture with its own large-scale ideological preferences. That is, the translator has not particularly attended to ST repetition that conveys the writer's ideology regarding such issues as 'honour', 'self-respect', and how, in the Arab mind, these are closely bound up with the concept of the 'land'. Instead, the preferences now are more target culture-oriented, and are pervaded with attitudes not only to style but to socio-cultural concepts such as 'land' and 'honour', shared not only by an entire translation tradition, but by an entire culture—the target's (Venuti 1995).

The Translation of Ideology

The facts of text as revealed by the kind of predominantly source-text analysis presented above are not sacrosanct. They can be and probably are often overridden by a number of factors to do with what we have labelled 'the ideology *of* translation' illustrated by the intervention we have just seen in the case of Sample 2b. It is, however, often difficult to separate the translator's ideological motives from those determined for him or her by an entire culture or translation tradition. Here, when it comes to individual motives, we would be talking about ideology *in* translation. This is the set of assumptions, beliefs and general socio-political and socio-cultural preferences which the text producer entertains vis-à-vis the world, and which may or may not be acceptable to the target reader. But as we suggested earlier, this is a process that is usually mediated by a translator with his or her own assumptions and beliefs to entertain. Ideally, this mediation should be least disruptive, and the target reader should be given ample opportunity to assess ST ideology without too much interference. But as we all know, this is a utopia since what happens more often than not is that we are left at the mercy of how a translator reads an ideology on our behalf.

To show the power of the word exercised by the translator that sometimes exceeds the requirements of a discourse, consider the following text samples. Elements in bold are original English, those in upper case are back-translated literally from Arabic.

Sample 3

- A **complete turnabout in political thinking**
  AN INTELLECTUAL COUP
- The 1999 report **provoked a heated controversy** among Egyptian intellectuals
  WAS IN THE EYE OF THE STORM
- The Kosovo crisis, which was portrayed as a **typical example of** ...
  A BLATENTLY GLARING MODEL
- Accusing them of **downplaying the facts**
  WILLFULLY SUPPRESSING THE FACTS
- The report further criticized **the opponents**
  THE REPORT CONDEMNED THE DISTORTERS

Context of Utilization

For the sake of the argument, let us now try to give both the translator and the target culture the benefit of the doubt and rule out even a whiff of conspiracy theory regarding an imperialist plot or onslaught on our cultural heritage, etc. Even so, translations would not be immune to undesirable interference. If the translator is not the culprit, who or what is behind the distortion, then? Sheer incompetence? It seems to be that the process of translation would still be hampered by constraints emanating from another important source—the context of utilization. Here, translators operate within parameters set by the professional setting in which the act of translation takes place (e.g. the courts), as well as by the nature of the skill in question (interpreting, etc.) Subtitling may be an ideal skill to illustrate this.

In practice, subtitling is not an easy task and, if we are to go by the kind of subtitled output we see on our screens day in, day out, the results are not always impressive. True, factors essentially to do with the skill involved conspire in shaping the textual outcome in particular ways. They tend to impose their own constraints that in the case of subtitling emanate from a range of sources:

- There will be difficulties to do with the shift in mode from source-text 'speech' (or a written transcript) to target-text 'writing'. It is difficult, for example, to preserve in the subtitled version certain features of the original message, such as non-standard dialect, style switching, emphasis.
- Subtitling is usually done within severe restrictions imposed by the medium itself. For example, there are physical constraints on available space (generally up to 33–40 keyboard spaces per line, and no more than two lines on screen). The pace of presentation is another factor that must be borne in mind by the subtitler: Subtitles can remain on screen for a maximum of seven seconds, for example.
- Another source of difficulty in subtitling relates to the need on the part of the subtitler to maximize retrievability of intended meaning. This is a challenge that arises primarily from such problems as the inability to convey source-text redundancy. Redundancy (or saying more than one normally needs) tends to give hearers more than one chance to understand the message.
- Although less stringently observed than in dubbing, the requirement that words should ideally match the visual image is nevertheless an important source of difficulty in subtitling. Coherence between the subtitled text and the moving image must always be maintained, otherwise confusion would set in and a comic effect inadvertently produced.

The Pragmatics of Sense

The preceding are real obstacles. However, the root cause of difficulty encountered in subtitling lies in a general failure to process texts adequately. By text processing we mean comprehending the ST, extracting the sense and shaping the outcome in a manner that is effective, efficient and appropriate. This brings to mind two major trends in the development of translation and interpreting theory and practice in the last 50 years or so: the incorporation of 'pragmatics' models and the formulation of a theory of 'sense'.

Deverbalization

In Translation & Interpreting Studies, an influential theory of text processing has for some time been the so-called 'theory of sense' (*théorie du sense*). A product of the ESIT (Paris School of Interpreting), the theory was put forward in the late 1960s almost exclusively as an account of what happens in conference interpreting (Seleskovitch 1968). In later years, however, the theory was extended to account for other forms of interpreting (e.g. **liaison interpreting**) and even for 'translation' of mostly non-literary texts.

Essentially, the theory of sense separates between meaning and language and suggests that what we do when interpreting is extract meaning out of linguistic expression, discard the linguistic 'shell' which envelopes it, and use the 'sense' which accrues as a basis for further reformulations in the target language.

The theory of sense thus strongly suggests that interpreting is essentially language-independent, that is, ST linguistic form is a disposable commodity that we deal with spontaneously and discard once the 'sense' is retrieved and retained. The retrieval and retention of sense are seen as a process that consists of three stages: interpretation or exegesis of the ST utterance, deverbalization and reformulation. This entails a distinction between two levels of message construction: a level of implicitness involving what the speaker (or writer) *intends to say*, and a level of explicitness involving what the speaker *actually says*. In this formulation of the deverbalization principle, sense straddles the implicit and explicit levels.

The Speech Act

The theory of sense begs several questions: deverbalize and reverbalize what exactly? Indeed, what does 'sense' consist of? To address these issues, let us now invoke pragmatics, the discipline that attends to the study of the purposes for which utterances are used (Stalnaker 1972: 380). Specifically, the foundational principle of pragmatics has been the simple fact that, while some 'sentences' do tell a story, describe a scene or state facts, others have meaning essentially by virtue of what they do and not what they describe, for example. These so-called performatives do not describe the world as true or false, but act on the world with practical consequences. When uttered in the right circumstances, the following utterance can 'open meetings':

I declare this meeting open

But the notion of performative may be less direct than this. It is this level of linguistic analysis that has given rise to the more general notion of the speech act that translators and interpreters, as well as users of language in general, find extremely helpful. For example,

Bush said that 'if Israel were to insist on ..., that would "complicate" matters'

This is a 'warning', an implicit, indeed euphemistic speech act in which ST *said* would be rendered 'warned' in Arabic.

Speech act analysis, then, somehow recasts the way performatives are distinguished from statements, and sees all utterances in terms of the dual function of 'stating' *and* 'doing things', of having a 'sense' and a 'force'. In fact, three things and not two seem to be happening simultaneously with any utterance:

(1) Utterances begin to have 'sense' or reference to specific events, persons or objects.
(2) Utterances also have functional or communicative 'force' which may override literal sense and thus relay added effects such as those associated with, say, a request, an admonition, etc.
(3) Utterances, finally, have overall effect or consequence which may or may not be of the kind conventionally associated with the linguistic expression or the functional force involved.

For example, *it is cold in here* is in a linguistic sense a statement (a 'locutionary force'). Uttered in the right circumstances, however, this statement could be construed as an imperative that could conceivably carry the instructional force of a request or an order. This is the 'illocutionary force' of the utterance. Still, the utterance in question could indeed be used simply to annoy the hearer. This is a level of the speech act known as the 'perlocutionary force' (for most authoritative accounts of 'speech acting', see classics such as Austin 1962 and Searle 1969).

The Functional Nature of Subtitling

The oft-discussed 'sense', then, is in reality multidimensional, and what we deverbalize must therefore be seen in this light—i.e. as multi-layered. There is:

(1) the 'sense' or reference to objective reality, signalled by the words and the grammar employed, and seen visibly on the surface of the text,
(2) the functional 'force' or what is achieved in and by uttering a string of words,
(3) the ultimate effect produced because of the speech act.

It is perhaps worth noting that the ultimate effect may be the same as the force conveyed, which in turn may be almost identical with the reference generated by the vocabulary and the grammar. This is when we say what we mean and mean what we say, in a direct and straightforward manner. In fact, the bulk of what we translate or interpret falls within this kind of language use.

However, effect, force and reference may diverge, sometimes drastically, and it is here that a multidimensional analysis of speech acts becomes necessary. To the three basic levels identified above, we need to recognize that utterances are linked to social activities via established routines that are sanctioned by a community of speakers, and which concern the correct sequence of events, the proper participants involved, as well as extralinguistic factors such as the feasibility of actions. Here, we would be involved in another dimension that a given utterance would take on relating to the level of the 'speech event', or the 'text'.

Thus, to reference, force and effect, we may add values yielded by other standards of textuality (which you recall had to be met for texts to be cohesive and coherent). For example, an utterance will contain:

- cohesive values and coherence signals (e.g. conjunctions which show if an utterance is an addition or a contrast to a previous utterance),
- situational markers (indicating the level of technicality, formality, etc.),
- indications of the intertextual links which an utterance has as part of a text, and which a text has in relation to other texts,
- elements of style that tend to be defamiliarizing, unexpected and interesting.

It is the cumulative effect that utterances produce within texts that we have to deverbalize, and it is these values that constitute what the *théorie du sense* generically refers to as 'sense'. Is it not a tall order to expect that the translator, let alone the subtitler or conference interpreter, render this rich array of meanings?

The kind of pressure subtitlers learn to cope with is certainly not as stressful as that common in such fairly demanding skills as simultaneous interpreting. Like translators, subtitlers can and often do work with tangible input: they can play a recording of the sound track repeatedly, they can use the official transcripts if such are available, or they can produce their own transcripts. The skill of subtitling, however, is unique, and the need to heed such pragmatic aspects of the utterance as 'force' is often overriding.

In a great deal of subtitling, not much attention is paid to the essentially functional nature of the interaction going on. Subtitling fails when merely seen as an exercise in 'translation', worse, in 'faithful' (i.e. literal) translation. The following extract from a subtitled Egyptian film is a good example of the kind of largely meaningless renderings we often get. For a clearer presentation, we include only the actual subtitles which appear on the screen, which invariably happen to be literal back-translations of the source text. To highlight the difference between what we see and what we should see, we provide a suggested version of what we think might be a more appropriate rendering (in italics).

Where the subtitling has gone wrong in this example can be identified not only in the sense, force or effect which have been erroneously reproduced, but also, and perhaps more significantly, in almost all the standards of textuality we have discussed so far: in the situationality, intentionality, intertextuality and informativity (the surprise element). These are invariably glossed over. Values from these text-in-context domains should have been heeded, alongside close attention to such features of subtitling as a context of utilization: economy, explicitness, and general transparency of form and content.

Sample 4

1. Source Text (ST):		أنا في عينيه
1. Target Text (TT):		I am in his eyes
1. Exegesis (E):		I am all he wants
1. Pragmatics-informed (PI):		*He's crazy about me*
2. ST:		ليلى! فين امال؟
2. TT:		Layla ... Where is Amal?
2. E:		Layla ... Where is Amal?
2. PI:		*Layla ... Have you seen Amal?*
3. ST:		أنا عارفة ... امال ... امال ...
3. TT:		I don't know. Amal. Amal
3. E:		Do I know? Amal ... Amal ...
3. PI:		*How should I know? Amal! Amal!*
4. ST:		كنت فين ؟
4. TT:		Where've you been?
4. E:		Where have you been?
4. PI:		*Just/Now/Well, what were you doing where you were?*
5. ST:		امينة كانت بتسألني عن جدول الأمتحانات
5. TT:		Amina asked me about exam program
5. E:		Amina asked me about the exam timetable
5. PI:		*Amina was asking about the exam dates*

To Conclude

In this chapter, with the practitioner in mind, three senses of purpose are distinguished. One is 'rhetorical' or what the text is intended to achieve macro-textually (e.g. counter-argument). The other sense is 'functional-linguistic' where elements of the lexico-grammar acquire a level of 'doing' that highlights the ideational, interpersonal and textual roles played at a micro-textual level (e.g. the passive structure). Finally, we have the 'translational' sense of purpose and here we would be dealing with ideology and discourse, whether *of* translation (e.g. domesticating Anglo-American preferences) or *in* translation (discourse critically analysed and translated). The chapter focuses on the theory of sense and applies this to the skill of subtitling, an activity seen within the remit of context of utilization. This is differentiated from the context of situation (basic register analysis) or the context of culture (applied pragmatics and semiotics).

9 The Status of the Paragraph as a Unit of Text Structure

Having dealt with the various strands of context (register, intentionality, etc.) and the manner in which these influence (and are influenced by) text-type focus, we can now move on to another aspect of the relationship between text and context—text structure. The structural organization of a text (i.e. its compositional plan) is related, on the one hand, to contextual categories such as text-type focus and the degree of text evaluativeness, and, on the other hand, to surface manifestations of cohesion serving as **cotextual** clues for underlying conceptual coherence.

The appreciation of text structure on the part of text producer and text receiver alike is one way of imposing order on how the various elements of a text concatenate to serve higher-order rhetorical purposes. In this chapter, the particular problem addressed relates to the paragraph as a unit of text organization beyond the sentence. The analysis firstly reconsiders the traditional distinction between the 'orthographic' or 'typographical' paragraph and the 'cognitive' or 'structural' paragraph, and seeks to demonstrate that it is the latter which contributes most to our perception of a text's hierarchic organization. Next, the topic-shift approach to the segmentation of discourse into structural paragraphs is considered and its shortcomings pointed out. This will lead into a discussion of text type and how this ultimately underpins our perception of 'rhetorical purpose' and the structural plan of a text.

Reading for Function

It has become clear by now that discourse context may best be seen in terms of the language user's intentionality (pragmatics), the status of the utterance as sign (semiotics), and a number of communicative factors such as subject matter and level of formality. For such contextual values to be realized in actual texts, however, a further category must be invoked—that of text-type focus. Text types are global frameworks utilized in the processing of rhetorical purposes in discourse. In what follows, this argument is further substantiated by the observation that text-type focus almost causally determines text structure and thus sets the parameters within which texts are organized as cohesive and coherent wholes.

When we first approach a text, we normally identify a series of linguistic elements (words, phrases, clauses) in the linear order in which they appear on the page (or as successive sounds in the air). However, this progression does not tell the whole story, and the sequence of the various elements is not, as is widely believed, entirely linear. Rather, the progression of the various elements is essentially hierarchic, with some elements enjoying a higher communicative status than others do. In ploughing through this hierarchy, we as text users are always conscious that each element is there to perform a particular rhetorical function. We are also conscious of the fact that each element enters into a discourse relation with other elements to perform rhetorical functions at a higher level of text organization (that of *chunk*). In turn, **chunks** (ideally of no less than two elements each) combine to serve an overall rhetorical purpose, ultimately realized by the unit text.

This 'Chinese boxes' image of the way a text is organized is apt here. Chinese boxes are a set of boxes of graduated size, each fitting inside the next larger box. This arrangement is exploited by both the critical interpreter as text receiver and the analytical composer or text producer. That is, whether we see it from the perspective of receiving a text as a finished product or that of actively engaging in the composition process, the hierarchic organization of texts is negotiated along lines that essentially group together a number of elements to make up a meaningful chunk, and a number of chunks to make up a text. Diagrammatically, this process of negotiation may be represented as in Figure 9.1.

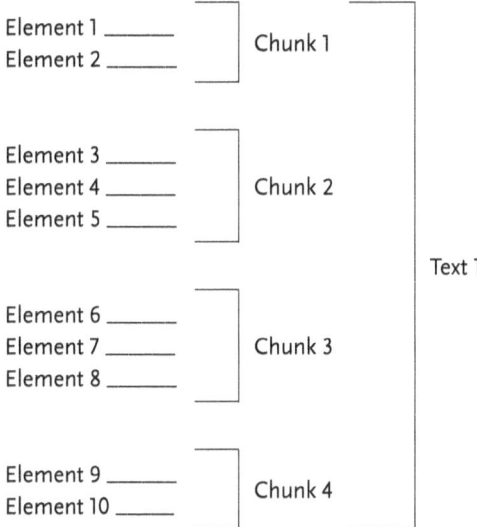

Figure 9.1 The negotiation of text structure

Text Structure: An Illustration

To illustrate the grouping of elements into chunks and, ultimately, into texts, let us first consider the following characterization of a possible context before it is transposed into text.

> Communicative **Transaction:** Locating the text within the appropriate **field of discourse** (e.g. Middle Eastern politics), 'tenor' or level of formality (semi-formal news commentary), and 'mode' or channel (the spoken-like quality of a magazine article).
>
> Pragmatic Action: Defending the premise that 'measures adopted by Israel are doing little to quash the Palestinian uprising in the West Bank'.
>
> Semiotic Interaction: Juxtaposing the **micro-sign** 'claim' and the two micro-signs 'counter-claim' and 'substantiation' ('Palestinians face a new deprivation—ban on fax. However, like other Israeli measures, this one will not work. This is because ...').
>
> Text Type: Counter-argumentation.

Let us now consider how the contextual values listed above are transformed into functional elements of texture within a given configuration of structural elements:

Element 1: Claim Cited: 'Palestinians face new deprivation'
Element 2: Enhancer: 'Israel has clamped down on the use of fax'
Element 3: Enhancer: 'Aim of ban: to stop transmission of leaflets'
Element 4: Counter-claim: 'Like other measures, this one is bound to fail'
Element 5: Substantiation as Evidence: 'Israelis tried same tactics with telephones'
Element 6: Further Substantiation: 'They gave up when Palestinians made calls from East Jerusalem'

Once pragmatic and semiotic values are properly negotiated to yield something like the meanings contained in the glosses suggested above, this sequential ordering of elements is then seen in terms of relations which obtain at a higher level of text organization, that of chunks [on this sample model of structure, a chunk may be realized by one element only]:

Chunk I: Elements 1, 2, 3: Claim Cited to be Opposed
Chunk II: Element 4: Counter-claim
Chunk III: Elements 5, 6: Substantiation

In turn, these sequences enter into other relations at an even higher level of text organization, ultimately reaching an appropriate threshold of termination and giving rise to the unit Text: Sample 1 below will be seen as a proper counter-argument.

Sample 1

Israel and the Palestinians
EXHAUSTION

Palestinians in the Israeli-occupied Gaza Strip are facing a new deprivation. Israel has decided to restrict their use of facsimile machines, in the hope of stopping the transmission of leaflets and instructions between activists in the occupied territories and the leadership of the Palestine Liberation Organization abroad.

Like many of the measures adopted by Israel since Palestinians started their uprising in December 1987, the ban on faxes looks pretty easy to circumvent.

> Israel tried to stop international telephone calls from the occupied territories early on in the Intifada, but gave up when Palestinians started making all their calls from East Jerusalem, formally part of Israel and therefore unaffected.
> *The Economist* (2 September 1989)

It is perhaps worth noting that the procedures for negotiating text structure outlined above are all part of a hypothetical model, a heuristic in search of empirical backing through further research. Nevertheless, this model of the way texts are hierarchically organized derives its basic theoretical validity from a number of studies of text structure (Sinclair and Coulthard 1975; Winter 1982; Hoey 1983; Crombie 1985; Hatim and Mason 1990). The model also represents a synthesis of insights gathered from practical experience of working with texts as text producers, receivers or translators.

The Paragraph as a Unit of Structure

> Were we to probe deeper into the linguistic nature of paragraphs, we would surely find that in certain crucial respects paragraphs are analogous to exchanges in dialogue. The paragraph is something like a vitiated dialogue worked into the body of a monologic utterance. Behind the device of partitioning speech into units, which are termed paragraphs in their written form, lie orientations toward listener or reader and calculation of the latter's possible reactions. The weaker this orientation and calculation are, the less organized, as regards paragraphs, our speech will be.
> V.N. Volosinov (1929/trans. 1973: 111)

It has long been recognized in discourse analysis that, in the segmentation of texts, an ability to identify the formal boundaries of chunks of discourse (i.e. the beginning, middle and end) is one way of lessening reliance on subjective, *a priori* specification of content (i.e. what the text is about). Formal markers of topic-shift, for example, have thus been used as a structural basis for dividing stretches of discourse. Brown and Yule (1982: 94–95) define this segmentation procedure in the following terms:

> Between two contiguous pieces of discourse that are intuitively considered to have two different 'topics', there should be a point at which the shift from one topic to the next is marked.

This approach to the analysis of written texts is extremely valuable in applied disciplines such as language teaching. One obvious strength of such a view of text organization lies in its effectiveness to distinguish between structural and orthographic paragraphs. In order to arrive at the true intentions of writers from a consideration of the way they develop their texts, we are no longer concerned merely with the identification of boundaries marked by indentations. After all, as Longacre (1979: 116) observes, orthographic paragraphs may be motivated purely by mechanical aspects of the writing process, such as 'eye appeal' or printing conventions, with little or no regard for the meanings being exchanged through texts.

From the perspective of contrastive textology in general and that of translation in particular, an awareness of the distinction between structural and orthographic paragraphs is essential. This is because, regrettably, it is the 'appearance' aspects of texts that all too often guide our search for their meaning. To illustrate this point, Sample 1 above was given to a group of postgraduate translator trainees as a translation assignment into Arabic (their mother tongue). The majority of those tested could not perceive the true development of the source text and thus did not preserve it in the target language. This was partly due to an inability to appreciate that the entire text was a single structural paragraph made up of two orthographic paragraphs. More specifically, the students taking the test were unable to make the appropriate connection between Chunk I (elements 1, 2, 3 as Claim Cited) and Chunk II (element 4, etc. as Counter-Claim). The problem is compounded by the fact that the signal of opposition (e.g. *but*, *however*), which would normally introduce Chunk II, happens to be **suppressed** in the English source text on this occasion.

The students assigned the task of translating Sample 1 committed another, more serious, error in reading comprehension. Basically, this too was related to their taking indentation as a marker of the boundary between one stretch of text and another and thus misreading the connection between them. The connection this time, however, was not between two complete orthographic paragraphs, but only between the final section of one such paragraph and the whole of the next one. That is, a new text emerged at the end of Sample 1, since, in fact, it was immediately followed—without an orthographic break—by Sample 2, cited below in bold, together with Sample 1 (repeated for context):

Sample 1

Israel and the Palestinians
EXHAUSTION

Palestinians in the Israeli-occupied Gaza Strip are facing a new deprivation. Israel has decided to restrict their use of facsimile machines, in the hope of stopping the transmission of leaflets and instructions between activists in the occupied territories and the leadership of the Palestine Liberation Organization abroad.

    Like many of the measures adopted by Israel since Palestinians started their uprising in December 1987, the ban on faxes looks pretty easy to circumvent. Israel tried to stop international telephone calls from the occupied territories early on in the Intifada, but gave up when Palestinians started making all their calls from East Jerusalem, formally part of Israel and therefore unaffected.

Sample 2 (a continuation of Sample 1)

(...) unaffected. Twenty months after it started, the Intifada is still unquashed. Even so, Israeli pressure is having an effect.

    The Palestinians have lately begun to show signs of stress, fatigue, even desperation. Until recently, Israeli officials who said it was only a matter of time before that happened were doing little more than thinking wishfully. Now some Palestinians are starting to question whether it is all worth it.

The Economist (2 September 1989)

Acting on the basis of orthographic features, the students added the meaning of the first two elements of Sample 2 to their already flawed comprehension of Sample 1. Overlooked in the process was an interesting feature of the evaluative journalistic paragraph in English, namely that the two elements concerned in fact perform a dual function: not only do they conclude the argument of Sample 1, but also initiate the argument contained in Sample 2.

In procedural terms, this functional duality could plausibly be explained in terms of the text producer initially intending to conclude a particular argument, but suddenly realizing either that the conclusion itself exhibits 'gaps' that have to be plugged by further discussion, or, as in this particular example, that the conclusion is too powerful and needs to be somewhat constrained. In either case, since to continue within the same orthographic paragraph would still be perfectly acceptable in English, it is mere orthographic considerations of 'appearance' (length, layout, etc.) that primarily motivate the decision to start a new paragraph.

Thus, from the point of view of comprehension, Sample 2 should preferably have been negotiated as an independent unit with its own counter-argumentative structure:

- Chunk I Thesis Cited to Be Opposed
- Element 1: Statement of a claim: Twenty months ...
- Chunk II Opposition
- Element 2: Counter-claim: Even so, Israeli pressure
- Chunk III Substantiation
- Element 3: Substantiator: The Palestinians have lately ...
- Element 4: Further substantiation, etc.

That is, instead of Chunk III being considered as the start of a new text (the reading which the students opted for), it should have been treated as a 'substantiator' of the 'opposition' (Element 2) to a 'cited thesis' (Element 1). In Arabic, this requires the use of a special substantiation signal (the particle *fa*), but not necessarily the start of a new orthographic paragraph.

Topic-Shift: An Assessment

Based on the definition of topic-shift cited above (the existence of a perceptible change of topic between adjacent portions of discourse), it could be argued that the only way to approach Sample 1 would be to see it as a single topic-unit, and that the mistake committed by the students was therefore not unavoidable. But would topic-shift help to explain the mistake made in translating Sample 2? We know that there is no overt topic-shift between the end of Sample 1 and the beginning of Sample 2—which in itself is sufficient ground for the two orthographic paragraphs to be seen as a single structural unit. Nonetheless, given the way the article develops, we feel, intuitively at least, that a new text has emerged at the end of Sample 1. If this is the case, the question now becomes: How is the emergence of that text signalled?

Of course, one could suggest that a formal signal (the adverbial expression *twenty months after it started* ...) is there to indicate that there is some kind of topic-shift. Such adverbial expressions, however, are not sufficiently reliable to be used consistently as a partitioning principle. Moreover, in terms of content, topic does not really shift in moving from Sample 1 to Sample 2. What, then, are the criteria for determining that one stretch of discourse (Sample 1) has ended and another has begun?

A Text-Typological Specification of Topic-Shift

While useful as a heuristic, the concept of topic-shift seems to suffer from a number of basic shortcomings. The first is the stipulation that shifts from one topic to the next are somehow formally marked. This condition may easily be met in narration or description, but it is not always recognizable in other kinds of discourse such as argumentation. How, for example, could one classify *twenty months after* ... in Sample 2: Is it a signal of a change of direction within a single argumentative text or between two argumentative texts? Even in our present, fairly well-developed, state of knowledge of how adverbials work, the question posed by Brown and Yule (1982: 98) has not yet received a satisfactory answer. They asked:

> Do all these adverbial expressions function in the same way? After all, we would like to distinguish between adverbials which indicate a connection between one sentence and the next and those adverbials used to link a set of sentences to another set.

A second weakness of the topic-shift approach is the implicit reliance on 'content', i.e. the *a priori* nature of topic. Two portions of discourse are felt to have two different topics somehow intuitively, and only then are formal signals sought to confirm such preconceived specifications of the way a text is put together.

Going by the kind of comprehension errors discussed above, it is clear that over-reliance on orthographic paragraphing did not help the students in approaching either Sample 1 or 2. Nor apparently did over-reliance on topic-shift as defined above. With the translator in mind, it is safe to conclude that, for the category 'topic' to be useful in determining the way a text is organized structurally, it has to incorporate more precise pragmatic and semiotic specifications of the way texts are structured. In addition to uniformity of topic, and the existence of certain lexical or syntactic partitioning signals, what essentially binds chunks I and II together (Sample 1 or 2), for example, is a series of important links including those of the writer's intention to 'rebut' a cited thesis and the requirement of the sign 'rebuttal' that a claim and a counter-claim be juxtaposed.

Such a combined semiotic–pragmatic specification of context gives rise to what we have termed text-type focus. In the case of Sample 1 and Sample 2, the counter-argumentative thrust determines both structure and texture. As competent users of language, our experience with texts has taught us that once, say, a counter-argument is perceived, we must, to maintain what Wienold (1990) calls 'text constancy', search for a claim, a counter-claim, a substantiation of the counter-claim and some sort of conclusion. This method of negotiating text structure is illustrated by Sample 3. Here, despite the fact that the example consists of a single orthographic paragraph, is devoted to a single topic (as hitherto defined by proponents of the topic-shift approach) and exhibits hardly any formal partitioning signals, two texts emerge:

Sample 3

The Prime Minister who betrayed her own Government

MARGARET THATCHER will never fully recover from the resignation of the Chancellor of the Exchequer. Last night, her method of running the Government had its logical outcome: an explosion. She could not indefinitely go on treating Cabinet ministers in the way she has done for a decade without at some point suffering politically disastrous consequences. Her manner of governing has been a means of infusing the administration with energy, and of carrying through vast and in many respects admirable reforms. It did not, however, involve winning the trust of colleagues, carrying them with her, proving to them that since she had appointed them, they could count on her support. Her method, whether conscious or not, has always been to manipulate subordinates and to stab them in the back when they had outlived their usefulness.

The Independent (27 October 1989)

At the risk of oversimplifying what in reality is a complex set of reception issues, the opposition may be taken here as an analytically convenient starting point:

It did not, however, involve winning the trust of ...

Within the conventions of the counter-argumentative text type, this condemnatory statement must be seen in opposition to a statement of 'facile praise', or a 'straw-man gambit':

Her manner of governing has been a means of infusing the administration with energy ...

By our own definition of 'topic', the apparent praise stands in contrast to the preceding discourse—eminently condemnatory in vein (... *She could not indefinitely go on treating ... without suffering politically disastrous consequences*). To be more precise, the fundamental contrast is not really one of topic, but of a shift in text-type focus from a through-argument about 'natural justice' to a counter-argument about 'winning votes vs winning trust'. Thus, a single orthographic paragraph yields two distinct texts differentiated not by their themes but by topic defined as the statement of a rhetorical purpose in a text. Such a differentiation is normally carried out in terms of our knowledge of how text types evolve, which provides us with the means to determine the intention of the text producer at any given juncture in the discourse as well as the text sign employed for that purpose.

To Conclude

In this chapter, we have argued that the inability to appreciate the distinction between orthographic paragraphs and structural or conceptual paragraphs is often the root cause of serious errors of comprehension committed at the level of discourse even by the advanced language user. The topic-shift approach to the analysis of discourse structure is shown to be valuable in making us less reliant on intuition and more on the evidence of formal markers. However, as our analysis of a number of texts has shown, for the notion of topic to be usable as a tool in the partitioning of discourse, it must be supplemented by a higher-level specification of text type. This is seen as a viable pragmatic, intentionality-based, as well as a semiotic, sign-related variable.

10 Signalling Background Information in Expository Texts

In dealing with the specific issue of text types, we have so far extensively discussed the issue of culture-specific modes of argumentation and the hierarchic organization of argumentative texts. This justifies that we now turn our attention to the other basic text type—exposition—and use this opportunity to illustrate multi-level text structure and well-formedness of texture. Within exposition, the sub-type narration will feature prominently. The discussion, however, will focus on genres other than literary ones. Specifically, we will deal with 'event reviews' such as those found in news reports. The discourse involved will therefore be of the more detached, non-evaluative type, and not of the emotive, fictional variety.

Still pursuing the topic of text structure, this chapter addresses the specific problem of how sequences of elements (or 'chunks') are sometimes embedded within larger stretches of text. When such embedding occurs, the embedded chunks begin to acquire prominence or a certain 'salience'. By 'salience' we mean that the embedded chunk stands out, displaying its own somehow independent context, structure and texture, while still being a part of the master or host text's global arrangement. To reflect the independent status that the embedded sequence begins to enjoy, however, language users (particularly translators) must first perceive the shift in text-type focus, and the concomitant variation in structural organization and cohesive harmony.

Particularly in translation, the shifts taking place within one and the same stretch of text can be a source of acute difficulty and must therefore be heeded if source-text integrity is to be optimally preserved. As demonstrated in the discussion of the paragraph, the problems are compounded when working into languages such as Arabic which, to reflect contextual fluctuations of this kind, tend to mark surface formats more explicitly than English, for example.

The Structure of Exposition

Seen from a socio-cognitive perspective, text types are global frameworks for the analysis and appreciation of rhetorical purposes. As such, text types are useful grids within which texts are produced, received and examined (in terms of both structure and texture). The various compositional plans are thus envisaged in the light of a range of specifications relating to text-type focus. To illustrate the process of negotiating text structure, let us remind ourselves of the kind of compositional plan typically displayed by the text type exposition (Figure 10.1).

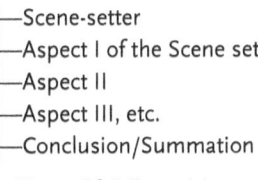

```
├─Scene-setter
├─Aspect I of the Scene set
├─Aspect II
├─Aspect III, etc.
├─Conclusion/Summation
```

Figure 10.1 Exposition

Beyond the surface sequence of words, phrases, clauses, etc. (conveniently referred to here as sentence elements), text users tend generally to negotiate higher-order relations on the basis of the rhetorical functions that a given element or a group of elements performs within a text. These functions are defined in terms of the contribution they make to the realization of the overall communicative goal or rhetorical purpose of the text (cf. Crombie 1985). As shown in earlier discussions of text type, they could be 'steps' in an argumentative plan, 'events' in a narrative, sets of **'attributes'** in a description, 'aspects' of a conceptual entity in an expository text and so on. Consider, for example, how coherence is lacking in the following text sample simply because the 'opposition' step, which is an essential ingredient of a counter-argumentative text, is not properly signalled:

Sample 1 (back-translated from Arabic)

> Travelling between the Gulf States is easy, and Gulf citizens do not need a visa to go from one Gulf state to another. And then (Ar. *thumma*), the passport is considered a proof of identity, and as such is indispensable.

The use of *and then*, instead of something like *but then*, has marred cohesion and compromised coherence in English. (For more on the ideological implications of such motivated departures from norms, see Chapters 16 and 17.)

Add-on Background Information

To illustrate the term 'rhetorical function' in relation to text structure, let us specifically consider 'background information' in expository texts. This is the kind of textual material commonly found in genres such as event reviews or news reports. The segment in italics in Sample 2 illustrates one way of presenting background information:

Sample 2

Moroccan Planning Minister Received

Morocco's Minister of Planning & Regional Development, Mr Taieb Bencheikh, visited the Arab Chamber of Commerce on 22 September 1981, for a reception in his honour. *Mr. Bencheikh, who was on his first visit to the UK, has been concerned with Moroccan economic planning for many years.*

Bulletin of the Arab–British Chamber of Commerce, November 1981

This is an example of the most basic type of background information in English: one or two elements are tagged on, normally at the end of the paragraph. Although often short and rather unimportant, this particular kind of 'background' information is nevertheless problematic when translating into languages which tend to signal function more explicitly. In English, this background function is not usually marked in any conspicuous way. But in Arabic, for example, this add-on piece of background information is frequently introduced by one of a number of conventional phrases such as *wa jadiirun bil dhikr* (lit. 'it is worth mentioning'). When translating into English, the Arabic background signal is normally dropped and the circumstantial detail is either incorporated parenthetically, or set off as a separate entity if it is of a substantial length. In fact, Sample 2 exhibits both types of add-on (the parenthesis and the complete sentence).

These are text production problems in the translation process. In reception terms, however, the background information in a text sample such as the above would be least problematic to process. As pointed out above, this kind of information is usually an extraneous, add-on sequence of elements serving a single rhetorical function which the main text happily accommodates as such. Diagrammatically, this may be represented as in Figure 10.2.

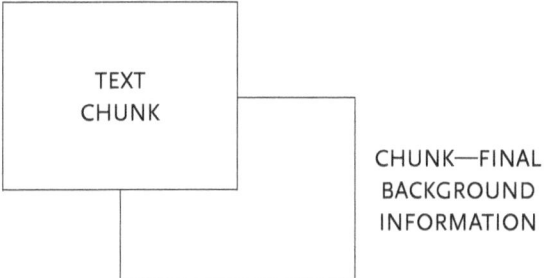

Figure 10.2 Add-on background information

Multi-Layered Background Information

Presenting background information is not always as straightforward as the add-on variety. It can be slightly more intricate and therefore more difficult to process both productively and receptively. Background information may be conveyed through a number of sentence elements or sequences of sentence elements. Each of these chunks caters for a particular aspect of background information (e.g. Background I, Background II, etc., often chronologically ordered). To illustrate the problems involved in the translation of this particular kind of background information (which we shall label 'multi-layered'), let us consider Sample 3 divided into three parts for easier reference.

Part I (3a) consists of the first six clause elements which together perform the single rhetorical function **'scene-setter'**. This is the initial chunk of an expository text reporting the macro-event of 'Greek freighter hit'.

Sample 3a

GREEK SHIP HIT

A Greek freighter was hit by Iraqi bombs on Saturday and ran aground off the Iranian port of Bandar Khomeini, a Greek shipping Ministry spokesman said. The 21 crew of the 10,000-ton Evangelia were all safe and awaiting repatriation, he added.

Part II (3b) consists of the two clause elements which immediately follow 3a and together perform a dual function: they provide us with a second aspect of the event being reported, and, at the same time, relay a useful chunk of background (Background One):

Sample 3b

Iraq said on Saturday that its aircraft sank an unidentified vessel in the Gulf.

The news report is finally concluded with Part III (3c) consisting of a further set of two clause elements which again perform the dual function of providing us with the third and final aspect of the event being reported, and relaying another useful chunk of the background (Background Two):

Sample 3c

It has declared the north-eastern sector of the Gulf a military zone and has threatened to sink any ship entering the area.

The Guardian

In presenting the text piecemeal like this, we are in effect reconstructing the reading process which we usually go through before embarking on any reworking of the text for purposes such as translation. A number of interesting points emerge from this text structure analysis. These may be seen against the background of a general point, namely that, while every single clause element individually has a role to play in shaping the overall rhetorical configuration of the text, and thereby helping us perceive the ultimate rhetorical purpose, to view the series of clause elements as enjoying equal weight, or as being equally important, is a monolithic, one-dimensional and utterly misleading approach to take (Beaugrande 1978). That is, the kind of relationship which ties Element 1 to 2 in Sample 3a (I below), for example, is different from that which ties Element 3 to Element 1 and 2 in Sample 3a, on the one hand, and to Element 1 in Sample 3b (II below), on the other hand.

Sample 3a Element 3 in relation to Elements 1 and 2 above it may be seen as ushering in background information (let us call it Background Zero). Sample 3b Element 1 seen against the backdrop of Sample 3b Element 2 and 1 would be what we may label Background One

I.
- (1) A Greek freighter was hit by Iraqi bombs on Saturday
- (2) and ran aground off the Iranian port of Bandar Khomeini,

II.
- (3) The 21 crew of the 10,000-ton *Evangelia* were all safe and awaiting repatriation (Background Zero)
- (1) Iraq said on Saturday that its aircraft sank an unidentified vessel in the Gulf. (Background One)

Two different levels within the unfolding narrative are thus involved: Sample 3a Element 3 is Background Zero, Sample 3b Element 1 is Background One. The same goes for the kind of relationships which tie the various elements of Sample 3c together and differentiate these from those of Sample 3b, providing us with Background Two. Schematically, the following sequence would be seen to function as three layers of background information:

Background Information Chinese Dolls

- The 21 crew of the 10,000-ton Evangelia were all safe and awaiting repatriation (Background Zero) (3)
- Iraq said on Saturday that its aircraft sank an unidentified vessel in the Gulf. (Background One) (2)
- It has declared the north-eastern sector of the Gulf a military zone and has threatened to sink any ship entering the area (Background Two) EVENT (1)

The situation portrayed in Sample 3c is thus different from that of Sample 3b. In 3b the rhetorical function 'background' is realized by a single element, albeit a complex one, which is attached to and can therefore be easily detached from the other adjacent elements. As pointed out above, Arabic handles the relationship by the use of the explicit background signal *wa jadiirun bil dhikr* ('it is worth mentioning'). In Sample 3, on the other hand, the background information is presented in a number of chunks, each of which is realized by a number of elements, a situation which gives rise to a status problem and makes a signal like *wa jadirun bil dhikr* possibly suitable but only for Background Zero.

This makes Sample 3 particularly difficult for the translator, who must here look for alternative signalling devices to mark Background One and Background Two. Such devices would not only cater for the background information scattered throughout, but would also mark the various levels of narration which distinguish the event related in Sample 3c from that of Sample 3b and both these events from that of Sample 3a.

What is more significant in all of this is the need both to perceive and to convey the various narrative levels outlined above. In languages such as English, mere sequencing without explicit linkage is often adequate for making distinct the various contours of texts. When a more explicative language such as Arabic is involved, however, special linking devices must be used to mark the various layers of background information and simultaneously indicate that we are operating on a particular level of narration or that we have moved on to another, more distant, narrative plane. To recap, Sample 3 Zero indicates minimal backgrounding, Sample 3 One, slightly further back, Sample 3 Two, furthest back.

There is no problem with regard to the first chunk (3a), including Background Zero, which could now optionally have *wa jadiirun bil dhikr* ('It is noteworthy') or simply left unconnected and thus remaining on the same narrative plane as the rest of chunk 1. The simple past which dominates the time-tense aspect of Sample 3a would be sufficient by itself to indicate that the narrative is progressing within what we shall call narrative Level I. However, a problem is faced in dealing with the second chunk—Sample 3b, and precisely with Background One. We need a connector which introduces this sequence as **'aspect of the scene** set' and at the same time pushes the narration back slightly from the basic level of Sample 3a, signalling in the process the emergence of narrative Level II: in Arabic, the particles *wa qad* can be used here for this purpose. Furthermore, to introduce the third chunk (Sample 3c), we need a connector that introduces another 'aspect of the scene set' and, at the same time, pushes the narration furthest back, signalling that we have moved on to narrative Level III: *wa kana ... qad* can be used here to relay this. Diagrammatically, the three levels of narration may be represented as in Figure 10.3.

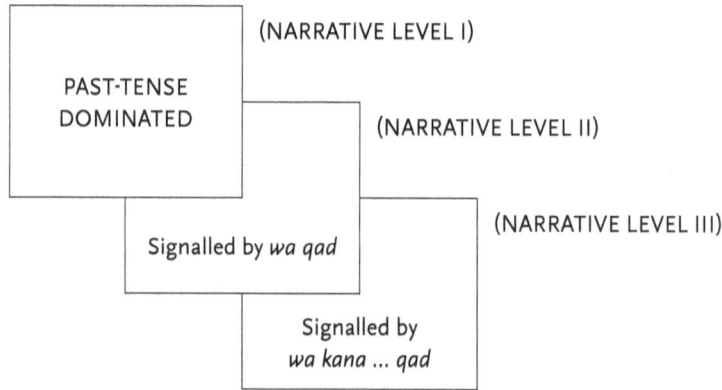

Figure 10.3 Three levels of narration

- *(Wa jadeerun bil shikr anna) (wa)* The 21 crew of the 10,000-ton Evangelia were all safe and awaiting repatriation. (Background Zero)
- *Wa qad* Iraq said on Saturday that its aircraft sank an unidentified vessel in the Gulf. (Background One)
- *Wa kana* X *qad* has declared the north-eastern sector of the Gulf a military zone and has threatened to sink any ship entering the area. (Background Two)

It is perhaps worth noting that, in dealing with a text like Sample 3 in the manner suggested above, translators should be aware that an element of evaluativeness inevitably creeps in, which shifts the genre and the discourse slightly. The shift indicates that we would no longer be dealing with a straightforward news report as a genre, or with detached reporting as discourse, but with an ideologically motivated use of language, in which the text producer is trying to apportion blame while ostensibly relaying a sequence of events.

To put this slightly differently, introducing Sample 3b as a stage 'once removed' from Sample 3a, and Sample 3c as a stage 'twice removed' from Sample 3a, pragmatically implicates someone or other for what happened to the Greek ship. Semiotically, Samples 3a, 3b and 3c thus become signs which, merely by being juxtaposed and set off from adjacent signs, begin to convey new meanings over and above those of their **propositional content**. This added 'ideological' meaning, which is expressed implicitly in English, must be made more explicit in languages such as Arabic. This highlights the need on the part of the translator to be vigilant and especially sensitive to how texture disguises all kinds of motives and how these are reflected in the compositional plans opted for, all in the service of relaying higher-level rhetorical purposes.

Embedded Background Information

The problems discussed above are by no means insignificant, and translators working into languages such as Arabic ignore them at their peril. In the texts analysed above, however, background information happened to be of a fairly straightforward nature—chunk-final (Sample 2) and text-final (Sample 3). More specifically, this information is relayed as the final rhetorical function of the 'biographical' chunk of text 2 where it is realized by a manageable sequence of elements. In Sample 3, although performing more than one rhetorical function and spread over more than one chunk, the background information also occupies final position in the text. In addition to such structural considerations, both texts similarly display sufficient cotextual clues (related to the texture of this kind of news reporting) to guide the translator and chart the routes through which the various rhetorical functions are to be negotiated with the aim of discovering the ultimate rhetorical purpose of the text.

But the hierarchical organization of texts can be far more opaque. Embedding of various kinds can often make the process of discovering the structural hierarchy of a text extremely difficult. Embedding is particularly problematical when a master or host (main) text (say, an expository event review) includes within it a subordinate element or sequence of elements which, while not different in overall function (i.e. still expository), nevertheless displays independent features of texture (tense and other devices of cohesion) which cater for a different, independent compositional plan (structural hierarchy) and serve a different, independent set of contextual instructions (text-type focus). For example, the subordinate element(s) could display a deeper, more distant level of narration (in italics) within a basic event review as in Sample 4:

Sample 4

BRIDGING THE GAP BETWEEN LOCAL VILLAGERS AND THE SPRAYING TEAMS

Extensive effort went into establishing channels of communication with the local chiefs. The consultants remained a month in the village of one chief who undertook to teach them the local dialect. *Proud of his guests, he spent many hours a day with them and invited visitors, including other chiefs and their captains, from his own and nearby villages.* The establishment of friendly relations in this way was accompanied by a free exchange of ideas about the government and the malaria eradication programme ...

WHO's Health Education: A Programme Review (1974: 59)

The difference between this form of embedding and that of Samples 2 or 3 above is that, while in 2 and 3, the rhetorical function 'background information' is realized by sentence elements which are accommodated as an add-on within one and the same text, background information in Sample 4 is relayed through elements performing more than one rhetorical function, none of which is part of the overall master text plan. In fact, the master text is resumed as though nothing has happened once the background intrusion (in italics) is out of the way. By the same token, removing the background chunk would not substantially harm the overall structural organization, nor indeed the cohesion of the text. This is primarily due to the capacity of the background information in question to be self-sufficient in both structure and texture, which enables it to acquire the status of an almost autonomous text. To appreciate the difference between the three texts, compare Figures 10.2 and 10.3 with Figure 10.4, which diagrammatically represents the relationship between main and subordinate (background) texts:

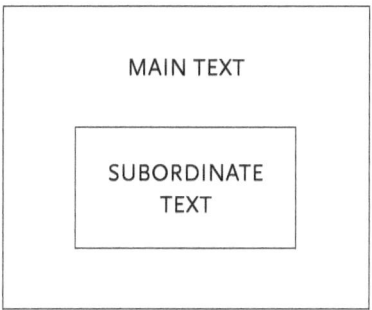

Figure 10.4 Main and subordinate texts

But it is this very autonomy which is perhaps at the root of the problems faced in working with a text like Sample 4. The texture of the English source text shows no marked differences when moving from main to subordinate text. However, the Arabic target text, for example, would have to distinguish between the two entities while not disturbing the overall patterns of cohesion. The separation is done through the use of explicit linking devices, which push the subordinate text into the background, leaving the main text very much in the foreground:

English source text	Arabic target text	Gloss
proud of his guests	kaana ya'tazzu	'had been proud'
he spent	kaana yaqDii	'would spend'
invited	kaana yad'uu	'would invite'

As the glosses above indicate, the mechanisms of marking these relationships are as available in English as they are in Arabic. In Arabic, however, this kind of explicit marking is essential and is required by the linguistic and the rhetorical conventions of the language.

Let us not forget that, while the conventional background signal *wa jadirun bil dhikr* was appropriate for Sample 2, and could conceivably be used in Sample 3, generic and discoursal constraints to do with the 'event review' as a main text and the 'personal narrative' as a subordinate text rule out the use of such a signal. Genres such as the 'personal narrative' and the evaluative discourse associated with them are conventionally distinguished from other semi-narrational types of text such as the 'news report'. Like all structural distinctions, however, this one is not without pragmatic or semiotic significance. As in the case of Sample 3, the shift from the 'main' event review to the 'subordinate' and to deeper levels of narration is motivated. The writer is inviting 'intimacy', which is sparked off by the signal 'the chief undertook to teach them the local dialect'. This kind of intentionality entails that the 'aside' is seen as a sign, self-sufficient and viable in its own right.

The appropriateness of texts is thus viewed not only in terms of extra-textual factors such as intentionality (context) which determine the way they are put together (structure and texture) but also in the light of a number of constraints, both generic and discoursal. It is only when the various pieces of the jigsaw are put in place that we can begin to talk about translations being faithful to the original.

To Conclude

In this chapter, we have examined text hierarchic organization and suggested that this is essentially determined by contextual categories such as text type. We have also suggested that text structure almost causally determines the kind of texture devices used to make texts operational as communicative occurrences. Perceiving text hierarchies in this way is shown to be an important aspect of the kind of text analysis which translators need prior to working with texts, particularly in languages with more explicit patterns of texture such as Arabic. The particular problem discussed here is a textual element or sequence of elements that is embedded within another master (host, main) text to serve a slightly different function from that of the main text. Translators into Arabic must identify the boundaries which separate one text from another and must use appropriate signals to ensure that such delimitation is made apparent to the target reader.

11 On the Interface Between Structure and Texture: The Textual Progression of Themes and Rhemes

In the previous chapters, we have gone some way towards demonstrating the relationship between text-type focus and text structure. Contextual factors such as 'monitoring' a situation in a fairly detached manner, and more involved 'managing', tend to find expression in how texts are ultimately organized in terms of both texture and structure. These two aspects of text constitution work in harmony. That is, for the compositional plan of a text to play its part in turning a sequence of separate sentences into a viable communicative occurrence that is effective, efficient and appropriate, the resources of cohesion or how text elements 'stick' together must be systematically tapped. Texture and structure thus ensure that a given sequence 'hangs together' as a cohesive and a coherent whole, as a series of 'steps' in an argument, 'events' in a narrative or 'instructions' in regulative discourse. However, whatever the text type, we would always be working towards achieving the ultimate goal of any text, namely, the realization of an overall rhetorical purpose (e.g. to narrate, to argue, to instruct).

To illustrate the role of texture in complementing the process of negotiating the structural design of a text, this chapter looks into one aspect of the interface between the two categories of cohesion and coherence—**thematic progression** in texts. This 'staging' or 'orchestration' of texts is primarily related to the choice and ordering of utterance points of departure or 'themes' within a given textual sequence. The concatenation of thematic elements in a text, we maintain, is not haphazard. On the contrary, 'thematic' elements seem to form patterns that, in highly complex ways, reflect higher-order contextual specifications such as text type and the hierarchical organization of text.

Sentence Typology in Arabic

By way of setting the scene, and to preview the kind of problems that will be addressed in the following discussion, let us briefly consider one aspect of Arabic grammatical analysis that is of particular relevance in this context. This is sentence typology.

Grammarians of Arabic, classical and modern, generally distinguish two basic sentence types. The **Nominal** or *al-jumla al-ismiyya*, where the subject precedes the predicate, e.g. *zaydun mariid* (Zayd is ill) or *zaydun inbaraa faSiiHan yudaafi'u 'anhu* (Zayd waxed eloquent in his defence), and the **Verbal** or *al-jumla al-fi3liyya*, where the predicate precedes the subject, e.g. *zaara zaydun 'amr* (literally 'visited Zayd 'Amr'). The problem confronting the student of Arabic as a native or foreign language is that accounts of the conditions under which either of these sentence types would be chosen are scarce and, when available, are plagued with vagueness. Operating within the sentence as the ultimate unit of analysis, grammarians of Arabic have plenty to say about the constitution of these types, but not much of particular significance about the conditions of use that regulate opting for this or that type. A contemporary linguist, A.F.L. Beeston, captured this air of ambivalence when he suspected that 'in literary prose the choice of a verbal sentence structure is the more favored', but immediately followed this with the caveat that 'the operative factor in the choice is still very obscure' (1970: 108).

Professionals working with texts in the general field of Arabic studies find the lack of coherent explanations of which sentence type to use, where and when, utterly frustrating. This is particularly the case when the translator or the advanced language user of Arabic is faced with the problem of having to make a choice between this or that sentence structure but finds no clear guidance. This becomes a real problem when experienced writers, translators, etc., perceive the difference only intuitively, respond to the various contextual requirements instinctively and invariably make decisions regarding the use of one or the other sentence type in a fairly ad hoc manner. For example, in translating Sample 1 and Sample 2 below, the majority in a group of postgraduate translator trainees used the Arabic Nominal and Verbal interchangeably and thus indiscriminately for the initial sentence of the two texts. When subsequently quizzed, those taking the test could not come up with a consistent explanation of why they opted for this or that structure, a situation that can only reflect the state of uncertainty surrounding this area of language use.

Sample 1

Much credit flows to the State of Israel for the vigor of the Kahan commission's enquiry and the rigour of its conclusions. There is not another country in the Middle East (and not too many beyond) where the rulers could be subjected to questioning of such a kind, and in Lebanon, at whose citizens' hands the massacres were committed, the parallel enquiry has turned into a charade.

The credit attaches to the state, though, and not the government that at first refused to have its complicity attainted ...

A *Guardian* editorial

Sample 2

Several consequences flow from this new proposal. One is that, if we are to have a site for the trace, a movement rule cannot obliterate the site from which something is moved ... Another consequence is that ...

Brown and Miller (1992)

Theme/Rheme: Current Conceptions

In an attempt to identify the 'operative' factors that regulate the choice of the Nominal and Verbal sentence types in Arabic, we will draw heavily on the classic Prague theory of theme and rheme and, in the process, suggest that, for this theory to have any practical value, it must be modified and essentially recast in text-typological terms. However, before we propose any modifications, it may be useful to summarize current views on theme and rheme.

The organization of the sentence in terms of theme and rheme has come to be collectively known as **functional sentence perspective** (FSP). The term is used to highlight the fact that sentence elements function within a certain perspective of communicative importance. In mainstream thinking by the Prague School of Linguistics, FSP means that in English:

(1) the basic sentence structure exhibits an order in which the theme (or what the sentence is about) precedes the rheme (or what is said about the theme),

(2) the thematic elements are identified as those that present 'known' information, while rhematic elements carry 'new' information ('known' and

'new' being a function of recoverability of information from the textual or extra-textual environment),

(3) 'context-dependent' theme elements are of lesser communicative importance than 'context-independent' rheme elements.

Thus, in the English sentence *He backed away slowly*, with *backed away* functioning as a transitional element, *he* would be identified as 'theme', as 'recoverable', as 'context-dependent' and as of lesser communicative importance than *slowly* (Firbas 1975: 318).

Sentence segmentation into theme–transition–rheme and the relative importance of these elements have been discussed under what is referred to as **communicative dynamism (CD)** (Firbas, e.g. 1975). This is the quality that pushes communication forward as the text unfolds. That is, certain known, context-dependent elements contribute less to the advancement of communication than other context-independent elements occurring subsequently.

Three principles are invoked in the determination of CD:

(a) gradation of position and an ensuing rise/fall in CD (e.g. *He backed away slowly* vs *He slowly backed away*),
(b) semantic content and a concomitant rise/fall in CD (e.g. *The boy stood at the corner of the street* vs *A boy was loitering nearby*),
(c) context-(in)dependence that, irrespective of position, can exercise a (de)dynamizing effect (e.g. *the boy* vs *a boy*).

From this brief outline of basic FSP theory, it is clear that, particularly in Firbas's formulation, context is posited as a crucial determinant of CD and the way it is distributed among the elements of the sentence. Yet, complex phenomena such as context 'dependence' (or independence), and a 'dynamizing' or dedynamizing effect, are all left virtually undefined, and the rich possibilities offered by the **marked/unmarked** distinction remain largely unexplored. In terms of CD, there is thus little if anything to distinguish the initial sentence of Sample 1 from that of Sample 2. Yet, even a cursory look at the two texts would reveal significant rhetorical differences that need to be explained more adequately. There is therefore an urgent need to re-examine the basic premises of grammatical theory in this area and to define the constraints under which clauses (and elements within) are put together. Textual phenomena such as these seem to transcend surface word order, ultimately linking up with deeper underlying factors of text coherence.

These shortcomings in theme–rheme analysis may in part be ascribed to an inherently sentence-oriented approach to the analysis of texts. As we have just pointed out, FSP theorists emphasize categories such as 'communicative purpose' as fundamental determinants of context. Nevertheless, like 'context' and related categories, nowhere are such notions satisfactorily defined. Circularity shrouds statements such as the following by Firbas (1975: 318):

> In deciding context dependence or independence, the last court of appeal is the communicative purpose imposed on the utterance by the immediate communicative concern of the speaker.

The missing link in formulations of this kind seems to be the relationship between contextual categories such as the communicative purpose and other aspects of contextual pragmatics and semiotics (intentions upheld or flouted, the intertextual potential of a given utterance, etc.). Once identified, these would have to be related to the hierarchic organization of texts (structure) and, ultimately, to the various mechanisms that lend texts the quality of texthood (e.g. theme–rheme progression, cohesion). The absence of such a comprehensive framework led Palkova and Palek (1977: 212–13) to conclude that

> Very generally, it can be said that the theories of FSP are directed to the description of the sentence from the point of view of its (potential) use in a message (framed in a text or a situation) while TG [Text Grammar] aims to describe the structure of texts in all its aspects. Whereas it may be deduced from this that some of the findings of FSP are of importance for TG, it must also be noted that there is a fundamental distinction between the two approaches: from the point of view of FSP theory, the sentence is the unit of the highest order, while in TG it is principally a fundamental component in a unit differently conceived.

While the general drift of such arguments is beyond reproach, one cannot but still feel slight unease with the establishment of a binary distinction between FSP and Text Grammar. FSP is a potentially useful analytical procedure and an FSP in which text and context are properly defined can be accommodated most happily within a comprehensive model of discourse processing. Armed with this general orientation, we shall now proceed.

Thematic Progression

Many attempts have been made at formulating FSP and at further developing the original theory, ensuring that it covered as many beyond-the-sentence phenomena as possible. Most notable in this respect is the set of procedures proposed by Daneš (e.g. 1974) under the label thematic progression (TP), which he defines as follows:

> By this term we mean the choice and ordering of utterance themes, their mutual concatenation and hierarchy, as well as their relationship to hyper-themes of the superior text units (such as the paragraph, chapter ...) to the whole text, and to the situation.
>
> (Daneš 1974: 113)

For Daneš, thematic progression yields a number of patterns. First, a simple linear TP with linear thematization of rhemes:

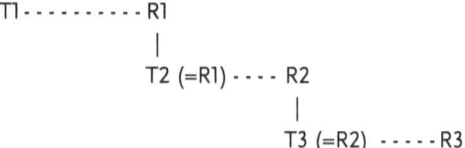

Figure 11.1 Simple linear TP

This pattern may be illustrated by the initial two sentences of Sample A above:

    S1 T1 (Much credit) >>> R1 (State of Israel)
    S2 T2 [R1] (There is not another country) >>> R2 (questioning)

Second, TP with a continuous theme:

Figure 11.2 TP with a continuous theme

The two initial sentences of Sample B above illustrate this pattern.

    S1 T1 (Several consequences) >>> R1 (proposal)
    T2 [T1] (One) >>> R2 (movement)

As will become clear in the course of the following discussion, the notion of thematic progression is a potentially useful analytic tool for unlocking texts and revealing their structure and texture. The analytical procedures suggested by Daneš, however, still suffer from the absence of any comprehensive, overall framework of text in context. That is, as it stands, the system of thematic progression is not variation-sensitive and cannot answer such questions as why Sample 1 and Sample 2, for example, display patterns 1 and 2, respectively.

Variety-Sensitive Approaches to Thematic Progression

One study which answers some of the questions raised by our critique of Firbas and Daneš is that conducted by Deyes (1978). Here, the analysis of theme and rheme is made more responsive to the way in which fluctuations in CD relate first and foremost to 'features which reflect varying contexts and situational parameters' (1978: 325). This is illustrated by focusing on the development of text structure in samples of English writing such as narration and argumentation.

Without doubt, Deyes' proposals have taken us a long way towards ridding basic FSP theories of their sentence-orientedness and introducing sensitivity to context and textual variation, elements glaringly missing in Daneš's formulation. However, the basic analytic tools used by Deyes were still informed by the standard theme/rheme conceptions current at the time. This is most evident in the treatment of 'transitional' elements where the procedures used neither reflect the degree of importance possessed by the verb as the 'fulcrum' of the clause (Halliday 1985), nor explain the basic text-typological differences engendered by factors such as rhetorical purpose. The difference in the verb element between the initial sentences of Sample 1 and Sample 2 above is a case in point. As will be made clear in the next section, *flow* in Sample 1 is a non-event and is there to support the evaluativeness of the rheme. In Sample 2, on the other hand, *flow* is very much an 'event' and is there to join forces with the theme, buttressing the unfolding narrative. Further substantiation of these and similar claims is needed, but this is our working hypothesis in a nutshell.

Towards a Text-Typological Redefinition of Theme and Rheme

In the model of text processing outlined in this book, texture is seen as providing the means of realizing in discourse a set of mutually relevant, interacting features of given register, intentions and signs. Together with an attendant text-type focus, these elements of context almost causally determine the hierarchical organization of texts or structure. Finally, texture charts the routes through which context is made more accessible and structure more transparent. For the text receiver, the negotiation of texture marks the transition from the stage of forming hypotheses about texts (e.g. the text likely to be this or that, as part of macro-processing) to the crucial stage of the step-by-step testing of hypotheses and the discovery of actual texts as meaningful units of communication (micro-processing).

In micro-processing proper, we usually begin with how the words, and even morphological elements within words, collaborate in realizing higher-order elements within the clause and beyond, and how these ultimately realize the unit 'text'. This process is constantly guided by top-down instructions (context to text) as well as bottom-up instructions (text to context). Top-down, text users generally concentrate on text-type focus, while bottom-up, users focus on the various elements of texture that contribute to the overall impression that a text coheres.

In the light of the foregoing, let us reconsider the following sentences, represented schematically in Figure 11.3. We recall, the initial sentence of Sample A sets the 'tone', whereas the initial sentence of Sample B sets the 'scene'.

1	Much	credit	flows	to	the	State	of	Israel
	i1	i2	i3	i4	i5	i6	i7	i8
			i3	i4	i5	i6	i7	i8
	i1	i2						
2	Several	consequences	flow	from	this	new	proposal	
	i1	i2	i3	i4	i5	i6	i7	
				i4	i5	i6	i7	
	i1	i2	i3					

In this representation, the letter i stands for 'item'. The figures (1,2,3 etc) indicate linear sequence. The middle line represents a hypothetical level below which items are perceived as communicatively less prominent ('thematic') and above which items are perceived as communicatively less prominent (i.e. rhematic).

Figure 11.3 The tone-setter and the scene-setter

In negotiating the texture of Sample A, micro-processing is set in motion by assigning values yielded by text-type focus to the first clause encountered (sentence 1 above). Item 1 is assigned the status 'thematic' and is thus taken to be communicatively 'least prominent'. However, and here is where we part company with mainstream FSP theory, a number of additional features manifest themselves and need to be accounted for.

(a) Given the contextual specification of the text (a rebuttal, a *Guardian* editorial, contentious discourse, etc.), and within the constraints of 'tone-setting' as part of an unfolding argument, *much* sparks off evaluativeness and joins forces with item 2 (*credit*), which is also assigned a thematic status, conveying the effect we associate with what may be described as a 'catalyst' to get the argument going, as it were.

(b) Being a 'non-doer', the thematic *much credit* searches not for an 'action' to be performed, thereby creating an 'event', but for what may be labelled a 'non-event'. This is located in an 'imagined' universe of argumentation, hypotheses, analogy, metaphor, etc. to be constructed and negotiated by both text producer and receiver as the text unfolds.

These interpretative procedures seem to point to a serious disruption of the theme–transition nexus. The item *flows* may be said to repel or be repelled by *much credit* and appears to join forces with to *the state of Israel* in what can be termed a progressive directionality (transition >>> rheme). This new alliance seems to dynamize the rheme maximally, presenting it as something that needs to be further developed lest the argument should weaken, if not fall through altogether. With this rhetorical aim in mind, and with the rhematic element having acquired sufficient communicative thrust, *flows to the State of Israel* becomes deployable as the theme of the subsequent element. In this way, communication is pushed forward and rheme-becoming-theme produces a **zigzag pattern** that reflects an element of 'turbulence' necessary for evaluative discourse to make an impact. In clause 2 of Sample A, *there is not another country* picks up the rheme of clause 1 and re-uses it as theme of clause 2.

The initial clause of Sample B (Sentence 2 above) seems to receive an entirely different treatment. Here, given the contextual specification of the text (summary review, etc.), and within the constraints of 'scene-setting' as the function of the initial utterance, the theme *several consequences* appears to defuse any potential tension between the actual text and the narrative context. Such tension would have been likely had the actual occurrence been situated within a more evaluative context (e.g. *No doubt, several consequences might flow from this formulation. However, focusing on consequences can only fudge the issue*). But, in Sample B, the process of monitoring is genuinely in evidence, upheld by the logic of the event, namely, that in a 'review', we have no trouble associating (metaphorically, of course) the action *flow* with actors such as *consequences*, and a theme–transition nexus is thus properly perceived.

The theme–transition nexus (as opposed to the transition–rheme nexus of Sample A) plays an important role in the processing of Sample B. It establishes a regressive directionality that may best be understood in terms of the narrative pull backward. It is the ability of an actor–action nexus of this kind (*Several consequences flow*) to take us back to a world of facts, happenings and assumptions valid for a familiar world already constructed—that of the narrative act. This is a world that is uniform and least turbulent, an iconicity which finds expression in a steady 'theme-staying-as-theme' progression. Unlike argumentation that relies on our **discursive competence**, exposition involves our narrative competence.

Diagrammatically, the discursive, **zigzag pattern** (Sample A), and the narrative, **uniform pattern** (Sample B) may be represented as follows:

Sample A

> Theme 1 *(Much credit)* >>> Rheme 1 *(flows to the State of Israel)*
> Theme 2 [Rheme 1] *(there is not another country)* >>> ...

Sample B

> Theme 1 *(Several consequences)* >>> Rheme 1 *(flow from this ...)*
> Theme 2 *(One ...)* >>> ...

Negotiating Texture

In the study of language in social life, it is almost a truism that interaction makes its own rules (Candlin 1976) and that these rules are usually discoverable and systematic (Stubbs 1983). Procedures for the negotiation of texture, and indeed of the various aspects of text in context, are thus necessarily a heuristic, a disciplined form of intuition. Text users embark on the negotiation process armed with a set of hypotheses about the way a given text is likely to be developed within a given context. These hypotheses are either confirmed and taken on as a basis for further hypothesis formation, or disconfirmed by the realities of the interaction and are therefore discarded.

Of course, it is a task for further research to test these interpretative procedures empirically. However, scattered bits of evidence already exist which, when pieced together, indicate that in making the claims we have so far entertained, we are certainly on the right track. For example, Deyes (1978: 323) points out that

> most notably in C [an argumentative text], the rheme of one field becomes the theme of subsequent fields.
> [NB: Insertions in square brackets are added]

Let us compare this with what Deyes has to say about 'exposition':

> The sequencing in passage B [an expository descriptive text] is much less pervasive, since rhemes tend to be thematized only in the immediately following sentence which generalizes rather than particularizes the information [a hybrid 'tone/scene-setter']. (p. 323)

On the distinction between a world 'yet to be constructed' in argumentation and a world 'already constructed' in the 'narrative' universe of exposition (progressive vs. regressive directionality, respectively), Deyes observes that:

> The communicative fields of A [an **expository narrative** text] produce the recurrent thematic question 'when?' On referring back to the opening, *Since early morning ...*, the identification of which morning is left unresolved, but only because this is an extract from a longer novel [i.e. is otherwise resolvable, which supports **backward directionality** and narrative competence]. (p. 322)

Finally, in dealing with the argumentative text in his sample, Deyes observes that

> The initial sentence still fulfills the thematic role outlined above, in that it answers 'under what circumstances the propositions are being made' [i.e. under what conditions the assertions made are to hold valid]. (p. 322)

The findings of Deyes' study thus support a number of the hypotheses with which we have been working. In particular, they lend empirical credence to two basic claims: that argumentative texts exhibit **'forward directionality'** towards a universe of discourse yet to be constructed (hence the unpredictable and therefore challenging nature of this particular text type), and that expository texts exhibit 'backward directionality' towards a universe of discourse already constructed (which is how we feel about, say, narration and its essentially familiar 'plots').

A Contrastive Slant on Thematization

The relevance of the above reformulation of theme–rheme theory, and its applicability to analysing the textual function of the Verbal and Nominal sentence types in Arabic, may be seen most convincingly in the process of translating the initial sentence of Sample 1 and that of Sample 2 above into a language whose texture tends to be more explicative than that of English. Let us first clarify what the choice involves when a language user or a translator is faced with the option of using either the Nominal or the Verbal in a language such as Arabic. These structures are not in free variation (i.e. interchangeable) as the general picture that emerged from our students' renderings in the above experiment (or the way the distinction is generally handled in day-to-day use of Arabic) would seem to suggest. Intuitively, textually competent language users would opt for the Nominal in rendering the initial sentence of Sample 1 above and for the Verbal in rendering the initial sentence of Sample 2. The reasoning behind this decision has to rely first on attested reactions of textually competent native speakers of the language. But there is also a text-linguistic explanation that relies on theme–rheme analysis of the kind proposed in the present study.

If it is correct to regard sentence 1 of Sample 2 as displaying a theme–transition nexus and a backward directionality towards the narrative act, then to ensure that this is maximally preserved, Arabic would opt for a Verbal sentence type (*wa yataratabu 'adadun min al-nataa'ij 'ala muqtaraHaatinaa haadhih*; lit. 'flow several consequences from our proposal'). In Arabic, the Verbal unequivocally assigns a thematic status to the verb and, with the subject as junctional, prevents any likelihood of a recourse to any context other than that of the narrative act's backward directionality. A text-typological commitment to an unevaluative, expository text is thus made and upheld.

In translating sentence 1 of Sample 1 into Arabic, on the other hand, the translator would be responding to a different set of contextual factors. Here, the thematic status is not assigned to an 'actor' as such, as the 'event' (if we could call it that) is not retrievable from a context already known as the narrative act would be, but from one yet to be constructed in some virtual universe of discourse which the arguer envisions. We live in a world in which not much is known about 'credits' of the 'praise' kind flowing, but we know enough about 'consequences' (as in results) flowing. The resulting forward directionality reflected in the transition–rheme nexus needs to be preserved and the Nominal structure in Arabic fulfils this role admirably (*saylun min 'ibaarati al-thanaa' yanhaalu 'alaa dawlati israa'iil*; lit. 'much credit flows to the State of Israel').

The marked status of this structure severs the theme–transition nexus and in so doing enhances the communicative thrust of the rheme by the addition of the transitional force.

To summarize, then, verbs in the Nominal format, unlike their counterparts in the Verbal format, no longer 'mean' what they 'say' they 'do'. Rather, they acquire an added text-semantic specification (**connotations**, if you like), which in the case of sentence 1 of Sample 1 runs something like: 'credit would continue to flow to the State of Israel rather undeservedly unless the statement were curtailed by the proviso that it is to the state and not to the government that credit must go'.

To Conclude

The aim of this chapter has been to demonstrate that theme–transition–rheme is a variety-sensitive variable of texture that responds to specific sets of demands made by specific text structures and by specific contextual directives. Like other aspects of texture, such as cohesion and kinds of information, for theme and rheme to provide us with useful analytic tools in dealing with texts, they must be seen as a realization of a higher-level semiology. This stratum of textual activity is no doubt seamless, fuzzy and 'nomadic', but certainly not formless. Thus, it is only templates such as text type that can provide us with the means of imposing order, controlling diversity and discovering patterns.

12 A Text-Type Solution to a Problem of Texture: Translating Cataphora

The model of text processing presented so far endorses the notion that, while contextual categories tend to be universal, linguistic realizations are usually language-specific. For example, we can 'counter-argue' in any language. Nevertheless, as a set of textual procedures, counter-arguments are realized differently in different languages. There will be variations both in the way the surface of a counter-argumentative text is made to 'stick together' (texture), and in how it is made to 'hang together' (structure), to achieve the rhetorical purpose intended.

This chapter, like the previous one, is primarily concerned with texture. The specific aim of the discussion which follows is to examine how variation in rhetorical purpose (text type), and the concomitant variation in the compositional plan (structure), play a role in the way linguistic expression is moulded to produce texts that are both cohesive and coherent. The particular aspect of texture to be focused on is **cataphora**—the use of a pro-form before a co-referring expression (e.g. 'In *his* speech, *Clinton* hinted that ...'). This is an interesting area of contrastive linguistics and one that can be particularly revealing when comparing those languages which tend to be more 'implicative' in texture, such as English, with those that tend to be more 'explicative'. Stated briefly, the specific issue addressed here relates to the translation of cataphora into languages that stylistically shun the use of this particular linguistic device (e.g. Arabic). This problem becomes particularly acute when cataphoric expression in the source language happens to be 'functional' and should therefore be somehow preserved.

Context, Structure and Texture

As has been made amply clear so far, context may be defined in terms of pragmatic notions such as intentionality and acceptability, in terms of semiotic categories like intertextuality, and, finally, in terms of the communicative transaction which frames both pragmatic 'action' and semiotic 'interaction' within the institutional parameters of 'who is speaking to whom, where, when and how'. Further, we have tried to demonstrate that the intention of a given language user to achieve rhetorical purposefulness, and thus to use a particular form of linguistic expression as a sign, within a particular communicative setting, almost causally determines text structure and texture. The text type counter-argumentation may be a good example with which to illustrate these constituents of textuality:

Sample 1

> The Arab East is a region with an unsurpassed ability to export wars and recessions. Yet, it is one whose inner workings the outside world understands only dimly. Because **their** history is interwoven with the history of Islam, and therefore sharpened five times a day by prayer, **Arabs** have a keen sense of the past. They exult in the memory of the seventh and eighth centuries, when they carried the word and the sword of Islam out of the Arabian fastness and built an empire from Persia to the Pyrenees.
>
> *The Economist* (6 February 1988); bold added

Following the statement of a claim ('The Arab East is an exporter of troubles'), the text producer of Sample 1 puts forward a mild counter-claim ('but it is a region little understood'). The grounds for this rather soft 'opposition' are then stated, and the counter-argument is somehow concluded. The semiotic interaction of these 'signs' (claim, counter-claim, substantiation, etc.) may be approached from the vantage point of intentionality (taking issue with the West's myopic view of the 'other'). Semiotics can also be defined in terms of the register membership of the text (*The Economist*'s expert in dialogue with Western policymakers). The text-type focus is very much on evaluativeness, which cumulatively determines that, for the text form 'rebuttal' to emerge as a successful token of the type 'argumentation', a particular structure format should be used: Claim–Counter-claim–Substantiation, together with appropriate texture devices that sustain cohesion and coherence (e.g. *yet, because, therefore*, which establish grammatical, as well as conceptual, continuity). It is perhaps worth noting that it is the substantiation part (*Because **their** history is interwoven ...*) that is the prime mover of rhetorical purpose in the present text and context. The use of the cataphoric construction is thus highly motivated, intended to 'foreground' the observation of where Western thinking may have gone wrong. (See Crombie 1985 and Hoey 1983 for alternative models of text structure.)

Thus, subject matter and other factors of register membership are only a minor part of the overall contextual specification. Even within the same subject area, the text producer's intentions can and often do vary. This entails having to function within different sign systems and ultimately leads to the emergence of different text types. Let us consider Sample 2 which illustrates this particular point:

Sample 2

> The Scottish Development Agency was set up in 1975 as the government's principal instrument of industrial and economic development in Scotland. As well as [having] **its** own wide-ranging powers to invest directly in new enterprise, **the Agency** provides factory space, industrial management advice and acts as a central Scottish information centre for international business ...
> Bulletin of the Arab–British Chamber of Commerce (1981); bold added

Theoretically at least, the intention of the text producer here is 'to define' an entity in a fairly detached manner: The signs used involve various aspects of a scene set in the first sentence, and, given the 'use' and 'user' normally involved in this particular kind of text, the text-type focus is on non-evaluativeness. For the text to be recognized as a successful token of the type 'exposition', it must first conform to the structure format Scene-Setter–Aspects of the Scene Set. Secondly, the text must exhibit the kind of texture that is appropriate for what we take to be a cohesive and coherent 'definition' as a text form. In Sample 2, texture patterns may be illustrated by the switch from the past tense (*was set up ...*) to the present tense, and the consistent use of the latter in relaying the various aspects of the Agency's work (*the Agency provides ...*).

Now, what could the status of the cataphoric construction in this kind of non-evaluative text and context be (in bold in Sample 2 above)? The cataphora here is largely cosmetic, a function of the convenience of the writing process to focus the reader's attention on the more noteworthy aspects of the work of the organization. On the other hand, doesn't the use of cataphora here not allow a slight element of public relations (PR) evaluativeness to creep in (e.g. advertising the Agency)? Probably, but not serious enough to justify flouting the rules of

Arabic stylistics. Or is it? These and related issues are bound up with translation *skopos* (purpose) and will occupy us shortly when we delve into the translation angle.

We recall that two basic text types are recognized within the model of text processing proposed throughout this book: involved 'counter-argumentation' and detached 'exposition'. As we have already shown, two basic structure formats are also recognizable as typical of the two types:

COUNTER-ARGUMENTATION (e.g. Rebuttal)	CONCEPTUAL EXPOSITION (e.g. Definition)
Claim	Scene-Setter
Counter-claim	Cataphoric Aspect I of Scene Set (functional or afunctional?)
Cataphoric substantiation (functional by definition)	Aspect II
Conclusion	etc.

Figure 12.1 Argumentation and exposition

Texture: Cataphora in English

To illustrate the category of texture with which the present chapter is primarily concerned, a theoretical overview of what is involved in the use of cataphora as a cohesive device might first be helpful. This is followed by a comparative statement of the way cataphoric constructions are used in the two text types, argumentation and exposition, and in the two languages, English and Arabic. With reference to Sample 1 and Sample 2 cited above, we will focus on the following examples of cataphoric use:

Sample 1 (part of substantiating the counter-argumentative 'opposition' to a 'claim'):

Because **their** history is interwoven with the history of Islam, and therefore sharpened five times a day by prayer, **Arabs** have a keen sense of the past.

Sample 2 (part of the 'first aspect' of the 'scene' described):
As well as [having] **its** own wide-ranging powers to invest directly in new enterprise, **the Agency** provides factory space.

Beaugrande and Dressler (1981: 61) define cataphora, after Halliday and Hasan (1976), as the use of the pro-form before the co-referring expression. The rhetorical rationale for the use of this mechanism is explained in the following terms:

> [In dealing with cataphora], processing would require the creation of a temporarily empty slot—a position on a hold stack ... until the required content is supplied.

The motivation for the use of such an anticipatory device, then, seems to be one of generating uncertainty and arousing the interest of the text receiver. This function of upholding stylistic informativity or unexpectedness is doubtlessly related to the notion of markedness and saliency (Prince 1981). But, like markedness, informativity seems to be closely bound up with 'text type' as a contextual category that determines the way texts actually emerge. That is, when dealing with cataphora, or indeed any other aspect of texture, receivers of different text types (argumentation, exposition, etc.) will perceive different degrees of markedness in some or other block of content. Markedness can thus range from minimal in texts that are meant to be least evaluative (detached exposition) to maximal in texts that are most evaluative (involved argumentation). Inevitably, there will always be cases in between: The use of cataphora in semi-evaluative exposition as in storytelling, for example, is bound to be somehow marked, impelling the reader to read on.

Text Type and Cataphora

The relationship between cataphora (referring forward), informativity (stylistic unexpectedness), markedness (motivated deviation from linguistic norms) and text type (rhetorical purpose) may now be illustrated from Sample 1 and Sample 2 above. In general, receivers of all texts expect that what they hear or read will be somehow structured. These text structure formats, though actually discovered only as one proceeds with the act of listening or reading, are nevertheless internalized templates cognitively stored as part of our textual competence, and usually 'cued' by all manner of signs and signals. To conform to the requirements of such global patterns and ultimately realize the overall rhetorical function of a text, sentences would singly or collectively perform various rhetorical functions, such as 'opposing a cited claim' in an argument or 'setting the scene' in an expository text.

The sequencing of sentences is only a partial representation of what actually goes on inside texts. True, what receivers first seek to discover in a text is some form of internal organization, with some elements contributing more and in a major way, some contributing less and in a minor way, to the achievement of a text's overall rhetorical purpose. As often happens in analysis, however, notions such as 'purpose' could easily be confused with 'content' and thus become misleading. A more adequate way of explaining these terms would be to view them in relation to deeper structures such as text types, macro-intentions, macro-signs.

Within an argumentative text, for example, what in 'formal' terms seems to be a minor element, making a lesser contribution to the sequential arrangement of the sentences, can within the unit 'text' take on added value such as 'making a concession', 'taking exception', 'anticipating attack' or 'trying to cover oneself by the provision of an important detail', and so on. That is, what on the surface may look like an inconsequential minor detail (say, a parenthesis) could in fact be an important 'step' in an argument. Given the primary objective of the text (for instance, to argue a point through), this becomes an important sign post which steers us in a direction most favourable to the text producer's goal.

The cataphora in Sample 1 may be taken as an example of this 'marked' (defamiliarizing, foregrounding) use of subordinate elements. The following is a representation of the various stages of the 'counter-argument', with the function of the cataphora highlighted in italics:

Claim:	'It is obvious that the Arab East is an exporter of troubles' >>>
Counter-claim:	'However, it is a region little understood' >>>
Substantiation:	'Given the prominence of Islam in the hearts and minds of all Arabs, *these people live in a past which they revere*' >>>

Figure 12.2 Cataphora in argumentation

It is safe to conclude this discussion of the counter-argumentative cataphora by suggesting that the use of this particular device here is stylistic and highly motivated, and should therefore be preserved in translation. But this would stretch and strain the stylistic resources of a target language like Arabic. Indeed, it will, but so be it. The payoff is more than worth it, in rhetorical terms. More on this shortly, in the translation discussion.

In detached exposition, on the other hand, formally minor elements actually contribute less to the overall rhetorical purpose of the text. They are genuinely subordinate elements in that they merely provide supporting details to prop up, say, the main narrative. They may well be 'making provisos', 'providing extra details', etc. but, unlike their argumentative counterparts, they are extraneous to the primary objective of the expository text. Exposition is to 'describe', 'narrate' or 'explain' in as detached a manner as possible. In including such minor elements, the text producer would thus be merely wanting to fill us in on the background, or provide an incidental detail.

The instance of cataphora in Sample 2 is an example of this unmarked (ordinary) use of subordinate elements. The following is a representation of the various stages of the 'definition', with the function of the cataphora highlighted in italics:

Scene-setter:	'The Scottish Development Agency was set up in 1975 by the government to be the principal instrument of industrial and economic development in Scotland' >>>
Detail:	'*in effect, this means having wide-ranging powers to invest directly in new enterprise*' >>>
Aspect I:	'One of the SDA's main functions is the provision of factory space'>
Aspect II:	'Another function is the provision of industrial advice' >
Aspect III:	'A third function is acting as an information centre' >

Figure 12.3 Cataphora in exposition

As we will strongly argue in the following translation aside, this kind of expository cataphora normally poses no problem and is usually ignored in target texts of a more explicative nature, that is, the use will be de-cataphorized. In the present text and context, and given the kind of publication where the text appears, an element of PR may (just may!) have to be catered for and some element of surprise may therefore have to be conveyed. But let us get into the details of the translation process first.

Cataphora in Arabic: The Translation Angle

Thus, to an arguer, cataphora would be a means of highlighting a particular detail. To achieve a variety of rhetorical purposes, a specific stretch of content is blocked, which makes what is formally minor substantively on a par with, if not slightly more prominent than, adjacent major elements. To the text producer engaging in detached exposition, on the other hand, minor elements de-emphasize both content and rhetorical value and prevent these from blocking the main flow of information. Here, the text producer attempts to make concepts less prominent; information and function are both shelved, as it were.

In Arabic, while the linguistic means of using pro-forms which point forward to a co-referring expression (i.e. cataphora) are formally available, the rhetorical norms and conventions of this language discourage the use of this mechanism to establish cohesion and coherence in the same way as it would do in English. Particularly in classical writings, grammarians of Arabic strongly advise against the use of cataphora, and classical stylisticians and rhetoricians almost categorically discourage its use. Only those uses of cataphora deemed to possess a high degree of stylistic informativity or unexpectedness (i.e. defamiliarizing, with a shock value) may be permitted, and this is only in a handful of cases, in an enormously significant work such as the inimitable Qur'an. A case in point is what is referred to in both the grammar and rhetoric of Arabic as the 'pronoun of prominence' (*Damiir al-sha'n*). But this use of cataphora is constrained by all kinds of genre and discourse factors which restrict it to the highly emotive or formal style of writing. Consider the following Qur'anic verse as an illustration:

innahu laa yaflaHu al-Zalimuun

'indeed it is that the wrong-doers never shall prosper'

At this point, it is important to raise the question of how Arabic, faced with the need to preserve functional cataphora, say, in English, and with stylistic restrictions that all but forbid the use of this linguistic device, will manage in this domain of textual activity. One way of handling English cataphoric elements in Arabic is of course to strip these of their cataphoric status by embedding them parenthetically and thus turning them into anaphoric elements. The cataphora in both Sample 1 and Sample 2 may be rendered as follows:

Sample 1 (Arabic)

aSbaHa li al-'arabi, wa li 'anna taarikhahum kaana qad iltaHama bi tariikhi al-islaam ..., Hassun murhafun bi maaDHiihim

Back-translation

The Arabs, because their history is interwoven with the history of Islam, came to develop a keen sense of their past.

Sample 2 (Arabic)

> wa taquumu al-wakaala, bi al-'idaafati ila al-SalaaHiyati al-waasi'a allati tatamata'u bihaa min Haythu al-mubaashrati bi al-mashaari'i al-jadiida, bi tawfiiri al-araaDHi li 'iqaamati al-maSani' wa taqdiimi al-mashuura

Back-translation

> The Agency, in addition to its own wide-ranging powers to invest directly in new enterprise, provides factory space and gives industrial advice ...

The solution of embedding cataphoric expression seems to be ideal in the case of translating Sample 2 into Arabic. The parenthetical anaphoric device appropriately subordinates the background information and thus leaves ample scope for a smoother progression of elements outlining the major aspects of the scene set by the 'definition' text. In Arabic, the flow of the actions *provide factory space, give industrial advice*, etc. should normally be allowed in an uninterrupted fashion, and this is precisely what happens.

One final point regarding Sample 2's PR slant in the source text, and how far the translator should be attentive to preserving it. A slight modification on the procedure suggested above would secure the added evaluativeness entailed by the PR element in question. As it stands, the sentence introducing the cataphora in Arabic is in the Verbal form (*al-jumla al-fi3liyya*):

> *wa taquumu al-wakaala, ...*
> Back literal translation: And provides the agency, ...

To allow some evaluativeness to creep in without compromising the non-cataphoric option selected, this Verbal sentence could painlessly be turned into a Nominal sentence type (*al-jumla al-ismiyya*):

> *wa al-wakaala taquumu, ...*
> Back literal translation: And the Agency provides ...

As indicated earlier, the introduction of such subtle modifications (namely the degree of evaluativeness to be allowed) is closely bound up with the *skopos* of a given translation commission. This together with the issue of 'literacy' and 'orality' of English or Arabic, is beyond the scope of the present discussion; this is to be picked up in greater detail in Chapter 16.

In dealing with Sample 1, on the other hand, the translator faces serious problems in simply adopting this particular de-cataphorizing procedure. Apart from the highly unidiomatic nature of the target rendering, the solution to embed the cataphoric element is surely a gross misrepresentation of source-text intentionality. Given its functionality in the English source text, the cataphora subdued in this way mars the general thrust of the argument and diminishes the rhetorical force of the text. For its success, the argument relies, among other things, on the sudden and emphatic 'intrusion' of the reasoning behind *because their history ...*

Thus, to preserve the role of cataphora in evaluative texts such as Sample 1 above and, at the same time, keep within the dictates of the grammar and rhetoric of the target language—Arabic—translators must seek an alternative solution. This may be illustrated by the following rendering:

Sample 1 (Arabic)

lamma kaana taariikhu al-'arabi multaHiman bi taariikhil islaami ... fa qad aSbaHa lahum Hassan murhafan bi maaDHihim

Back-translation

Because the history of the Arabs is interwoven with the history of Islam, they have developed a keen sense of their past

In this way, we manage to preserve the dynamism of the 'highlighting' function that the cataphora performs in the source text and at the same time avoid using the pro-form to refer forward. In adopting this procedure, however, the translation would still suffer, but only because the textual status of the source-text cataphoric element is not preserved: we no longer have the informativity of the element in question intact. The source text impels its readers to figure out the co-referent for *their*, but this is somehow lost in the translation.

But, is it always important or indeed possible to achieve this close degree of both formal and dynamic equivalence? The answer obviously depends on the kind of text, or the kind of context, one is dealing with, which are issues that may ultimately be settled by appealing to text type and degree of evaluativeness. These variables would provide us with reasonably rigorous criteria for deciding when to insist on equivalence of both 'what' is said and 'how' it is said. Sample 1, for example, is an argumentative text, which belongs to the genre 'article in prestigious weekly magazine', and which utilizes evaluative but balanced discourse. This makes it slightly less emotive than, say, a text that belongs to a genre such as the 'editorial in a national daily newspaper' that uses highly emotive discourse. In dealing with contexts such as the latter, a different solution to the problem of cataphoric expression would have to be found in order to preserve the added generic and discourse significance.

Preserving cataphoric use in maximally emotive contexts may be achieved by resorting to what might initially strike us as a violation of the rules of Arabic 'usage'. Nevertheless, given the specific generic and discourse considerations that distinguish one text from another even within the same text type, the use of forward-pointing pro-forms could indeed be justified. This sensitive response to the subtleties of context, however, is not the same as the willfully negligent kind of writing we sometimes find, especially in journalistic Arabic, that is heavily and uncritically influenced by Western text conventions.

The option proposed and the one which, it must be stressed, should be sparingly used, and only when generically, discoursally and textually appropriate, brings us to an area of language use that we can only allude to here. It relates to the distinction introduced by Arab rhetoricians between what we might rather freely translate as 'cohesion' (in the sense of 'usage'—*fasaha*) and what we might refer to as 'coherence' (in the sense of 'use'—*balagha*). This distinction, liberally reinterpreted here, is made in the following way in the manuals of rhetoric: What is 'cohesive' may or may not be 'coherent', but what is 'coherent' is almost always in some fashion 'cohesive'. That is, rendering English cataphoric expression in highly emotive discourse, for example, by actually making pronouns function cataphorically in Arabic, could constitute a **violation** of the rules of cohesion (usage) though not of the rules of coherence (use) which are ultimately overriding. In such contexts, coherence itself begins to have a text grammar of its own in which new standards of cohesion are set to be upheld or flouted in a motivated manner. Apparent violations, if sufficiently motivated, would be tolerated and permitted.

To Conclude

In this chapter, the function of cataphora as a device which contributes both to the cohesion and the coherence of texts is examined. In addition, the basic difference between the use of cataphora in evaluative argumentation and its use in detached exposition is discussed. Given this text-type perspective, informativity or stylistic shock value, one of the standards of textuality that is upheld by the use of cataphora, can consequently be designated as text type-sensitive:

it is maximal in texts that are more evaluative, and minimal in texts that are less evaluative. Finally, the problems faced in this respect by translators working into Arabic, a language in which almost all forms of cataphora are discouraged, are presented. The translation procedures suggested for dealing with cataphoric expression vary from 'neutral', in which the form of the cataphora is modified but its function retained, to 'fully involved', which necessitates that target-language rules of cohesion (usage) be stretched, even strained, to accommodate cataphorizing in the interest of text coherence and optimal preservation of source-text intentionality.

13 Degree of Explicitness as a Distinctive Feature of Texture

Texture, or the way texts hang together as cohesive and coherent units, has been the theme of the last two chapters. In this chapter, we continue with the discussion of texture manifestations and examine how the degree of explicitness in the linguistic realization of various contextual categories (e.g. register, emotiveness) can vary from one text type to another within and between languages. Of particular relevance to this domain of (con)textual activity is the issue of how this aspect of variation can be problematic in translating from relatively more 'implicative' languages such as English into markedly more 'explicative' languages like Arabic.

In the following discussion, a number of specific lexico-grammatical structures (e.g. the correlative subordinate clause *whether X or Y*) are analysed in terms of their English–Arabic translation equivalence across a number of text types. It is found that, while one and the same surface form (*whether X or Y*) is invariably used in both evaluative and non-evaluative (con)texts in English, there are two forms for realizing the correlative linguistic function in Arabic—one evaluative, the other non-evaluative. The task of the translator working into Arabic must therefore be to recognize and respond to text function in source languages that opt for a higher degree of implicitness. It is only in the light of such a recognition that informed decisions may be made regarding which form to use and in which context. From this perspective, notions such as **'literal'** vs **'free'** translation come to be seen not as static 'either–or' options but rather as a dynamic and variable set of strategies. In this respect, text type, once again, seems to provide an ideal framework to inform the translator's choice of expression and to which appeal is constantly made.

Texture, we recall, relates to the cohesion and coherence of utterances in texts. Furthermore, for these standards of textuality to be upheld, utterances must also have a role to play in the hierarchic organization of texts (structure). However, it is text type that is the single most important factor in determining how contextual instructions are enacted, yielding actual structures that are efficient, effective and appropriate. That is, text users (e.g. translators, interpreters, advanced language users) seem initially to react to context in terms of the text type selected. In the processing of texts, this organizing principle appears to inform the majority of decisions we take in using language across linguistic and cultural divides.

Particularly crucial for translators working into Arabic from, say, a European language such as English is an appreciation of the fact that Arabic seems to utilize a much more 'explicative' texture, a pragmatic tendency which constitutes one of the main problems of establishing adequate levels of equivalence. The often-opaque relationship between form and meaning which characterizes expression in languages such as English thus becomes an area fraught with difficulties for translators working from or into this language. The aim in the following discussion is thus to suggest a framework within which translators may be able to develop their own text strategy and make more appropriate choices.

A Grammar of Texts

On a number of occasions in previous chapters (e.g. Ch. 11), a case was made for the need in English, despite time-honoured beliefs about the structure of the clause being an invariant Subject-Verb-Object (**SVO**), to distinguish between sentences such as the following, with those elements in italics being especially noteworthy:

Sample 1

> Created by the IMF, *Special Drawing Rights are an international currency*. They can formally be used by the Fund's members for making international payments ...

Sample 2

> *Certainly tomorrow's meeting of OPEC is formally about Saudi Arabia's determination to keep prices down*. But this meeting is primarily about the future cohesion of the organization itself.

The grounds for the need to make such a distinction between two types of SVO structure, we suggest, are text-typological, with serious implications for aspects of text constitution such as 'staging', 'thematic progression' and so on. The initial sentence of Sample 1 simply 'sets the scene' for a detached expository report, while that of Sample 2 'sets the tone' for an involved argumentative rebuttal and is usually followed by the 'opposition' to the 'thesis cited'. The point worth recalling from the earlier discussion of these textual manifestations is that such distinctions can be systematically made only when text-type considerations are invoked. Furthermore, it is of paramount importance that translators working into a language such as Arabic make these distinctions and appreciate their significance in the text. A text grammar of Arabic, if such were to exist, would stipulate that one or the other of the two major clause types (the Verbal VSO or the Nominal SVO) be used, depending on what the apparently invariant English SVO pattern is pragmatically 'doing' and in which text type.

Thus, Sample 1 would be initiated in Arabic by a Verbal clause type (*jumla fi3liyya*) (one beginning with a verb, *tu'tabaru huquuq al-saHb al-khaaSa wiHdatan naqdiyyatan dawliyya* ..., lit. 'considered (V) the SDRs (S) an international currency (O)') which ushers in non-evaluative exposition and has the following text structure format:

Scene-setter > Aspect I of the scene set > Aspect II, etc.

Sample 2, on the other hand, would be initiated by a Nominal clause type (*jumla ismiyya*), one beginning with a noun, seemingly like its English counterpart surface structure (*inna ijtimaa' OPEC ghadan*, lit. 'tomorrow's OPEC meeting ... is about ...'), followed by the opposition (also in the Nominal: *illaa anna haadha al-ijtimaa'*, lit 'but this meeting ...'), ushering in evaluative counter-argumentation and displaying the following text structure format:

Thesis cited > Opposition > Substantiation

In terms of texture, the Verbal clause type which will predominate in the Arabic rendering of Sample 1 as a whole exhibits a degree of detachment compatible with the contextual specification of the source text (namely, conceptual exposition). The Nominal clause type, on the other hand, relays an element of involvement essential for the way arguments are normally put together.

In concluding the earlier argument regarding sentence types in Arabic, we must emphasize that it is not grammar alone that is involved in the production of discourse meanings, but also, and perhaps more significantly, language systems such as intonation, semantics and a host of textual considerations having to do with the cohesion and coherence of the unit text. That is, concomitant with discourse intonation and text-syntactic distinctions such as the mainly expository Verbal and the mainly argumentative Nominal construction, other text-semantic distinctions are always made and upheld by the language user. Examples of these inter-systemic phenomena at work are the two readings that the lexical item *formally* in Sample 2 above yields, depending on the text type in which it occurs, and on the position of the sentence in the text in which it occurs: *shakliyyan* (lit. 'to do with mere formalities') and not, say, *rasmiyyan* (lit. 'formally'), the latter being a rendering that would be more appropriate for expository contexts.

Thus, it is often difficult to separate between the various language systems, an issue best illustrated by the interaction between semantics, syntax and text grammar. Within this network of relationships, the lexico-grammar would be informed primarily by higher-level contextual factors.

Explicit and Implicit Texture

The various choices that translators make regarding the grammar and lexis of source and target texts, then, are closely bound up with the notion of text type and related matters. This added level of meaning is so subtle that it is often overlooked by translators and other text users. To illustrate the need on the part of the translator to be extra vigilant when switching from a literal mode to a freer one or vice versa, let us consider the following text segments drawn from two different text types:

Sample 3

> Health education is concerned not merely with the prevention of disease but with achieving balance and harmony between all the factors that affect the health of human beings, *whether biological, psychological or social*.
> World Health Forum, Vol. 5, 1984; italics added

Sample 4

> **BACKGROUND**
> **Children in Circumstances of Armed Conflict and other Disasters**
> *Whether they involve armed violence or natural phenomena*, disasters are growing both in number and in the severity of their impact. They are occurring

more frequently ... They may now directly threaten the lives, health or development of millions of children.

From a United Nations Policy Review; italics added

The particular structure selected for analysis here is genuinely lexico-grammatical, i.e. involving both grammar and lexis. It is the *whether-* correlative subordinator used to indicate 'equality of options'. A formally and substantively isomorphic structure is available in Arabic to relay a similar function:

Sample 3 (Arabic)

sawaa'un 'a biyuuluujiyyatan kaanat haadhihi al-'awaamilu am nafsiyyatan am ijtimaa'iyya

Sample 4 (Arabic)

sawaa'un 'a naajimatun 'anil 'unfil musallahi awil Zawahiril Tabi'iyyati fa 'innaal kawaaritha tashhadu ziyaadatan fi 'adadiha wa fi khuTuurati nataa'ijiha 'ala Haddin sawaa'

But failing to discriminate between the rhetorical force of the English *whether-* subordinate clause in Sample 3 and that in Sample 4 by slavishly adhering to the surface manifestations in the source text, and opting for the same surface form in Arabic when handling the two text types, is a basically flawed strategy in appreciating text function. Sample 3 is intended to be an argument in which an 'assertion' is made and then 'argued through' (a through-argument). Here, the *whether-* element occupies a prominent place in the realization of this argumentative procedure. Given the overall text strategy, it is important in this particular text to recognize that a set of alternatives is available, and that opting for either one or the other is not meant to be taken lightly (i.e. in a literal sense). In this kind of text, the text producer is seeking to convey some rhetorical effect by sensationalizing the issues involved. In text-type terms, the *whether-* structure in question here is what we shall label 'evaluative'.

The expository text in Sample 4, on the other hand, is performing an entirely different function. It is intended simply to review a series of events, starting with a 'scene-setter', and moving on to tackle the various aspects of the scene. Here, the *whether-* element is not used to juxtapose two variants of a given situation in a pointed way. As far as the overall text function is concerned, it is true that 'disasters cannot simply be just disasters' and that it is not immaterial to distinguish between those involving 'armed violence' and those involving 'natural phenomena'. However, in this type of text, the text producer is not trying to gain any rhetorical mileage out of what is and what should be an off-handed listing of alternatives. The *whether-* structure in question here is what we shall, in text-type terms, call 'non-evaluative'.

Thus, it is the degree of evaluativeness exhibited by English using the same structure but with two different functions to serve most subtly, that must somehow be reflected more explicitly in Arabic. The use or absence of the correlative is strictly governed by text-type considerations. The *whether-* structure in Arabic is appropriate only in evaluative contexts such as that of Sample 3. An alternative rendering that strips this structure of its evaluativeness, however, would have to be found in dealing with Sample 4. This would simply be opting for a bare *or-* structure:

Sample 4 (Arabic)

> *tashhadul kawaarithu al-naajimatu 'anil 'unfil musallahi awil Zawahiril tabi'iyati ziyaadatan fi 'adadihaa wa fi khuTuurati nataa'ijiha 'alaa Haddin sawaa' ...*

Back-Translation

> Disasters involving armed violence or natural phenomena are growing both in number and in the severity of their impact ...

It is interesting to note that a proper appreciation of the function of Sample 4 would entail the non-evaluative handling not only of the *whether-* structure, but also of the structure of the clause (opting for the Verbal clause type) and the cataphora (which is embedded in this text).

Handling More Opaque Structures

As far as English as a source language is concerned, then, dealing with text samples such as 3 and 4 above is problematic. Retaining the *whether-* structure indiscriminately is a problem in working into Arabic. But a more serious difficulty is when evaluativeness in English happens to be even far more implicit, and the evaluative surface form *whether-* is actually suppressed. In Arabic, this 'correlative' signal would have to be retrieved. To illustrate this textual phenomenon, let us consider Sample 5 below, and compare this with the relatively more explicit Sample 3 above:

Sample 5

> To the Arab intellectual versed in international law or the peasant whose orchards were bulldozed, there seemed no justification in Israel's maneuvers to make Jerusalem the de facto Jewish capital of Israel.
>
> From Kate Maguire's *The Israelisation of Jerusalem*

This argumentative text adopts a similar structure format to that of Sample 3: a thesis (assertion) is cited to be extensively defended. The *or-* structure cited here states such a thesis. Essentially, a set of alternatives, the marking of which is crucial for the rhetorical development of the argument, is put forward by the author. The function of *or* must thus be seen as maximally 'evaluative'. The success of the text's rhetorical strategy depends to a great extent on appreciating that 'it does not in the least matter whether the person one was talking to happened to be a peasant or a professor of political science, this feeling is shared by everyone across the board'.

Thus, while *or* can have the dual function of evaluative and non-evaluative in English, Arabic, as we have seen, reserves this particular device for the non-evaluative function only. Opting for a straightforward *or* in Arabic would thus strip the element in question of its essentially evaluative nature and therefore mar the flow of the argument as this unfolds. Here, translators must make the choice of activating a latent *whether* in the following manner:

Sample 5 (Arabic)

> *sawaa'un 'a muthaqafan dali'an fil qanun al-dawli kaan al 'arabiyu am falahan sahaqat al-jarraraat al-isra'iliyatu basatinahu, fa'innahu laa yara mubarriran ...*

Back-translation

> Whether an intellectual, well-versed in international law the Arab is or a peasant whose orchards were bulldozed by the Israelis, he sees no justification ...

The 'Literal' vs 'Free' Translation Debate

Problems like those discussed above open up the age-old debate concerning whether translation should be free or literal. Some translation theorists present these two aspects of the translation process as though they were mutually exclusive alternatives, one or the other of which is to be opted for at any one time, depending on the translator's own brand of theory or the prevailing orthodoxy. Nevertheless, as Hatim and Mason (1990) make abundantly clear, 'literalness' and 'freedom' are part and parcel of the whole process of translation-text strategy, translator decision-making, etc. It is also generally emphasized that opting for one or the other alternative must be undertaken in the light of the requirements of the type of text or part of the text being translated. That is, it would be misleading to talk about a 'literal' or a 'free' translation of, say, an entire editorial or news report. Instead, it would be more appropriate to talk of a less literal (or a freer) translation of certain parts of an editorial, or a more literal (or a less free) translation of certain parts of a news report. Text type, at both micro- and macro-levels, is thus the last court of appeal in determining what forms of expression are to be retained, shelved, modified or jettisoned altogether.

In conclusion, it may be helpful to put the explicit texture hypothesis to the test by considering the following two examples. Sample 6 is taken from an expository text, Sample 7 from an argumentative text. It is perhaps worth noting that, while in both texts *as a consequence* means 'as a result', the focus in Sample 6 is on the 'temporal' and that of Sample 7 is on the 'logical'.

Sample 6

As a consequence, a WHO Regional Seminar on School Health Education was held in Kuwait in 1966 ...

Sample 7

As a consequence, fewer people were eligible for government aid ...

An indiscriminate, literal approach to these samples would distort the true force of the utterance in context. But more seriously than these problems of 'comprehension' are the more concrete choices of 'texture' which have to be made in a language such as Arabic. The following is the translation into Arabic of Samples 6 and 7:

Sample 6 (Arabic)

wa qad 'aqadat munazamat al-sihat al-'alamiyya 'ala 'ithri dhaalik fi al-kuwait 'aama 1966 'alaaqatan diraasiya iqliimiya 'anil tarbiyat al-sihiya fi al-madaaris

Back-translation

The WHO, in the period following that, convened ...

Sample 7 (Arabic)

wa natiijatan li dhaalik, fa'ina 'adada ...

Back-translation

As a result, the number of ...

Thus, the explicative nature of texture in Arabic demands that the focus on the 'temporal' or the 'logical' be thrown into sharp relief, actually using a different wording to produce a given effect.

Regarding the issue of explicitness, one final point must be stressed, namely that 'explicitness' should not be confused with 'absence of subtlety'. In explicative languages such as Arabic, intentions can be and often are expressed as opaquely as in any of the more implicative languages. Within a given range of expressions (e.g. the numerous ways of referring to such words as 'sword', 'camel'), the choices made could themselves contain deeper levels of indirect meaning. True, by not opting for cataphora or the use of an explicit correlative construction, for example, the text producer would indeed be signalling that he or she intends to serve one rhetorical purpose and not another (say, inform and not argue). But, the text receiver would still have to look beneath this or that choice, whether lexical, syntactic, or rhetorical, for the motivation behind particular modes of expression. Take irony as a case in point. As Chapter 19 will make clear, the very explicitness of saying more than one needs (as opposed to being deliberately cryptic) could relay sarcasm in Arabic. That is, intentionality remains to be a matter open for negotiation beyond the particular specifications of a given text type. This does not in the least make having two separate expressions for two separate intentions any less or more accessible and therefore less or more subtle than having one particular form for the expression of two separate intentions.

To Conclude

In this chapter, texture is once again seen as almost causally determined by contextual specifications relating to higher-order contextual categories such as text type. Elements of both grammar and lexis are shown to yield a number of readings, only one of which is appropriate for a given text type. The problem arises when the various readings are conveyed by one and the same surface structure in the source language text (e.g. English), while various alternative formulations are available in the target language (e.g. Arabic). Decisions regarding what a given item would actually be 'doing', or which alternative form of expression is the most appropriate, all seem to be almost always regulated by the text type.

14 Emotiveness and Its Linguistic Realization in Texts

We now come to the concluding part of our discussion of texture, a subject with which we have been concerned in the last three chapters. Having tackled various devices used in making texts both cohesive and coherent (e.g. background information, cataphora, theme and rheme), we can now examine more closely how texture responds to extra-textual factors such as power and ideology. In this chapter, the specific topic addressed is emotiveness and its linguistic realization in texts.

Like all other facets of texture, the expression of emotiveness is closely bound up with semiotic constructs such as text type, genre and, perhaps most significantly, discourse. Emotiveness is first and foremost a textural phenomenon whose primary domain is the set of relationships obtaining between ideological meaning and the lexico-grammar (i.e. between form and function). In the course of discussing such interrelationships, we will briefly broach the issue of the multi-functionality and consequently the variable and hybrid nature, of all texts. The aim here is to reiterate important arguments presented in earlier chapters on cotext and texture, and to present more concrete proposals for the assessment of the degree of emotiveness generally present in evaluative language use.

The present proposals owe their main theoretical thrust both to text linguistics and to notions developed over the centuries by classical rhetoricians (both Arab and Western). As we have seen in Chapter 5 (where we introduced a contrastive-rhetorical slant to our analysis), the Arab rhetoricians' concern with text in context gave rise to what may be regarded, even by today's standards, pioneering attempts at theorizing such processes as cohesion and coherence, text and discourse, cotext and context. Of immediate relevance for our purpose here is the specific issue of the assessment by the text producer of the likely reactions of the text receiver and how this set of insights is used in motivating decisions regarding the appropriate degree of evaluativeness with which the utterance or the text is imbued.

A combination of rhetorical insights from both Arab and Western rhetorical traditions will thus yield a set of criteria that can inform decisions regarding textual appropriateness. Such an approach will enable us to describe texts not only as belonging to one of two major types (exposition and argumentation), but also as displaying various degrees of 'detachment' or 'involvement'. These subtle shifts in text function are elusive, yet highly significant elements of text meaning.

Macro- and Micro-Processing of Texts

As we have already established, the various contextual values accruing from the various domains of context combine to yield what may be termed a 'dominant contextual focus'. This is defined by Werlich (1976: 19) in the following way:

> Texts distinctively correlate with contextual factors in a communicative situation. They conventionally focus the addressee's attention only on specific factors and circumstances from the whole set of factors (e.g. the chronology of events in a narrative).

In the text-type model developed here, this 'focus' is fully recognized initially at a 'micro' level, accounting for text function element by element (i.e. clauses, sentences, etc.), and next at the level of how this correlates with context. Only when this initial stage is completed (to varying degrees of success, of course) can the various elements be seen together as establishing an orientation or a text slant towards a particular 'macro' text function. As will be argued shortly, the degree of evaluativeness displayed by this macro function can be rigorously determined on the basis of the contribution that the various elements make to the overall rhetorical purpose of the text. Consider, for example, sentence (1) below. It is a statement by the British Foreign Secretary, made just before the execution of one British national and the 15-year imprisonment of another, both accused by the Iraqis of spying. This utterance is seen to display a particular rhetorical force that we might label 'serving notice', 'warning', etc.

(1) The death and imprisonment sentences, if carried out, are bound to have a far-reaching effect on bilateral relations between the two countries.

But this pragmatic reading, which can never be definitive and may at a later stage be retained, modified or even jettisoned in the light of the unfolding textual evidence, could only be reached through a process of accumulating relevant textual and contextual information. This involves negotiating pragmatic micro-intentions within a particular social semiotics (ideational, interpersonal and textual meanings) and other domains of textual activity such as 'use' and 'user' of language. The escalation of 'serving notice' to 'warning', and even to 'threat', is perceived as complete only when sentence (1) is seen against the background provided by the preceding discourse:

(2) Our objective now is to concentrate on the immediate future, the immediate next few hours, to try to get the death sentence lifted.

Some languages would make the relationship between the various speech acts more explicit. In Arabic, for example, the initial sentence (2 above) would be introduced by the verb of saying: *SarraHa* (lit. 'he stated') and would be linked to the sentence which follows (sentence 1 above) by an explicit adversative (e.g. 'but'), together with a 'warning' verb of saying: *illa annahu hadhdhara qaa'ilan anna ...* ' (lit. 'But he warned by saying that ...').

The Multi-Functionality of Texts

Thus, for a given text to emerge and be recognized as a successful realization of a given text type, a number of elements would singly and collectively be made to function in such a way as to ensure the smooth implementation of an overall rhetorical plan or purpose. It is true that evaluativeness is an all-pervasive phenomenon in all texts and that, ultimately, no text is free from a certain amount of involvement. Yet, text hybridization, inevitable as it is, should not provide licence for an 'everything goes' attitude. Texts must ultimately be made to address a single predominant purpose, and the question becomes not 'either this or that type' but rather 'which type is predominant and which is subsidiary'. Here, the key concept is 'predominant', and text processing would be specifically aimed at discovering (a) what motivates a given pattern of predominance and (b) where, when and how texts cease to be effective, efficient and appropriate as a result of employing this or that degree of evaluativeness, detachment, etc. That is, as competent users of language, we must watch out for when, for example, news reports lapse into editorializing by becoming too involved, or editorials fail to achieve the desired goal by becoming too detached. The following, seemingly detached 'background' note (together with the highlighted phrase in scare quotes) which follows sentences (1) and (2) cited above, is surely not inserted in the news report without ulterior motives:

(3) Under the present system there is no legal appeal, though the President can commute sentences 'for humanitarian reasons'.

This shift in rhetorical purpose from involvement to detachment is rarely if ever unmotivated and must therefore be as far as possible preserved in translation. To pursue this point further, we should recall a point made in Chapter 7 that, in Arabic, 'background' notes as in sentence (3) are usually introduced by a phrase such as 'it is noteworthy that': *wa jadiirun bi al-dhikr anna* .... This signal has a dual function, depending on the degree of text emotiveness: it may either be void of evaluativeness, an empty cliché which competent translators into English, for example, normally discard, or it may be fully evaluative, as is the case in sentence (3) above.

The degree of evaluativeness admitted is usually motivated by a variety of factors surrounding the text. Functional shifts can therefore never be determined with absolute certainty. After all, interaction makes its own rules, albeit within limits that are both discoverable and describable. In this connection, we reiterate that, while hybridization is the rule rather than the exception in the design or retrieval of a given text as a token of a given type, it should not be used as an argument against text classification (cf. Emery 1991). As Hatim and Mason (1990: 148) conclude:

Hybridization, then, is a fact of life and the very fact that it exists lends credence to the notion that we do indeed perceive texts as belonging to recognizable types.

Put differently, how can deviations ever be determined if we are to deny the existence of 'norms' in the first place? With this in mind, it is to this dynamic and variable nature of texts that we shall now turn our attention. For the purpose of this analysis, two text samples are subjected to an assessment not so much of their text-type membership (they are both predominantly expository news reports), but of the degree of evaluativeness which is displayed by each of them. The two samples cover the news of a British journalist's conviction for spying in Iraq. Sample 1 is from *The Observer*, Sample 2 from *The Independent*. It may be relevant to point out that *The Observer* is the newspaper for which the journalist in question worked and which engaged in an intensive campaign to secure his release. The following are relevant extracts from both texts.

Sample 1

An *Observer* journalist, Farzad Bazoft, was yesterday sentenced to death by an Iraqi military court after being found guilty of espionage. A British nurse, Mrs Daphne Parish, accused of helping him, was given 15 years' imprisonment and an Iraqi co-defendant 10 years. There is no appeal and only the Iraqi President Saddam Hussein can commute them.

The evidence presented in the military court against Mr Bazoft, aged 31, and Mrs Parish, who is 52, failed to substantiate the charges against them. When the verdicts were handed down at about 10 a.m., London time, there was no translation and the defendants were still confused about their fate as they were led away.

The spying charge relates to Mr Bazoft's inquiries into a major explosion at a military complex south of Baghdad, where up to 700 people are reported to have been killed. Mrs Parish's offence was to give the reporter a lift to the area in her car last September.

The lawyer would not confirm whether, at his trial, Mr Bazoft repeated his defence that a videotaped admission to being a spy—produced by the Iraqi authorities after he had been in isolation for seven weeks—was made after intensive interrogation and threats of violence.

The Observer (11 March 1990)

Sample 2

The British government last night sent an urgent appeal for clemency to President Saddam Hussein of Iraq after a Baghdad court sentenced Farzad Bazoft, a journalist working for *The Observer*, to death on spying charges.

Mr Bazoft, 31, born in Iran, went to Iraq on British travel documents. A British nursing officer, Daphne Parish, who drove Mr Bazoft to a secret military complex near Baghdad, was sentenced with him to 15 years in prison.

Mr Bazoft and Mrs Parish were arrested last September, and in November Mr Bazoft was shown on Iraqi television confessing to spying for Israel. At the time the editor of *The Observer*, Donald Trelford, said he was certain the 'confession' was made under duress. Yesterday, Mr Trelford pointed out that he had been denied permission to attend the trial, *The Observer* was not allowed to give evidence, and an application for a British lawyer to be present was refused. The trial was attended by the British Consul-general in Baghdad.

The Independent (11 March 1990)

The hypothesis advanced here regarding the degree of evaluativeness in the two texts is straightforward: we react to the two texts differently, an impression that might have something to do with the degree of emotiveness which seems to be glaringly present in Sample 1, and conspicuously absent from Sample 2. But what textual evidence can there be for the way we react, and can there be textual proof for how the sense of involvement exhibited ultimately reflects higher-level contextual specifications? That is, what criteria can we devise for confirming or refuting such first impressions? In the following, we will try to answer some of these questions by reviewing proposals from both modern text linguistics and classical Arab rhetoric put forward for the identification and description of the elusive 'subjectivity'. In the process, we will conduct an analysis of the two texts, then define and illustrate the various categories of the evaluative use of language involved.

A Text-Linguistic Model of Evaluative Texture

As argued earlier, the way texts are put together as cohesive and coherent entities is primarily determined by a diverse range of contextual factors surrounding the text. As a contextual variable, evaluativeness is analysable in terms of the various manifestations of texture as this is manipulated to accommodate a variety of emotive values. The degree of evaluativeness is therefore bound to vary in response to whether and how far the text is intended either to 'manage' or to 'monitor' a given situation (cf. Farghal 1991). In the analysis of texture in this way, a number of categories may be identified within an eclectic model of evaluativeness that draws heavily on proposals put forward within linguistic stylistics (e.g. Fowler 1986/1996) and systemic linguistics (e.g. Martin 1985).

1. Lexical Processes

(1) Over-lexicalization is an evaluative device intended to underline the prominence of given concepts in the thinking of a particular individual or community of text users. For example, the term *nurse* and the network of semantic relations conjured up, is an over-lexicalization intended by *The Observer* (Sample 1) to stress values such as 'compassion', 'self-denial', etc., with which the British reader is bound to identify. Compare this with *British nursing officer*, the more official title used by *The Independent* for Mrs Parish (Sample 2).

(2) Referentiality determines whether concepts are abstract and general or

concrete and specific. Abstract and general concepts are intrinsically more evaluative as they show intellectual superiority and institutional power. For example, *espionage*, the abstract 'officialese' term used in Sample 1, may be compared with the more colloquial *spying*, the more specific and thus less evaluative term used in Sample 2.

2. Ideation

Textual ideation (or the 'ideological' stamping of the text) is realized most notably by the lexico-grammatical system of transitivity. Here, different world views are conveyed by the different patterns of participants (designated by nouns performing specific agency roles) and predicates (designated by verbs or adjectives communicating specific actions, processes or states). For example, interesting distinctions may be discerned at the level of transitivity *between Mrs Parish's offence was to give the reporter a lift to the area* in Sample 1, and *Daphne Parish, who drove Mr Bazoft to a secret military complex* in Sample 2. While the former manages to underplay the action by nominalizing it (*offence*) and by relegating it to 'state or process undergone', the latter *Independent* rendering categorically states that an agent has deliberately performed an action. Given the thematic arrangement of the two utterances, the former is by far a more evaluative structure.

3. Deletion

(1) **Ellipsis** is used for the expression of brusqueness, emphasis, shared knowledge, etc. Such attitudes emanate from the fact that an ellipted second sentence relies for its interpretation on a preceding sentence. For example, in Sample 1, the meaning of the truncated *and an Iraqi co-defendant 10 years* is recoverable only when reference is made to the preceding utterance *Parish was given 15 years' imprisonment*. The element of 'brusqueness' emphasizes the ad hoc nature of the trial procedures.

(2) Nominalization involves rendering the meaning of a verb in the form of a noun, thus dispensing with both 'agency' and 'modality'. This evaluative device is very effective in masking real intentions, as we have seen in the use of *offence* (under 'ideation'). Another example of this in Sample 1 is *admission to being a spy*. This packages experience in a way that deflects attention from who, if any, admits what, a linguistic pattern better suited for the leftist leanings being served here.

4. Sequencing

This involves the order in which information is presented. The choices made can reflect various degrees of evaluativeness as they selectively determine what objects are to be the focus of attention:

(1) Passivization evaluates by suppressing or de-emphasizing certain elements of the sentence for a particular purpose. For example, in terms of the order of elements and their informational value, *An Observer journalist was yesterday sentenced to death by an Iraqi military court* in Sample 1 is far more evaluative than *a Baghdad court sentenced Farzad Bazoft to death on spying charges* in Sample 2. The evaluativeness of the passive structure emanates, among other things, from the marked status of the sentence structure and the deliberate fronting of certain elements and not others. In languages such as Arabic, passivization of the evaluative type discussed here becomes particularly significant. Stylistically, Arabic has a preference for the active voice thus dispensing with the need to use a 'by-agent' passive. In dealing with evaluative uses of the passive, the translator into Arabic should therefore opt for either:

(a) altogether abandoning the 'active' stylistic preference in the interest of preserving the evaluative rhetorical function involved (e.g. *wa quDHiya al-amr*—'and the will [of God] was done') (as in the Qur'an: Hud:44), or

(b) manipulating word order and exploiting other syntactic and semantic possibilities in such a way as to ensure that any loss incurred by the non-permissibility of the passive construction is compensated (e.g. *Let us see how this might pan out in practice*).

(2) Word order subsumes the various devices used in manipulating texture and in the process underlining topic salience within the sentence. For example, an adverbial phrase may be taken out of its normal, unmarked position and placed in an unusual and therefore marked position. Consider, for instance, the position of adverbials in English news reporting (*In the midst of recession, X did Y* vs *X, in the midst of recession, did Y*). True, this is fairly flexible and adverbials could be sentence-initial, sentence-medial or sentence-final. Within this variability, however, norms develop which may either be upheld or flouted (see Enkvist 1991). In Sample 1, reserving initial position for an element other than the adverbial, particularly when one is somehow expected, is not insignificant. The sentence is worded in the following way: *An Observer*

journalist was yesterday sentenced ..., leaving the reader to react to and interact with an 'absent' adverbial element, conspicuous by its absence from initial position.

(3) Interruptions of a sequence evaluate discourse by the use of parenthetically inserted linguistic elements. Of a number of parenthetical constructions used in a single paragraph in Sample 1, one is highly significant:—*produced by the Iraqi authorities after he had been in isolation for seven weeks—*. This is an insertion intended to cast serious doubt on the authenticity of 'the videotaped admission'.

(4) Order of paragraphs or of any other chunks of information beyond the boundaries of a single sentence can relay an element of evaluativeness. The decision in Sample 1 to have the 'court sentence' as the initial chunk of information is revealing when compared with the more sedate choice in Sample 2 of the 'British government reaction' theme for initial position.

5. Complexity of Syntax

Complex syntax is intrinsically evaluative in that it normally relays attitudes of knowledgeability and authority. For example, as Sample 1 goes on to relate: *the confusion which arose from the Iraqi lawyer's reluctance to confirm whether Bazoft repeated his defence that the videotaped admission produced by the Iraqis was made after intensive interrogation* is, perhaps not unintentionally, a highly complex structure. To break the sentence up into more manageable units when, say, translating into languages that do not readily tolerate this degree of complexity is to lose an important element of evaluativeness.

(1) Subordination of clauses implies complexity of logical relationships and thus acts as an evaluative device. Coordination, on the other hand, relays a more sedate attitude to the sequencing of ideas, paradoxically a naive or primitive mode of discourse. Sample 1 is highly subordinative, to avoid relaying a smooth, detached progression of events. (See Chapter 17 for a discussion of orality and the predominance of the paratactic style.)

(2) Complexity of noun phrases, in terms of what and how many premodifiers and postmodifiers there are, may in itself be significant for the perception of evaluativeness. Compare, for example, *aged 31* and *who is 52* in Sample 1 with the unmodified *31* in Sample 2. In the latter instance, the phrase is for information only and carries no evaluative weight whatsoever.

6. Modality

This includes a variety of intrinsically evaluative devices which indicate the speaker's attitude both to the utterance and to the addressee. For example, the highly charged use of modality in *The lawyer would not confirm* in Sample 1 is effective in relaying the feeling of a terrified judiciary. In Arabic, *wa lam yakun bi istiTa'ati al-muHaamii an yu'akkida* (which may be glossed as 'he was somehow impeded'), will get round this subtle use of the modal 'would' and thus relay the meaning of inhibition.

7. Speech Acts

Utterances do not only communicate propositional content but also perform actions. The degree of opacity which the meaning of these actions normally exhibits will obviously vary from text type to text type. In this respect, intentionality in evaluative texts tends to be far more opaque than that encountered in non-evaluative texts. This confronts the translator with added layers of meaning, the subtlety of which must somehow be preserved in the target text when translating.

The distinction 'opaque' vs 'transparent' may be illustrated by the degree of indirectness exhibited by a given utterance. Evaluative discourse tends to favour indirectness as a way of capturing the attention of the text receiver (e.g. *was given 15 years' imprisonment* [Sample 1]). More direct utterances, on the other hand, predominate in non-evaluative contexts as they are generally easier to process and are thus more compatible with the air of detachment characteristic of expository texts (e.g. *was sentenced to 15 years* [Sample 2]).

8. Implicature

Implicatures are unstated propositions that lurk between the lines of discourse. This highly evaluative way of speaking is not accidental, but the product of an intentional act. Also, the propositions that are implied may be consistent with one another and add up to a set of ideological commitments. Note, for example, the use of 'irony' in Sample 1: *There is no appeal and only the Iraqi President Saddam Hussein can commute* [these sentences]; *Mrs Parish's offence was to give the reporter a lift*. The implicates in both these utterances enhance the ideological stance being propounded.

9. Address, Naming and Personal Reference

In the discussion of evaluativeness, a feature worth noting in Sample 1 is the mention of Bazoft's and Mrs Parish's professions (*journalist, nurse*) before citing their names. This relays a specific attitudinal stance and thus carries ideological meaning.

The above checklist is by no means intended to be an exhaustive catalogue of all the evaluative devices which language users in general and translators in particular work with. The catalogue of features, however, underlines the need to bear in mind that evaluativeness is in fact an all-pervasive phenomenon and is not restricted to aspects of text constitution such as emphasis or word order, and that awareness of these subtle aspects of texture, which are crucial to an appreciation of discoursal meanings in texts, goes beyond basic, primary meanings of utterances.

The Text Receiver in Rhetoric

In the discussion by classical Arab rhetoricians of the interrelationship between communicative purpose and linguistic realization, the text receiver consistently acquires supreme importance. However, the text producer is not lost sight of altogether. As judged by the text producer, the receiver's state of preparedness to accept or reject propositions put forward is the basis on which utterances and texts are designed and moulded. In fact, what is referred to in Arabic rhetoric as 'the science of meanings' is entirely devoted to tracking down those patterns of correspondence between speech and contextual factors such as the degree of receiver certainty regarding the truth value of a given proposition, and the way this interacts with linguistic expression.

As explained in Chapter 5, three degrees (or 'states') of text receiver certainty may be identified in calibrating choices made by the text producer: the state of the 'denier', that of the 'uncertain' and that of the 'open-minded', justifying maximal, moderate and minimal emphasis respectively. But, for the Arab rhetorician, a far more important issue than these unmarked situations of receiver stance and text producer action is perhaps motivated violation (or rather, flouting) of what the norm dictates. In a purposeful manner, text producers can break the rules creatively and still keep within the bounds of rhetorical appropriateness. For example, the text producer may simply monitor a situation non-evaluatively while in fact addressing a denier, or manipulate language evaluatively when the person addressed is actually open-minded. Let us reconsider the 'background' sentence (3) taken from *The Independent* text (Sample 2) which is highly evaluative:

(3) Under the present system there is no legal appeal, though the President can commute sentences 'for humanitarian reasons'.

Sentence (3) functions as a 'managing' device, normally catering for a high degree of denial on the part of the addressee. However, given the essential function of both the text and the utterance itself (expository, background information), norms dictate that the addressee in this context should be treated as entirely open-minded, and minimal evaluativeness should therefore be opted for. In fact, both Sample 1 and Sample 2 flout the 'evaluation' **maxim** for a good reason (to be interesting, witty, more persuasive). As the above analysis shows, Sample 2 is particularly adept at deliberately assuming an element of 'doubt' on the part of the receiver when, in theory at least, none is to be expected.

The Translator at Work

In this final section, an attempt will be made to highlight a number of features from Sample 1 and Sample 2 and to discuss these from the perspective of translation. While translation into Arabic will obviously be the focus of our attention, it is hoped that the discussion will also be of interest to those working with other languages. Subjected to this kind of analysis will be the initial paragraph of Sample 1 only, with Sample 2 providing backdrop material as appropriate. Lack of space prevents a more detailed analysis. As will become apparent shortly, however, the guiding principles suggested, together with the illustrations in the above checklist of evaluative devices, should prove helpful in tackling the rest of the text. Furthermore, it is initial 'scene-setters' which normally encapsulate the gist of the ideological stance that will unfold as the text develops.

Sentence 1, The Observer

> An *Observer* journalist, Farzad Bazoft, was yesterday sentenced to death by an Iraqi military court after being found guilty of espionage.

Given that this is the initial sentence of an expository text (news report), neutral style is normally called for in Arabic (e.g. the use of the detached Verbal sentence structure (*al-jumla al-fi3liyya*) and not, say, the evaluative Nominal sentence structure (*al-jumla al-ismiyya*)). However, an important contextual factor at work here is the remarkably marked discourse of the source text, which is to be read not for its informational value only, but for the ideological stance being negotiated throughout. *The Observer* is trying hard to shake its Sunday morning readers out of their slumber and alert them to the plight of the journalist in question.

To resolve the tension between the requirements of the text (detached expository news report) and those of the discourse (highly evaluative and committed plea), the translator could opt for a compromise: choose the format of the Verbal sentence structure (verb first) and at the same time manipulate the order in which the information is presented. This conflation of rhetorical functions would ensure that the required degree of evaluativeness is generated. Within word order manipulation:

(i) One could highlight the adverb of time *yesterday* (*yawma ams*) by using it anywhere except at the first possible opportunity immediately after the verb-subject sequence, a slot strictly reserved in Arabic for unmarked adverbial elements. Manipulating the position of the adverbial in this way ensures that a reasonable degree of marking is preserved.

(ii) One could also choose an additional 'verb of beginning' which will prop up the verb *sentenced* (*hakama*) by nominalizing it thus, *aSdarat hukmaha*, 'issued its judgement'. This would relay an additional effect, namely drawing attention to the 'harshness' of the sentence.

(iii) Another evaluative device would be circumlocution to get round the compound in English, *An Observer journalist*, thus, *Sahafiyyun ya'malu fi Sahifat al-observer* ('a journalist who works for the *Observer* newspaper'). This sentence is linked to the preceding name of the journalist by *wa huwa* ('and he is ...') which underlines the emotive element intended by the source text.

(iv) Finally, appending the minor sentence *after being found guilty of espionage*, to the emotive device *wa dhaalika ba'da an* ('and that was after ...'). Strictly speaking, the phrase signals 'logical consequence', which if used here could misrepresent the text producer's intention. But when immediately followed by *being found guilty* rendered in terms which preserve as much of the meaning of 'whim' as is required by the source text, the overall effect would be magical and more in line with the text producer's intention. With the implicit meaning of 'only after' already present, one way of rendering the element of 'ad hocery' could be to select 'the court' as the agent of the passive construction, thus *wa dhaalika ba'da an athbatat al maHkama idaanatahu bi al-tajassus* ('only after the court found him guilty of spying').

In full, sentence (1) would read as follows in Arabic:

yawma ams aSdarat maHkamatun 'askariyyatun 'iraaqiyya Hukmahaa bi al-'i'daami 'alaa farzad bazoft wa huwa SaHafiyyun ya'malu fi SaHiifat al-observer, wa dhaalika ba'da an athbatat al-maHkama idaanatahu bi al-tajassus.

In back-translation, the Arabic rendering reads as follows:

Yesterday, an Iraqi military court issued a judgement on Farzad Bazoft, a journalist working for the Observer, and this was only after the court found him guilty of espionage.

Sentence 1 The Independent

The British government last night sent an urgent appeal for clemency to President Saddam Hussein of Iraq after a Baghdad court sentenced Farzad Bazoft, a journalist working for the Observer, to death on spying charges.

One striking feature of this text is its almost totally stable texture: an expository news report, more in harmony with detached discourse than anything else. While the narrative is not altogether indifferent, and evaluativeness does creep in, the text is certainly not a passionate appeal to reader sensibilities or anything of the sort. In translating the above-cited scene-setter into Arabic, using a non-manipulative Verbal sentence structure would thus be sufficient to relay the predominant element of detachment.

Thus, none of the cotextual problems encountered in translating Sample 1 above is likely to arise in dealing with Sample 2. For example, the adverbial *last night* would be embedded immediately after the verb–noun sequence, an unmarked position in Arabic. There would be no need for a verb of beginning to precede *Hakamat*, as the sentence is straightforwardly descriptive. Though circumlocution ('working for *The Observer*') is resorted to, this is more to do with idiomaticity in the Arabic way of handling such compounds than with a functionally motivated choice. Also, given the context of 'appealing for clemency', the identity of the journalist would be more formally presented (*an Observer journalist called X*). Finally, though the linker *wa dhaalika ba'da an* can still be used, it is here a logical connector which in any case is optional. When used, the linker would not be as indicting as it is in *The Observer* text since the sentence continues in a way which does revolve round the element of whim.

In full, the *Independent*'s initial sentence will read something like this in Arabic:

taqaddamat al-Hukuuma al-bariiTaniyya laylata ams bi Talabin 'aajil ilaa al-ra'iis al-'iraaqi Saddaam Husayn taltamisuhu al-ra'fa wadhaalika ba'da an Hakamat maHkamatun 'iraaqiyya bi al-'i'daami bi tuhmati al-tajassus 'alaa SaHafiyyin yud'aa farzad bazoft wa ya'malu fii SaHiifati al-observer

To Conclude

In the evaluativeness scheme proposed in this chapter, features 1–9 above would mark *The Observer* sentence under analysis as a highly evaluative utterance. Tabulating the various evaluative devices in use throughout the text would yield both a quantitative and a qualitative assessment of the degree of emotiveness which the text carries. These indicators can then be taken as an objective set of criteria for assessing the state of the text receiver as envisaged by the text producer and for distinguishing this text from other comparable texts such as *The Independent*'s.

The phrase 'as envisaged by the text producer' is very important here. It is immaterial whether, on that quiet Sunday morning, the majority of *The Observer*'s readers were up in arms, showing extreme resentment at what the Iraqi President had done or not done. What is of more significance is that someone envisaged them to be that agitated and that resentful of what had happened to Bazoft. To fulfil this communicative brief, that 'someone' visualized *The Observer*'s reader as a 'denier' (as opposed to the 'open-minded' receiver of an innocuous news report) and in effect provided him or her with what deniers normally require: a highly emotive run-down of a sequence of events.

There is nothing particularly remarkable about stressing the role that the reaction of the text receiver plays in the way texts are put together. This has been the subject of discussion since the beginning of rhetorical inquiry. Moreover, as translators, we have also always done well in this respect, intuitively reacting to text nuance and subtleties. What is truly remarkable about a scheme such as the one suggested here is that we are now nearer to being able to use a set of criteria with which to measure attitudinal response to texts fairly objectively. The elusive nature of 'what the text producer is getting at' can now, I hope, be made somewhat more accessible, an important step towards the fulfilment of the trust which target-language readers have placed in us as translators.

15 Translating Direct and Indirect Speech and the Dynamics of News Reporting

The aim of this chapter is to re-examine the well-established distinction between direct and indirect or reported speech, and to suggest that the use of one or the other carries wider implications for the way rhetorical purposes are pursued in texts. Of immediate relevance in this respect are the findings of an informal survey of reporting modes in newspaper Arabic in which it is established that, in this domain of language use, there is a distinct preference for indirect forms of reporting. In carefully examining the use of indirect speech, the survey further reveals that a number of 'tones' or different 'harmonies' are normally relayed within this mode of reporting in Arabic. In translation, whether the source text is in the direct or indirect mode of reporting, the indirect form likely to be adopted when working into Arabic would thus have to be multi-functional, communicating the various subtle shades of meaning of the original. Using the indirect in Arabic is therefore not as straightforward a matter as one might initially think.

Multiplicity of Tones

When translating direct speech into Arabic from a language such as English, the translator faces a dilemma: the need to preserve the autonomy of the utterance precisely as it was expressed in its original direct mode, and, at the same time, work with rhetorical norms that encourage 'indirectness'. As will be argued in the course of the following discussion, a third form of reported speech, which may best be termed 'quasi-direct', may have to be distinguished in situations like these. Though indirect in form, this kind of reported speech would be direct in function. To relay the 'directness' of the source and the 'veiled' evaluativeness of the original discourse, a variety of syntactic and semantic means are normally employed in the target Arabic text. This is in order to preserve in the target discourse the 'tone' of the original, while at the same time inhabiting a predominantly indirect textual environment in the target language. The task of the translator, in other words, is to allow at least two distinct rhetorical functions to co-exist in one and the same stretch of textual material that ultimately serves a single rhetorical purpose.

With modes of reporting in mind, let us now consider discourse Sample 1, divided for ease of reference into five major parts. As a journalistic text, Sample 1 is typical of the kind of material regularly translated from English into other languages, and can thus adequately illustrate the kind of problems faced in the translation of direct speech:

Sample 1

> I The Defence Minister, Yitzhak Rabin, has repeated Israel's denial of allegations that it has collaborated with South Africa in developing a long-range nuclear missile.
>
> II He told the cabinet Israel had transferred no technology to South Africa, least of all technology acquired from the United States for the Lavi fighter-bomber project.
>
> III However, the denials have not stopped Israel feeling diplomatic fallout from the allegations on relations with the US.
>
> IV Israeli papers reported prominently President Bush's comment on Saturday that such a project, if true, could 'complicate' US–Israeli ties.
>
> V 'I hope our position is clear on transfer of any military technology that should not be transferred. If that's taken place, it would not enhance relations between us ... It would complicate things. There's no question about that.'
>
> A *Guardian* news report

It should be noted at the outset that, while translators of this text into other European languages may face no particular problem with the direct and indirect modes of reporting, the translator into Arabic is considerably more constrained. Of course, like any other language, Arabic has the formal and rhetorical means of using either mode of reporting as a distinct form. One only has to cite the Qur'anic text that abounds with examples of direct speech. And, indeed, *The Arabian Nights* is a good example of the quite normal use of direct speech in that kind of storytelling.

However, in dealing with the kind of texts illustrated by Sample 1 above, the translator into Arabic has to work within parameters set by the news report as a genre, which imposes its own constraints that are different from those set by, say, storytelling as a generic structure. To complicate matters further, the news report as a generic structure is not usually a 'pure' form, but a hybrid at best. That is, in addition to news reporting as a major function, other subsidiary communicative goals are also in evidence. The translator has thus to deal with the co-existence of different (often opposing) contextual values in one and the same text:

(a) 'report' vs 'comment' (genre),
(b) 'detachment' vs 'involvement' (discourse),
(c) 'narration' vs 'argumentation' (text).

In this kind of predominantly reporting genre, detached discourse and expository text type in Arabic, such hybridization exists alongside a linguistic-stylistic predilection for one form of speech reporting—the indirect. As has already been pointed out, despite the fact that Arabic recognizes direct speech formally, there is a tendency in this kind of text to favour indirect forms. The preference for the indirect form is partly due to the intrinsic 'orality/aurality' of Arabic (texts must be heard as well as seen; see Chapter 17) which has rendered ancillary systems of representation such as punctuation and the usual diacritical marks virtually redundant.

Let us focus briefly on punctuation. Though outside the language system proper in most languages, punctuation and other orthographic devices are always of considerable help: They aid in shifting the burden of marking the various 'tones' (e.g. detachment vs involvement) away from the 'textual' to the 'visual' level of texts. In Arabic, while such marking of intentionality continues to be of primary importance, the means of going about the process would no longer be purely 'visual' but rather a matter of actual wording or texture manipulation. The meanings normally relayed by quotation marks, say, in English would in Arabic have to be made more explicit through verbalizing (i.e. spelling out) what quotation marks normally do: (e.g. *wa Hadhdhara qaa'ilan* ..., lit. 'And he warned saying ...' dispensing with the English quotes).

When working into Arabic as a target language, translators must therefore ensure that the kind of reported speech rendered exhibits two different kinds of tone:

(1) subdued, when the source language utterance is indirect (e.g. II in Sample 1),
(2) more pointed when the source language utterance is fully-fledged direct (e.g. V in Sample 1).

Given this discourse diversity, the question to be addressed now is how are we to discern, in the absence of conventional signals such as quotation marks, meanings of distinct contextual values such as evaluativeness (normally more compatible with direct speech), and non-evaluativeness (best relayed through the indirect). This is quite a challenge to face when all such values usually get transposed into a single option, namely indirect text in the target language (Arabic in this case).

This is precisely what happens when rendering speech such as that reported in Sample 1 into Arabic. Capturing the intricacy of this context switching requires skill and sensitivity to text in context, an important challenge in the training of contrastive linguists in general and of translators in particular.

Text in Context

The definition of context adopted in this study rests on three basic premises. Firstly, lexical and syntactic choices are dictated by contextual variables such as 'field of discourse' (including social processes and institutions), 'tenor of discourse' (including relations of power and solidarity), and 'mode of discourse' (including channel or physical distance separating text production from reception)—which we have collectively labelled the 'institutional-communicative' dimension of context (register, etc.). The second premise relates to how these register membership variables determine, and are ultimately determined by, 'pragmatic' considerations to do with the purposes for which utterances are used, real-world conditions, and so on. For example, consider the following elements from Sample 1:

(1) 'If that's taken place, it would not enhance relations between us ...'
(2) 'It would complicate things ...'

In terms of register membership, these display the following contextual profile:

Field: Journalistic account of international politics (e.g. *relations*)
Tenor: Semi-formal (e.g. *us, enhance, complicate, that's*)
Mode: Written to be read as if heard as an off-the-cuff remark (e.g. *things*)

This way of identifying the register membership of a given text is an essential part of the translator's (or interpreter's) preparatory work. Problems involved in translating Sample 1, for example, include locating equivalent terms in the appropriate field and achieving target-language 'equivalence' in the appropriate mode and tenor. Much more than this, however, is involved in reconstructing context and in tracing the ways in which contextual values are reflected in actual texts. The meanings of elements (1) and (2) above are ultimately determined by the pragmatic action involved, namely, 'warning' in the two examples. It is only when this pragmatic focus is retrieved, and intentionality properly perceived, that meaning is appropriately conveyed. The translation of direct and indirect speech is certain to benefit from such perceptions.

The third and final premise adopted in the definition of context is that, in order to appreciate the full communicative thrust of an utterance, we need to appreciate not only the so-called illocutionary force of the utterance (e.g. to warn), but also its status as a token of a given type of sign. This semiotic dimension of context regulates the interaction of the various discourse elements within a socio-cultural system of meanings. For example:

(3) Such a project, if true, could 'complicate' US–Israeli ties.

This speech act may be labelled 'warning'. But this has taken on the meaning it has only by virtue of the interaction between this particular utterance as a sign and the surrounding utterance signs, for example:

(4) Israel feeling diplomatic fallout ...

(5) 'I hope our position is clear on transfer of any military technology.'

Semiotic interaction takes place at various levels of sign work. There is the conventional interaction between speaker (writer) and hearer (reader). There is also an interactive relationship between the speaker and his or her utterance (the way meanings are teased out of different wordings). Finally and perhaps more significantly, there is the way an utterance relates to other utterances (intertextuality). As will become clearer later in the discussion of direct and indirect speech, these various semiotic interrelationships have a bearing on the inter-semiotic transfer which translation necessarily involves.

Mode as a Communicative Factor

Of immediate relevance to the problem of reported speech is the variable 'mode'. Essentially, this refers to the 'physical distance' between text producer and receiver, and to the 'conceptual distance' between producer or receiver and whatever is being talked about—the actual text message. These values manifest themselves in the kind of interaction that emerges as texts unfold. Mode is thus the linguistic manifestation of the interactive code in use. The basic distinction here is that between speech and writing and the various permutations on such a distinction (direct quotation, written to be spoken, etc.). Overlapping considerably with mode are, of course, both the field and tenor of discourse. As explained earlier, these respectively relay technicality and formality that collectively characterize the relationship between the addresser and the addressee.

In Sample 1 above, the shift from the authorial (journalist's) speech (I, III) to the 'reported' speech (II, IV), and finally to the 'direct' speech signalled in English by quotation marks (V), involves subtle variation in field, tenor and, more importantly, in mode. In attempting to relay these shifts in a language such as Arabic, the translator must learn to function within the following kinds of constraint. Firstly, while the English source text tends to be syntactically and semantically implicative (subdued) in marking the mode 'written to be read as if heard or overheard' (IV), a tendency which can create difficulties for text comprehension, Arabic is much more explicative (vocal) in articulating such distinctions, which, in turn, creates difficulties for translation.

The latter kind of problem which the shift in mode may cause is that the translator into Arabic would have to mark the text for mode 'twice' as it were: to overcome the problem of stylistic implicitness of the English source text and to try to capture the tone of the direct speech. As an illustration, let us consider Sample 1, Part IV, reproduced here for easier reference:

> IV Israeli papers reported prominently President Bush's comment on Saturday that such a project, if true, could 'complicate' US–Israeli ties.

The opaque use of *could complicate* is spelt out in Arabic to read something like 'likely to exacerbate the situation' (*min sha'nihi ann yufaaqima al-wad'* ...). The modal element 'likely to' properly signals that the journalist has shifted onto Bush the responsibility for his own words.

Speech Act Sequence as a Pragmatic Factor

Particularly in the translation of linguistic forms such as direct and indirect speech, the problems faced by the translator into Arabic transcend mode to include a pragmatic component. In the analysis of Sample 1, for example, a fundamental question is: What is the difference between, say, I and III, on the one hand, and II and IV, on the other?

TRANSLATING DIRECT AND INDIRECT SPEECH

SET 1

I The Defence Minister, Yitzhak Rabin, has repeated Israel's denial of allegations that it has collaborated with South Africa in developing a long-range nuclear missile.

III However, the denials have not stopped Israel feeling diplomatic fallout from the allegations on relations with the US.

SET 2

II He told the cabinet Israel had transferred no technology to South Africa, least of all technology acquired from the United States for the Lavi fighter-bomber project.

IV Israeli papers reported prominently President Bush's comment on Saturday that such a project, if true, could 'complicate' US–Israeli ties.

Reproduced here for easier reference

The two sets would be lumped together by mode analysis and labelled simply as authorial intervention and reporting, respectively. But this captures the difference only partially. From the perspective adopted here, we focus on 'speech act sequence' as one of the more important elements of pragmatic meaning. As an important indicator of overall intentionality, this is the cumulative effect of a series of speech acts leading to the perception of a predominant pragmatic force in a given stretch of discourse.

We have distinguished two basic strategies for processing speech act sequences. One is situation monitoring, the other situation managing. For example, in Sample 1, Part I:

(6) The Defence Minister ... has repeated Israel's denial of allegations that it has collaborated with ...

is a clear example of 'monitoring' by the journalist, while:

(7) However, the denials have not stopped Israel feeling diplomatic fallout ...

in Sample 1, Part III, is an example of 'managing' intended to steer the receiver into adopting a position favoured by the text producer. This manipulation of discourse, which is fairly innocuous in this case of journalistic intervention, can lapse into a more tendentious form of managing as in Sample 1, Part V:

(8) 'There's no question about that', said Bush.

Transposing into the indirect form the force of the direct speech in element (8), as Arabic is likely to do, and allowing this 'quasi-direct' speech to co-exist with a genuinely indirect authorial context as in (6), and a 'less' genuinely indirect context as in (7), involves perceiving and relaying pragmatic values of monitoring and managing, which tend to be generally implicit in English.

The translation of Sample 1, Part V may be taken as an example that illustrates the role of pragmatics in dealing with direct speech in English. The speech act sequence involved is reproduced here as a series of speech acts:

(a) 'I hope our position is clear on transfer of any military technology that should not be transferred.
(b) 'If that's taken place, it would not enhance relations between us.
(c) 'It would complicate things.
(d) 'There is no question about that.'

The choice of the reporting verbs to introduce indirect speech in Arabic will be determined by the need to capture the very pragmatic import of the sequence in question. Here, it is 'He signalled, confirming that ...'. This incorporates the 'warning' that cumulatively emanates from *hope, is clear, that should not, if, would not enhance, complicate things, no question*. Once introduced in this way, the sequence will undergo two basic modifications within and between the various speech acts, one semantic and the other syntactic. The Arabic translation will read something like this:

Sample 1 (Back-translation from Arabic)

And President Bush in his statement signalled, confirming that he hopes that the position of his government is clear regarding the transfer of any military technology, a transfer which is banned. And he added that, if that were actually to happen, he has no doubt it would not strengthen the relations between the two countries but would undermine them.

Notice how, in addition to the slightly more emotive lexical and syntactic choices made throughout the text, the Arabic text manipulates the speech act sequence in two ways:

(1) conflating (b) and (c) and turning the additive relation into an adversative one,
(2) paraphrasing (d) and using it to introduce this adversative relation.

Intertextuality as the Driving Force of Signification

To impose order on this seemingly unmanageable situation of discourse diversity, we need a framework within which the various communicative and pragmatic values may be processed as 'signs', in both socio-cultural and socio-textual terms. An important principle to be focused on in the analysis of this semiotic dimension of context is to do with the way we relate textual occurrences to each other and recognize them as triggers that evoke whole areas of previous textual experience. This is 'intertextuality', a mechanism through which textual occurrences are recognized in terms of their dependence on other relevant prior texts. To illustrate this phenomenon of dealing with signs, let us compare an utterance from Part IV of Sample 1 with one from Part V in the same sample. Both instances are reproduced here for easier reference:

Part IV

(a) Israeli papers reported prominently President Bush's comment on Saturday

(b) that such a project, if true, could 'complicate' US–Israeli ties.

Part V

(a) If that's taken place, it would not enhance relations between us.

(b) It would complicate things.

Element (a) Part IV is an intertextual signal evoking previous textual experience with news reporting as a professional pursuit (genre), journalistic neutrality as a discourse attitude, and the narrative as a text form. Element (a) or (b) Part V, however, conjures up a different image—probably that of a 'public statement' delivered with a maximal sense of force and commitment. Translation equivalence is achieved by evoking in the target-language reader similar experiences stored and retrieved by language users as a series of signs that are in constant interaction with one another.

In the elements of discourse under consideration (Part IV and Part V), perhaps a more interesting phenomenon is the semiotic difference between Part IV (b) and Part V (a). The two elements express the same propositional content and they are both 'warnings'. In semiotic terms, however, the two tokens are different. The difference lies in the intertextual potential that they are bound to display as signs. Token (b) Part IV refers us to a 'polemic simply and neutrally reported in a narrative'. Token (a) Part V, on the other hand, refers the reader intertextually to a 'polemic created subjectively and afresh in an argument'. The striking nature of the difference may be clearly illustrated by a comparison of *complicate* (IVb) with *complicate* (Vb). These two propositionally identical utterances, which belong to the same sign type 'warning', are nonetheless different tokens. The grounds for establishing the difference are the same as for the previous two examples: the two occurrences of *complicate* are used by different people for different purposes (a journalist reporting vs the President of the United States arguing).

Here, it may be helpful to note that, in the analysis of intertextuality, the term 'textual' is used in a fairly general way and rather liberally. In reality, such occurrences are not restricted to the level of 'texts' as defined technically (e.g. narrative, the counter-argument), but also cover the other two basic categories: 'discourse' (e.g. journalistic neutrality) and 'genre' (e.g. the news report). All of these semiotic structures are capable of displaying intertextual potential, imposing their own constraints on the inter-semiotic transfer entailed by translation.

As we have already pointed out, genres are conventionalized forms of texts that reflect the functions and goals involved in particular communicative events, as well as the purposes of the participants in such events (Kress 1985b). These semiotic structures impose their own constraints on the process of translation. In this respect, it is perhaps useful to note that generic constraints emanate not only from a single genre seen to predominate on a given communicative occasion (e.g. the news report), but also from a number of minor ones usually deployed to make the **master genre** operational. This is most relevant in translating direct/indirect speech. In Sample 1, for example, there is the predominant genre of news reporting, within which we have a periodic switching from the authorial/journalist's contribution (an interventionist **sub-genre**), to the reported speech (a straightforward reporting sub-genre) and to the direct speech (a polemical sub-genre).

Through intertextuality, the lexico-grammatical wording of the message would have to reflect the subtle differences that exist between the various generic structures. That is, lexical and syntactic choices are made ultimately in the light of considerations of genre membership. In the case of Arabic, noted for its explicitness, this manipulation of texture in the service of higher semiotic considerations (e.g. generic) is of crucial importance. As has been shown above, the reader of the translation will be guided from 'tone' to 'tone' by different wordings, serving different genres and highlighting the various contours of the text.

Furthermore, the participants in the communicative events reflected in genres are bound to be also involved in attitudinally determined expression characteristic of these events. For example, the news report as a genre involves journalists in conveying typical attitudes towards their subject. In this case, the mode of expression tends to be 'non-evaluative'. Nevertheless, the journalist is not tied to one and only one mode of operation. He or she may at times find it more appropriate to engage in evaluating the news as well as reporting it. Journalists may also sometimes rely on 'invited' speakers (e.g. an authority on the subject) who may engage in an objective review of events or in a polemic or comment (i.e. altogether different sub-genres to that of the 'dominant' news report). A different attitudinal expression emerges with each of these fluctuations. Two basic shifts may be distinguished. The journalist yields the floor either to a different persona (him or herself as a commentator) or a different person (the invited speaker).

In a language such as English, the shift to a different persona is relayed subtly (e.g. through understatement), while the shift to a different person is signalled by quotation marks. In Arabic, however, the various sets of attitudinal expression are conflated, and it is the task of the translator to make sure that different intertextual tones are faithfully reflected through all kinds of syntactic or semantic means. These will sometimes have to point to the discourse of detachment (the journalist's), at other times to the committed discourse of the polemicist or commentator from within or from outside. Skill and sensitivity in handling discourse expression are called for in dealing with intricate situations like these.

Finally, within discourse and genre there are fluctuations that have to be accounted for in the reworking of any text. In the genre of the news report, for example, differences arise when the discourse of 'objective reporting' gives way to 'subjective evaluation'. The latter varies in intensity from the mildly evaluative sections of the journalist's own mainly objective discourse to the highly evaluative argumentation likely to dominate in, say, the committed discourse of the 'comment' as an intruding genre. Here, there could always be a subjective 'element' set against the background of an objective exposition. These differences give rise to rhetorical intents such as 'counter-argumentation', 'narration'. Counter-arguments, narratives, etc. are what we have been technically calling 'texts'.

In dealing with the problem faced by the translator in rendering direct speech, the textual dimension is of crucial importance. So-called journalese (which is a misleading cover term for what may more rigorously be defined only in terms of genre and discourse) is nothing but a body of mutually relevant texts, each with its own specific rhetorical purpose. It is this sense of textual purposefulness which the translator must make sure to convey when the news report slides, say, from objective narrative (the journalist's), to subjective evaluation (which could also be the journalist's or that of the invited speaker), to even more extreme forms of evaluation (which are most probably the invited speaker's, but could also be the journalist's). In fact, viewing Sample 1 in terms of the relative degree of evaluativeness as distributed among the various parts of the text, we can see a systematic build-up from least to most evaluative, beginning with Part I through to Part V. That is, the direct speech quoted in Part V, functioning as the 'substantiator' of the opposition to a 'cited thesis' in the unfolding argument, marks the highest point of evaluativeness.

This switch from one rhetorical intention to another, both at micro-level and at macro-level, may distinguish one text from another (with macro-rhetorical intention then matching the rhetorical purpose of the text) or one part of a given text from another part (with micro-rhetorical intention seen as the same as local discourse function). The direct speech cited in Sample 1 is an example of one such discourse function. Figure 15.1 represents the discourse functions in Sample 1.

Thesis Cited To Be Countered	The Defence Minister Yitzhak Rabin has repeated Israel's ... denial of allegations ...
	He told the cabinet ...
Opposition	However, the denials have not stopped Israel feeling diplomatic fallout ...
Substantiation	Israeli papers reported prominently President Bush's comment on Saturday ...
Substantiation Enhancer	'I hope our position is clear ...'

Figure 15.1 Text structure of Sample 1

While quotation marks play an important role in English, setting off the various texts and text segments one from the other, Arabic (and therefore the translator into Arabic) has to rely solely on other appropriate textual resources as and when required for text development. In Arabic, all of this is ultimately reflected through actual wording as opposed to punctuation that, although formally available, is, to all intents and purposes, functionally redundant (diehard punctuation fans should never fret; they can still use quotation marks in Arabic!). Within the text strategy illustrated in Figure 15.1, Bush's comment takes on the textual value 'enhancer of a substantiation'. In Arabic, the substantiation and the enhancer, which are more appropriately rendered as indirect speech, are respectively marked with a substantiation particle (*fa*) ('thus') and an additive particle (*wa*) ('and').

The Text–Discourse–Genre Chain of Interaction

Genre and discourse strategy, then, informs textual strategy. But texts, in turn, modify the specification of the genre and, consequently, of the discourse within a given communicative transaction. This may be illustrated schematically in Figure 15.2 for Sample 1 above.

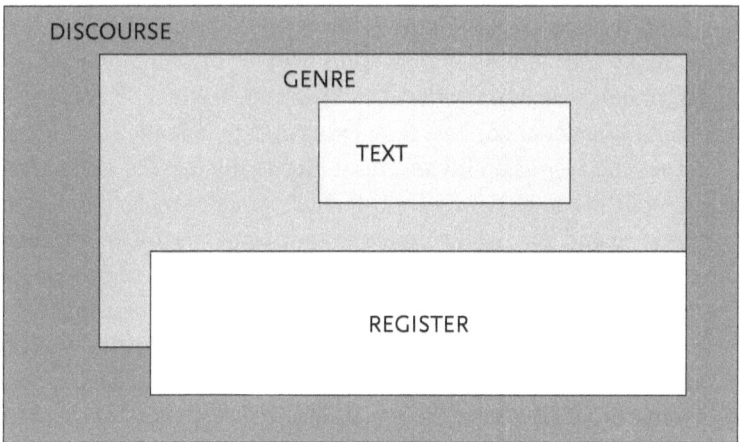

Figure 15.2 Text–discourse–genre chain

Thus, the type of juxtaposition displayed by the semi-evaluative discourse of this investigative news report may be distinguished from the counter-argumentative text format found in the highly evaluative discourse of the genre Letter to the Editor, for example. That is, the opposition, signalled by *however* in Sample 1, is different from a similar opposition in Sample 2 below.

Sample 2

> KENNETH CLARKE, Health Secretary, is reported (*Guardian*, November 14, 1989) as saying that the inclusion of a question on ethnic origin in the 1991 census 'would yield valuable information in the fight against racial discrimination.' The census will not, however, yield any information about the discrimination faced by Irish people in Britain.
>
> The Irish community is the largest ethnic minority in Britain ...
>
> *The Guardian*

In Sample 1, the opposition is somewhat veiled. It is, as it were, held at some remove from the author. In Sample 2, on the other hand, it is more 'up front'.

These distinctions have a bearing on the way we perceive the wider implications that the direct speech has for the structure of the entire text.

Direct, Indirect and Quasi-Direct Speech

We have thus far discussed the difficulties faced by the translator in rendering direct and indirect speech into Arabic. We have also shown that such difficulties are not normally encountered by translators working into, or producers of texts in, English, or indeed in the majority of European languages. In these languages, a conventionally sanctioned, time-tested system of punctuation and quotation marks carries the responsibility of presenting as distinct the various modes of speech reporting in text. Here, within each mode of reporting, aspects of genre, discourse and text, while present as they would be in any language, are nevertheless realized implicitly. Context, tight text structure and opaque texture together relay subtle pragmatic, semiotic and other kinds of meaning.

An analysis of Arabic textual conventions would certainly reveal that almost all of these aspects of text constitution are present. Nevertheless, such an analysis would only focus on formal aspects, barely touching on the underlying functional significance of surface realizations. True, the choice between direct and indirect speech is formally available in Arabic. Furthermore, a system of punctuation has been 'imported' from English and other European languages by certain Arab neo-rhetoricians. And, as we have made amply clear, generic, discourse and textual constraints operate in Arabic in more or less the same way as they do in other languages. A closer examination of these phenomena in actual use, however, would reveal that the analogy between Arabic and these other languages is far from complete. First, while the means of expressing direct and indirect speech is no doubt formally available, the deployment of such means is not unconstrained. A number of factors render the use of the direct in a genre such as news reporting in Arabic rare indeed. This is borne out by day-to-day experience with texts and by an informal survey of modes of reporting in newspaper Arabic which conclusively points to the remarkable frequency of the indirect form (almost 98 per cent).

The second area in which the comparability between Arabic and Western European languages in this respect is likely to be partial relates to the fact that the system of punctuation outlined in modern manuals of Arabic style has been wished on Arabic by those in a hurry to see Arabic capable of responding to the demands of a modern age. In surveying a number of these manuals (e.g. Nu'aimi and Kayyal 1984), one cannot but note that, even when the so-called punctuation marks are removed from the various textual elements cited, those textually well-formed examples tend to stand up to scrutiny for cohesiveness. By the same token, with or without punctuation, those cited examples which are ill-formed simply do not work. That is, when standards of textuality are met, these marks become redundant, serving decorative, easy-readability purposes only. Cohesion in Arabic is maintained through text syntax and semantics, and not by the use of marks that artificially set off parentheses (the use of which is rare in any case) or unnaturally separate the various elements of the clause, the sentence or the text (which are intrinsically additive in a predominately paratactic, not hypotactic, language). In the final analysis, the test of a cohesive text in Arabic is that it should display continuity of sense (coherence) if heard or seen.

Finally, while generic, discoursal and textual considerations are no doubt as important in Arabic as they are in any other language, the relationship between the contextual level of a given generic specification and the textural level or the linguistic realization of that particular specification is much more explicit in Arabic (explicative) than it is in other less 'oral/aural' languages (which tend to be largely implicative). In fact, it is this very explicit and almost causal relationship obtaining between text and context that may help us explain 'why' users of Arabic opt for indirect speech in texts, as the present analysis has amply demonstrated, despite the formal availability of the choice of direct or indirect speech, and of punctuation.

The Grammarian's Position

Typically, Arabic grammarians, classical and modern, adopt a narrowly focused, system-oriented stance towards aspects of language use such as the choice of direct or indirect speech under consideration. A. Hasan (1975), for example, fully discusses the phenomenon under *al-Hikaaya* (narration) and points to the availability of the choices alluded to earlier. However, like all system-oriented grammarians, the description is restricted to the 'what' and to the 'how', but often does not deal with the 'why'. Moreover, the description is restricted to the level of the sentence and below, almost in total obliviousness to considerations of genre, discourse and text.

Inspired by valuable insights yielded by Arabic rhetoric (*balaagha*) into the relationship between text and context (see Hatim 2010), we would suggest that the constraints on the use of direct speech are related to the admissibility or otherwise of such rhetorical devices as reference-switching, say, from direct to indirect quote or vice versa *(al-iltifaat)*. This restriction is closely bound up with modes of expression (e.g. sacred texts, sensitive texts, run-of-the-mill newspaper Arabic), and could explain the predominance of the indirect in Arabic texts such as Sample 1 in translation. The genre of news reporting does not permit the reference-switching allowed by other genres (e.g. the Qur'an as a unique genre or the traditions of the Prophet Mohammed *Hadiith* as a sensitive genre). This shift is appropriate only when the context's genre, discourse and text happen to be creatively 'turbulent' and 'restless', performing a managing act of persuading and not simply a monitoring act of informing.

To Conclude

In this chapter, it is established that the stylistic conventions of Arabic tend to favour the use of indirect speech in genres such as news reporting. This is partially due to genre, discourse and text constraints which are related to certain rhetorical modes of expression such as 'reference-switching' being the preserve of certain registers found in literature. For example, the shift of reference from, say, the 3rd person to the 1st person which would be entailed by the use of direct speech within reporting is reserved for more elevated forms of expression and not, say, the more pedestrian occasions such as that of reporting the news. But whatever the cause, the translator's responsibility when working into Arabic is to preserve the 'immediacy' of direct speech in the source text while at the same time operating with textual conventions which generally encourage the use of indirect forms. The way to reconcile these seemingly conflicting goals resides in tapping the resources of semiotics manifested by the use of genre, discourse and textual strategy which play an important part in making maximally interactive the pragmatic purport of the direct quote when this is used in a predominantly indirect reporting situation in the source text. Pragmatic action, in turn, motivates the use of a particular mode of discourse for direct speech. When the direct is turned into indirect in Arabic, preserving these pragma-semiotic properties ensures that the direct speech of the source text, while most certainly losing its form, does not necessarily lose its original tone and thrust.

16 A Text-Type Perspective on the Pragmatics of Politeness

A general aim of this chapter is to extend the basic theory of pragmatic politeness originally developed by Brown and Levinson (e.g. 1978/1987) and to apply it to the analysis of monologic (i.e. non-dialogic), and written (i.e. not just spoken) discourse. Like a number of other studies (e.g. Myers 1989), this investigation is not intended as an assessment of the basic theory of politeness, but rather as a case study to ascertain whether the original model of politeness is sufficiently flexible to handle entire stretches of monologue and not just separate conversational dyads. Unlike the majority of other applied-linguistic studies of politeness, however, the present enquiry will be concerned both with written and with spoken texts, and will define text rather restrictively in terms of rhetorical purpose.

A more specific aim of this study is to test the hypothesis that politeness *of*, and not simply politeness *in*, texts (Sell 1993) is closely bound up with text-type variation. It will be argued that the choice between exposition and argumentation or, within the latter, between counter-argumentation and through-argumentation, is regulated by an array of contextual factors relating to the text 'act'. Such acts are envisaged as 'signs' intended to perform given rhetorical functions as part of achieving a diverse range of overall rhetorical purposes in texts. It will be further argued that this pragmatic and semiotic specification of the utterance or of the text could be usefully explained in terms of politeness strategies. To take science as a field of communication, for example, it is our contention that the scientist, just like the civil servant or the cookery writer or any text producer one cares to name, has available to him or her the whole gamut of choices from wanting to engage in detached exposition, to getting involved in argumentation, to issuing instructions just like a legal expert. Within, say, argumentation, the choice is also wide open as to which form to use (explicit or implicit counter-argument, through-argument, etc.). Which text type and which specific text form to use is not haphazard, and to make the wrong choice would be to threaten personal **face** (a politeness variable, as we shall see shortly). This unmasks the fallacy of viewing science communication as a monolithic discipline comprising terminology and favoured grammatical structures such as the passive voice.

A Recap of the Semiotic Triad: Discourse–Genre–Text

From the perspective adopted in this study, spoken or written communication among scientists, for example, is seen in terms of the way text users utilize a number of different genres, each with its own characteristic discourse style and types of text. In the 'academic article' as a macro-genre, for instance, the largely committed and involved discourse of the 'discussion' part (a micro-genre) is distinct from, say, the predominantly detached discourse of the 'literature review' part (another micro-genre). And, even within the literature review, the explanatory synthesis will be different from the persuasive synthesis (or critique). However, as we have seen on a number of occasions so far, the characterization of discourse and, perhaps to a lesser extent, that of genre, tends to be diffuse and in parts almost seamless. For this essentially open-ended nature of discourse or genre to be brought under control and made more accessible (to writer, reader or analyst), some other more concrete system of textual practice must be exploited. That is, for **discourse statements** and generic structures to be perceived as viable coherent wholes, relatively less intangible units of communication must be employed to perform the various rhetorical tasks. The 'sites' in which rhetorical purposes are negotiated are what we have been referring to as 'texts'.

Thus, the detached discourse of the scientist finds concrete expression in the text type 'exposition'. Exposition is in turn realized by sub-types such as conceptual exposition, description, narration. To convey detachment, a number of genres are also deployed: the 'summary', the 'abstract', etc. This chain of realization may be illustrated as in Figure 16.1.

>Discourse (Detached vs Committed)
>Genre (e.g. the Abstract vs Critique)
>Text type (Exposition vs Argumentation)
>Sub-type (Conceptual Exposition vs Counter-Argument)

>Figure 16.1 From discourse to text forms

The choices that are made by one and the same text producer and that normally cover the full range, from discourse, to genre, to text type, to sub-type, to forms and tokens, seem to be closely bound up with relationships of 'power' or 'solidarity' (mostly in relation to ideology), and also with 'distance' or 'proximity' (mostly related to spoken- or written-like modes). Ultimately, of course, all these layers of meaning link up with the set of dos and don'ts that is regulated by such pragmatic constructs as politeness. Therefore, any assumption indiscriminately entertained about subcultures like those of scientists, civil servants or whomsoever, as if these were self-contained, monolithic entities, is essentially ill-conceived and unsustainable. Variables such as 'power' will fluctuate as the language user switches from one rhetorical purpose (i.e. text) to another. Genre- and discourse-switching may also be heavily involved in the process, and, given this multifaceted activity of doing things with texts, the question of 'face' and 'politeness' is bound to figure prominently. To pursue this line of enquiry and to try to substantiate some of these hypothetical statements, we will address a question not substantially different from the one originally raised in relation to politeness strategies by Brown and Levinson themselves in their classic work on politeness (1978: 62): 'What sort of assumptions, and what sort of reasoning are utilized by participants to produce such universal strategies of verbal interaction?'

Politeness of Texts: An Example

Before presenting a detailed account of the implications that text typologies can have for a pragmatic theory of politeness, it may be helpful to illustrate the main issue of text type politeness by means of a simple example that was discussed in Chapter 2 from the standpoint of the semiotic triad discourse–genre–text. This is briefly recalled here simply to introduce the new research theme: 'text politeness'.

Sample 1

> The University of X and Y University have a proven track record ... that this collaborative venture *can only enhance.*

Sample 2

> The University of X and Y University have a proven track record ... that this collaborative venture *is intended to enhance.*

In considering these sample texts, what is particularly relevant for the present discussion is the use of 'emphasis' (*can only*), which strikes us as a communicative privilege that can be enjoyed by the speaker in Sample 1 but is normally denied to the speaker in Sample 2. That is, one could not envisage the producer of Sample 2 as generally engaging in anything approximating to the kind of 'evaluativeness' which is almost part and parcel of the discourse we associate with the language of Sample 1.

For rhetorical purposes such as 'persuading' (e.g. Sample 1 above) or 'informing' (e.g. Sample 2) to be properly pursued, and for role relationships such as 'university dean arguing a point' or 'PR Office journalist reviewing an event' to stabilize within text in some context, they would have to be dealt with by language users engaging in a process of meaning negotiation through texts and thus reacting to context in a highly interactive and goal-directed manner. As Hatim and Mason (1990: 64–65) point out from the perspective of discourse and the translator:

> Seeing the meaning of texts as something which is negotiated between producer and receiver and not as a static entity, independent of human processing activity once it has been encoded, is, we believe, the key to an understanding of translating, teaching translating and judging translations.

Thus, almost universally, utterances in context seem roughly to fall into two major categories: persuasive or informative. As explained in great detail throughout this book, it is almost as though 'arguers' have declared some area of textual activity as their own turf, most familiar to them and where they feel most confident. And the same may be said of the other side—the 'expounders' have a turf of their own to cherish and protect. Any encroachment on the arguers' turf by expounders or by the arguers on the expounders' turf will be discouraged, shunned, resented. Arguers would be labelled 'too coy' if they were to cross over to the other side inappropriately, and expounders would be seen as 'over to the top' if crossing the line uninvited. This is where text politeness enters the equation, as we shall see shortly.

Interestingly, literary theorist Britton (1963: 37) captures these distinctions from the perspective of creative writing and literary discourse, thus:

> If I describe what has happened to me in order to get my hearer to do something for me, or even to change his opinion about me, then I remain a participant in my own affairs and invite him to become one. If, on the other hand, I merely want to interest him, so that he ... appreciates with me the

intricate patterns of events, then not only do I invite him to be a spectator, but I am myself a spectator of my own experience ... As a participant, I should be planning ... As a spectator, I should be daydreaming ...

Certainly, more than daydreaming is involved in what 'expounders' do when imparting information, or even describing a scene or narrating a story. Granted, one cannot completely 'persuade' without using at least some 'information' in a text; however, the general drift of the argument is clear enough: 'to inform' is qualitatively different from 'to persuade'. In the desire merely to inform, the producer of Sample 2 above remains a spectator among spectators of the way a sequence of events has unfolded. The producer of Sample 1, on the other hand, seeks to persuade and wants to invite everyone to take part in the construction of a universe of discourse of which he himself approves. The two activities of being a participant or a spectator are kept somehow distinct in the socio-textual practices of a linguistic community, and it is the intriguing question of what it is that regulates such practices that will occupy us in the remainder of this chapter.

Politeness Recast in Text-Typological Terms

Before embarking on the details of how the two major text types exposition and argumentation can account for subtle differences in politeness *of* texts (as opposed to *in* texts), a recap of text-type terminology is in order. We adopt the position that argumentation and exposition are distinguished one from the other by the relative presence or absence of the element 'evaluativeness'. This text quality subsumes a set of textual properties to do with emotiveness, commitment, focus, etc. Argumentative texts are taken to be intrinsically evaluative, an orientation which manifests itself in one of two basic text formats:

(1) through-argumentation, characterized by extensive substantiation of an initial thesis (for an example, see Sample 7 below),
(2) counter-argumentation, involving the rebuttal of a cited claim (e.g. Sample 6 below).

In counter-argumentation, two further forms may be distinguished:

(A) explicit counter-arguments, where the opposition to the cited adversary is signalled either by:
  (a) overt markers such as *Although ..., X decided ...*; or by

(b) claim presented subtly, then rebutted by an explicit adversative such as *however*, *but*, etc. (e.g. Sample 6 below)
(B) implicit counter-arguments, where the opposition is signalled implicitly, i.e. by contrastive content and not by an explicit conjunction.

In politeness theory, the text user (producer or receiver) may be seen as a Model Person (MP): 'a willful fluent speaker of a natural language' (Brown and Levinson 1978: 63).[1] MPs have at their disposal, 'a precisely definable mode of reasoning from ends to the means that will achieve those ends' (p. 63), that is, they exhibit 'rationality'. For example, producers of a text like that of Sample 2 usually operate within a context such as the 'event review' in a manner that may be described in the following terms. They first negotiate a text-initial element that 'sets the scene'. They then cover, in as much detail as is deemed appropriate (in a Gricean fashion, see later), the various aspects of that scene. The process is continued until a threshold of termination is reached, i.e. a point where text production is seen to be complete.

Nevertheless, the same text producer of a review, on the same or on a different occasion of text production, could also perceive a 'claim' that is open to question. In order to rebut such a claim, he or she needs to operate in a different capacity—that of an arguer. In situations like these, text producers switch to a different mode of reasoning but only by first discharging current responsibilities and signalling their new intentions. The latter task of engaging in a new intentionality can be achieved in a number of ways, one of which may be by first 'citing an opponent's contentious claim', then 'opposing' it and finally 'substantiating' the claim put forward, a text form we have labelled 'counter-argumentation'. Alternatively, as in Sample 1 above, a thesis may be put forward and extensively defended or argued through, a text form we have called 'through-argumentation'.

Whether responding to the expository context of a review, to the counter-argumentative context of a rebuttal, or to yet another kind of context that calls for through-argumentation, text users are all the time trying out various plans. They would assess the different means by which to reach a given end, eventually opting for one set of means that seems to be optimally effective, efficient and appropriate in reaching the desired communicative goal (in a Gricean fashion again). In all of this 'practical reasoning', text users are constantly guided by a basic principle, first proposed by Jiří Levý in his 1969 theory of 'minimax': 'not

---

1 Unless otherwise indicated, bracketed page numbers in this chapter refer to Brown and Levinson (1978).

to waste effort to no avail' (p. 70), a theme which we pick up in this book under 'relevance'.

These goals and the means to achieve them as illustrated by Sample 1 and Sample 2 above, thus relate to two different types of focus that cater for different kinds of context and involve different kinds of producer–receiver relationship. As we have made clear on a number of occasions so far, any transgression involving an unsanctioned switch from one contextual domain to another (e.g. when news reports lapse haphazardly into editorializing) is deemed textually inappropriate. To avoid what can and does at times amount to a breakdown in communication, text users are endowed with another property, namely 'face', involving either 'honour' or 'shame' and various degrees in between. They have 'two particular wants—roughly the want to be unimpeded and the want to be approved of in certain respects' (p. 66). The desire on the part of an MP to be left alone and free to do as he or she wants is called 'negative face'; the desire that others actually approve of him or her is 'positive face'.

That is, as text users, we seem to have textual rights and obligations. Unless motivated by context, news reports displaying a degree of evaluation which goes beyond the expected limits are condemned as 'over the top'. Conversely, editorials that sound too measured and factual are condemned as overly reserved, or 'coy'. In effect, what seems to be happening in either case is that a particular text receiver is being somewhat thwarted (the dreaded reaction of writer and reader alike: 'So what?!') or, alternatively, disregarded (a comment all too familiar here is: 'this is an insult to my intelligence'). At stake is 'the basic claim to freedom of action and freedom from **imposition**' (negative face) and/or 'the positive consistent self-image or "personality" (positive face)' (p. 66).

The textual stance adopted by the producers of Sample 1 and Sample 2 above is a case in point. These texts demonstrate how smooth interaction necessitates that text users behave as cooperative, rational, face-possessing agents. Our proposals have so far re-examined rationality and face and recast these in terms of textual competence, viewing the mechanisms in use from the perspective of being able to 'do things with texts'. Face (and rationality) will be perceived differently in different cultures. Moreover, within the framework adopted here, 'culture' is no longer seen merely as a catalogue of static socio-cultural features (e.g. address forms, modes of dress) but will include textual practices pertaining to the limits to personal territories and, perhaps more significantly, 'textual turfs'. As explained above, turfs have to do with the mutual knowledge of individuals' self-image, and with the social necessity to orient oneself to current norms of interaction.

All these facets of the communicative act ultimately relate to individuals in their capacity as competent users of texts. The kind of community of text producers and receivers that emerges will thus be multicultural as well as multilingual. However, these terms are to be understood not in their traditional meanings but rather in the sense of an individual, intuitively or professionally well versed in a variety of modes of speaking and writing, and also willing and able to cooperate in upholding the text conventions sanctioned by the culture in question.

Text-Type Controls

The kind of community of text producers and consumers we have portrayed is not always as harmonious. To return to our example briefly, had the speaker in Sample 1 (the university dean) violated the norms of argumentation, he would have only produced a weak-kneed, faint-hearted comment on the future of the new venture. Similarly, had the writer of Sample 2 (a PR Office journalist) been too emotive, trying to whip up support for the joint venture and what it stands for, he would have been ticked off for speaking out of turn, for being linguistically cocky, for having the cheek to tell his readers what to do and how they ought to think.

These and similar verbal 'misdemeanors' can and often do happen, particularly in cross-cultural communication. In terms of politeness theory, the transgressions committed would belong to the class of acts which 'intrinsically threaten face, namely those acts that by their very nature run contrary to the face wants of the addressee and/or the speaker' (p. 70). Acts that can threaten both negative face and positive face are called **Face-Threatening Acts** (FTAs). These might include orators or reporters not operating by the rules of customary communicative practice, and thus leaving the audience of receivers gasping for more (or less), feeling somewhat disoriented, even frustrated or angry. In either of these hypothetical situations, the text producer would be considered essentially uncaring about the addressees' wants and feelings.

Thus, text-type controls provide us with the first set of tools for policing this linguistic community of 'model text users'. The seriousness of an FTA is assessed in the light of upholding or violating generic, discourse or textual conventions, which directly or indirectly relate to the context, structure and texture of 'text' as a communicative occurrence. Cohesion, coherence, the linguistic manifestations of attitudinal meaning and the various rules and principles which regulate the membership of a given text within a particular type of language events, are some of the areas that could be at risk and are therefore heavily implicated.

Distance, Power and Imposition

At a slightly higher level of contextual negotiation, text-type criteria will involve observing another set of instructions. These specifically regulate the process of assessing the seriousness of an FTA from three points of view: distance, power and imposition.

Social Distance

The social distance (D) between the text producer and the text receiver is 'a symmetric social dimension of similarity/difference within which [co-communicants] stand for the purpose of the act, based on the frequency of interaction, the kinds of material and non-material goods exchanged ... and [a number of other, more] stable social attributes' (p. 82). Although for fundamentally different reasons, the producers of Sample 1 and Sample 2 above, for example, could under this definition both be assumed to display great distance with their respective audiences. Status as a stable social attribute (e.g. university dean) and the kind of goods exchanged (e.g. the news) can have a bearing on the variable distance.

    This kind of distance analysis, however, is not sufficiently delicate or dynamic to stand up to scrutiny, particularly when text-type fluctuations have to be accounted for in the analysis of politeness. In Sample 1, status is a minor factor, and what is central to the question of distance is, paradoxically, the need on the part of the speaker to be more approachable, to be close to 'Mr and Mrs Average', to identify with the masses. By lowering distance, the arguer can enhance his or her credibility and consequently chances of success as an arguer. In situations like this, distance tends to be lessened rather than increased.

    This would be the case particularly if we were to assume that the predominant mode of persuasion involved in Sample 1 is actually one of 'counter-arguing' (Claim–Counter-claim–Substantiation). If, on the other hand, the context specified for Sample 1 called instead for 'through-argumentation' (Assertion–Substantiation), then the distance could safely be presumed to be greater, if only slightly so. It is hard to imagine that through-arguers are prepared to relinquish distance drastically. But try as they might to hold on to a greater distance, the desire to succeed as arguers, which necessitates that distance be prevented from becoming forbiddingly too great, remains fairly high on their list of priorities.

In the case of Sample 2, the kinds of 'goods exchanged' are no doubt a relevant factor. However, what is essentially at stake in the way the text producer goes about his or her textual business is the fact that news reporting is ideally always in the service of the truth. It is this received wisdom, conventionally enshrined in societal norms that regulate the acceptability of certain modes of writing (e.g. journalese), which may more helpfully account for distance being great: ideally, the news reporter does not feel the urge to impress, nor is such impression making expected by his or her audience.

Thus, unlike those of the sociologist, these ratings of distance are purpose-specific and have little if anything to do with social status as such. University deans, for example, can and often do modify their assumptions of distance and adjust it accordingly. Similarly, distance would be lessened when deans deal, say, with the situation of having to win over their audience in speaking on issues such as cuts in higher education. For the same reason, daily reporters attending to the business of news dissemination of a type not as institutionalized as that of covering a formal ceremony for a university bulletin may find themselves adjusting distance slightly by lessening it to allow a certain amount of evaluativeness to creep into their reporting.

Relative Power

The relative power (P) of the text producer and text receiver is an 'asymmetric social dimension [which calibrates] the degree to which [the receiver] can impose his own plans and his own self-evaluation (i.e. face) at the expense of [the text producer's] plans and self-evaluation' (p. 82). Given the context of a formal address by a university dean, for example, the producer of Sample 1, particularly when 'through arguing', can be assumed to display greater power than that possessed by his audience of receivers. Reporters, in turn, also wield power, but of a different kind to that of the arguer. In order to win over their audience, arguers tend (or pretend) to share power with the addressee, i.e. to empower him or her to become a participant in condoning or condemning the state of affairs being depicted. Reporters, on the other hand, tend to assume a more authoritative stance that is least concessive. Such reporter authority derives its main thrust from similar factors to those that has engendered distance. As servers of the truth (as they see themselves), they feel that they can afford to entertain a 'take it or leave it' attitude.

It has to be noted that, while attributes to do with 'deanship' or 'reportership' are no doubt in evidence, the real reason behind power being relinquished, shared or adhered to in language use is primarily text-typological. Whether they happen to be deans or cookery writers, arguers share (or even relinquish) power on the basis of rights and obligations entailed by the argumentative context and type of text. Reporters, on the other hand, deal with a community of text receivers whose relationship with the producer of the texts they buy solely relies on the assumption that 'truth' (or the commodity offered by the text type exposition) is more powerful than anything else.

As with distance, it is perhaps worth noting too that the two particular contexts of argumentation and exposition, and the power differences attached to them, are also purpose-specific. That is, they are in no way permanent attributes of deans or journalists. When deans perceive the need to engage in a detached review of a sequence of events, they immediately reverse roles and adjust the degree of power on display to be at a higher level acceptable to the larger and more powerful community of 'truth-seekers'. By the same token, when reporters feel that what is at stake is an issue which goes beyond the bounds of 'detachment', they too can switch over, this time to the 'inciting of emotions', adjusting their power accordingly and pitching it at a lower level which puts their audience in tune with the ensuing evaluative slant. In this case, the receiver will no longer be one to be informed, but one to be won over. For this reversal of roles to be sustainable, however, sufficient contextual motivation must be provided, otherwise each and every one of these new roles would be a monumental communicative disaster—an FTA.

Ranking of Imposition

The absolute ranking of impositions is 'a culturally and situationally defined ranking ... by the degree to which [impositions] are considered to interfere with an agent's wants of self-determination or of approval (his negative and positive face wants)' (p. 82). Rephrased in terms of our text-type model, impositions will be ranked in a way that reflects whether and how far power and distance are effectively and justifiably used, by certain users, in certain contexts, and for certain rhetorical purposes. Ranking of this kind is, in a sense, a balance sheet showing the credits and debits accruing from the interface of text type with power and distance.

But it is not only considerations of text type or power/distance/rank of imposition that determines the relative weighting of an FTA. Avoiding the FTA altogether, or adopting strategies to minimize it, which are all courses of action open to any rational, face-possessing agent, may be seen in the light of 'the relative weightings of (at least) three wants' (p. 73):

(a) The want to communicate the content of the FTA. For example, the use in a news report of evaluative text structure (say, an opaque metaphor or some subtle use of epistemic modality, or a cleft sentence) is an FTA forced by the text producer on the text receiver in the light of circumstances surrounding the communicative event in question (e.g. the event could be the subject of a raging controversy at the time).
(b) The want to be efficient or urgent, as when switching to a detached, balanced review of events is seen to have high stylistic 'informativity' (an element of surprise, some unexpectedness, shock value, etc.) which can only enhance an argument.
(c) The want to maintain the receiver's face to any degree, a state of affairs which should be sought (i.e. FTA minimized or avoided altogether) unless (b) is greater than (c).

The key want in politeness is not to commit an FTA. But, if such an act has to be committed (and often to get anything done, one would seem to always have to), then a number of strategic orientations are available to the text producer. He may do it:

(1) On Record, when 'it is clear to participants what communicative intention led the actor to do the act' (p. 74), that is, when contextual and, to a greater extent, cotextual clues are clear for all to see as justifying the transgression. Explicit flouting (as opposed to breaking or violating) any of the **Gricean maxims** is a case of an on-record FTA. An ideological 'hobby horse' or 'an axe to grind' in, say, a literary narrative, if sufficiently motivated by the presence of adequate textual and contextual clues, is also an example of an on-record FTA.
(2) Off Record, when there is 'more than one unambiguously attributable intention so that the actor cannot be held to have committed himself to one particular intent' (p. 74). The more opaque the motivation is for flouting the Gricean maxims referred to above, the more 'off record' it becomes: 'linguistic realizations of off-record strategies include metaphor and irony, rhetorical questions, understatement, tautologies, all kinds of hints as to what a speaker wants or means to communicate, without doing so directly so that the meaning is to some degree negotiable' (p. 74). Contextual and, to a lesser extent, cotextual clues are the key factor in the success of doing FTAs off record.

On-record FTAs and off-record FTAs may be placed on a continuum. Doing an FTA on record baldly without redress is the most extreme of on-record acts: an FTA is done 'in the most direct, clear, unambiguous manner' (p. 74). Doing an FTA on record with redress, on the other hand, is the least extreme of on-record FTAs: 'action that gives face to the addressee, that is, that attempts to counteract the potential face damage of the FTA by doing it in such a way, or with such modifications or additions, that ... indicate clearly that no such face threat is indicated or desired' (p. 75).

Similar variation within off-record acts may be discerned. But the more significant point about all kinds of redressive and non-redressive off-record and on-record FTAs is that FTAs, wherever they emanate from, are regulated by the variables of power, distance and, consequently, rank of imposition, which are in turn themselves regulated, on the one hand, by text-typological criteria to do with (non-)evaluation, and on the other, by the set of basic kinds of 'wants' to communicate content efficiently and so on.

Politeness and Text Types: The Case of Exposition

Pragmatic notions such as politeness could thus be usefully invoked to make sure that text-type transgressions are avoided or kept under control. Face becomes a property of context, and face-threatening action the dividing line between textually competent and textually incompetent use of language. In doing 'exposition' as a text type, rational and non-face-threatening action entails that distance be increased. Readers of an academic abstract, for example, are essentially there to be informed, in as efficient a manner as possible, of the contents of, say, an entire annual report. This justifies the blandness and pro forma nature of this text form. To illustrate distance as an aspect of politeness in exposition, consider Sample 3:

Sample 3

INTRODUCTORY NOTE

Volume I contains the Final Act, the resolutions adopted by the Conference, and the Draft Additional Protocols prepared by the International Committee of the Red Cross. Volume II contains the rules of procedures, the list of participants, the report of the Drafting Committee and the reports of the Credentials Committee. Volumes III and IV contain the table of amendments.

Volumes V to VII contain the summary records of the plenary meetings of the Conference. Volumes VIII to X contain the summary records and reports of Committee I. Volumes XI to XIII contain the summary records and reports of Committee II. Volumes XIV and XV contain the summary records and reports of Committee III, and volume XVI contains the summary records and reports of the Ad Hoc Committee on Conventional Weapons. Volume XVII contains the table of contents of the sixteen volumes.

From the UN's *Documents of the Diplomatic Conference* (1974)

For the mechanisms of polite exposition to run smoothly, maximal distance must be accompanied by an equally high level of power. Receivers of ultra-detached academic abstracts, for example, are hardly the kind of audience to impress with a quaint turn of phrase, emotive use of language or graphic metaphor. The content itself is invariably colourless, normally possessing a sense of urgency that demands a to-the-point account. Furthermore, the producer of the expository text rarely sets out to persuade or try to form any future behaviour. Abstract writers are debarred from engaging in the business of manipulating language for effect.

Thus, to violate the normal pattern of lexical cohesion in this type of text unnecessarily by, for example, opting for lexical variation as opposed to the expected strict reiteration or repetition is to compromise the distance and/or the power variables, and ultimately to flout the conventions of the genre, the discourse and the text type in question. Such violations would, we argue, be face-threatening and reader-disorienting acts that, in the absence of extenuating circumstances, will render the text in question lacking in coherence.

To illustrate such transgressions, consider Sample 4 (a published translation of an academic abstract from Arabic) which we cite here with two purposes in mind: to show that different cultures handle text-type politeness differently (that is, text forms not judged 'polite' in English could be tolerated and accepted as 'polite' in Arabic, and vice versa) and to show that the expression of pragmatic politeness is an important aspect of text meaning which must therefore be heeded in translation. It must be preserved and, if necessary, adjusted in such a way as to be compatible with target-language conventions. Regrettably, such goals do not seem to be achieved in the following rather unidiomatic, flawed rendering:

Sample 4

Patterning in Pre-Islamic Love Poetry

No doubt, the sentimental dialogue is one of the sources of aesthetic values that portray the similarity of the human intellect and its universality in the world of sensations. The paper attempts to observe the expressive methods of patterning these sensations through spiritual meanings and psychological and religious content as well as personal and non-personal experiences. This research also tries to establish a pattern for the world of sensations in pre-Islamic love poetry: a pattern that combines Arabic sentiment in the pre-Islamic period ... with its counterpart in Babylonian love poetry ... Moreover, this research tries to mark the beginnings of the love poetry of the Arabs ... This is made possible owing to the similarity of the human, intellectual and religious content ...

If instructions to maximize both power and distance in relation to the text-type exposition were adhered to, the rank of imposition would inevitably be slight and FTA thus avoided. But this description of politeness is idealized, portraying what could be considered as the benchmark, default, unmarked case. Subsidiary functions such as evaluativeness could in varying degrees be allowed to creep in. Only when motivated, however, would these transgressions be tolerated and the threat to face minimized. By motivation is meant purposeful manipulation of the levels of distance and power, such that distance is not lesser than, and power not greater than, the levels allowed by the textual conventions of the relevant genre and the relevant discourse associated with the text type in question (i.e. the expository text form abstract in this example). If such violations were to occur, a series of FTAs would most certainly ensue, and the identity of the text form abstract would be obliterated, as is made clear by Sample 4.

As an example of how distance and power are manipulated for effect and within the limits suggested, consider Sample 5. This is an abstract of the 'attention-getting' type, normally provided by editors to 'advertise' what is on offer (a blurb):

Sample 5

The Influence of Culture
[ABSTRACT]

A society's attitudes to health and disease are closely bound up with its culture. However, this culture is rarely static and can usually accommodate new ideas if they do not appear to threaten it. Whatever changes health workers introduce, they should always harmonize their activities with the culture in which they find themselves.

World Health Forum Vol. 5 (1984)

Sample 3 above may be considered typical of the text form abstract. It is an example of unmarked exposition, which relays an appropriate level of text politeness through the display of maximal power and distance. Sample 4, on the other hand, is flawed as an abstract: the levels of power and distance are compromised in a manner not deemed appropriate for the text form in question. Finally, Sample 5 handles politeness in more or less the same manner as 4, but, we suggest, can nevertheless be tolerated and is deemed appropriate in its own context. Here, the FTAs in evidence are motivated (cf. the attention-getting 'editorial' intervention), and the text form in question is acceptable as a marked variety of expository abstracts.

Counter-Argumentation and Politeness

Sample 5 is interesting for yet another reason. It vividly illustrates the kind of constraints imposed by the macro-sign genre on both the discourse and the text as units of semiotic interaction, and ultimately on what constitutes face-threatening action in politeness terms. In a motivated manner, both the discourse and the text of Sample 5 are shifted away from their unmarked status, in the direction of more evaluativeness. But genre sets limits on how far the shift can go. Power and distance are minimized but not so much as to obliterate the identity of the genre in question. Had generic constraints not been heeded in this context, we would have ended up with a totally different genre (e.g. a rebuttal), and expository politeness would have been irreparably harmed. That is, had power been raised and distance lessened more noticeably than they are at present, the generic structure of the abstract would have been irredeemably compromised.

This brings us to a consideration of politeness in counter-argumentation, where power is normally maximized and distance minimized far beyond what is admitted by a text such as Sample 5. Within the unmarked form of this type, text producers try to accommodate counter-views but still hope to give due prominence to their own claims. This text type is a variety of argumentation, which builds on the 'citation of the opposite view' before countering it. To achieve this in a way that does not threaten face, text users opt to part with distance and continue to hold on to the power of the arguer. Thus, while the power of the arguer is kept maximal, distance would be lessened to facilitate getting through to a sceptical audience assumed to entertain counter-beliefs that even the arguers themselves found worth citing. This is exactly the opposite of what actually happens in exposition. As an example of a through-the-back-door persuasive strategy, consider the counter-argumentative Sample 6 and compare it with Samples 4 and 3 above in terms of the gradients of both power and distance:

Sample 6

The Influence of Culture

Asked to provide an example of the relationship between culture and health, many professional health workers would point to the persistence of certain time-honoured medical procedures in some simple rural society. However, culture may shape and fashion attitudes and responses to health and sickness in any society, whatever the level of sophistication. An awareness of the ways in which it can do this is of the highest importance, not only in promoting health in the community but in understanding disease processes ...

World Health Forum, Vol. 5, No. 1 (1984)

Thus, through the appropriate use of power and distance, the producer of Sample 6 has managed successfully to keep within the unmarked form of the 'rebuttal' as a genre, with its own evaluative discourse and counter-argumentative text strategy. Had the text been envisaged within a lower level of power and a greater level of distance, it would have become essential that a different generic structure be used in order to maintain the appropriate level of politeness. Put differently, had Sample 6 maintained the level of power (or raised it slightly, which is more likely) but raised the level of distance too, the result would have been a series of FTAs as far as the genre 'rebuttal' is concerned. But, as will be explained in the next section, displaying maximal power and a fairly high level of distance is a precondition for the success of another form of argumentation—through-argumentation.

Through-Argumentation and Politeness

Texts that belong to the through-argumentative variety, we recall, build on a premise which the text producer posits and supports wholeheartedly and extensively. Such texts derive their distance, which tends to be slightly higher than that of counter-argumentation, from the fact that they are 'masked expositions'. That is, these texts are expository in 'form', which provides distance, and argumentative in 'tone', which neutralizes such distance. This tension is manifested in the logical analysis normally provided by the text, which tends to be biased one way or another and which dominates the reasoning throughout. The maximal power in these texts, on the other hand, is derived from the authoritative air assumed by the text producer in his capacity as arguer/persuader. To illustrate this text type with its maximal power and fairly high level of distance, consider Sample 7 and compare it with its expository counterpart (Sample 3) which also displays maximal power and distance.

Sample 7

> Sickness introduces an entirely new dimension into any society. It is an unwelcome intruder, it threatens people, and it may lead to death. A society's attitudes and practices in respect of the sick reflect its understanding and interpretation of the causes of disease. In some societies, it has been the custom to isolate the sick and take no care of them. This practice probably originated with infections such as smallpox or pulmonary tuberculosis, which were often transmitted to members of the patient's family or others living in the same compound. In many places, a basic reluctance to go near the sick can still affect the behaviour of members of the health team, inclining them to neglect their patients. (...)
>
> *World Health Forum*, Vol. 5, No. 1 (1984)

The hallmark of this kind of through-argumentation, then, is its reliance on a premise accepted and defended categorically by the text producer. The systems of **evidentiality** (the indication of the nature of evidence for a given statement) and modality (calibrating degree of certainty) in evidence in this kind of committed discourse, which tends towards down-toning and tentativeness, may at first give the impression of intimacy, even weakness. This may be seen in a surface reading of *may lead to death, in some societies, this practice probably originated, often transmitted,* and so on. In reality, however, these are important characteristics of science as a discipline and contribute little to the distance and the power which the producer has claimed for himself.

To Conclude

We have examined rational and face-saving (i.e. polite) message construction, and viewed the process from the standpoint of text types in actual language use. Politeness is shown to manifest itself through the appropriate handling of two variables: distance and power. Misperception of the relationship between distance and power, on the one hand, and type of text, on the other, is claimed to be an important source of FTA. Schematically, politeness interrelationships may be represented as follows:

Text type	Power	Distance
Exposition	Fairly high	Maximal
Through-argumentation	Maximal	Fairly high
Counter-argumentation	Maximal	Fairly high

Figure 16.2 Text type, power and distance

Within this 'idealized' matrix, it is argued that any transgression, unless motivated by factors such as genre and discourse or the need to be communicatively efficient, would constitute an FTA.

The chapter also attempted to extend the theory of politeness to use in the analysis of entire texts. In dealing with the politeness of text, a text-type orientation was adopted revealing that the variables power, distance and imposition vary as the type of text varies. The proposals put forward here are not intended to be a prescriptive set of rules, nor indeed a descriptive statement of what actually happens. We simply do not know enough at this stage. Nevertheless, there are sufficient indications that enable us to present our scheme as a set of hypotheses to be confirmed, modified or discarded, once tested against authentic data. If shown to be sustainable, these insights into textuality should prove helpful to users of language in fields as disparate as translating, interpreting, academic writing, and the general field of foreign language teaching.

17 Cultures in Contact and What People Do with Their Texts: An Applied-Linguistic Perspective

It is established that discussing the notion of culture per se, let alone cultures involving contact and perhaps even conflict, is a daunting task. The scope of this investigation will therefore have to be curtailed in a number of ways. Firstly, primary attention will be given to what members of two particular cultures (loosely referred to here as Western and Islamic-Arab) do with their own texts and those of each other. Secondly, the focus will be on how literate members representative of either sociolinguistic grouping (i.e. Western and Islamic-Arab) actually engage in handling one particular rhetorical purpose, namely that of arguing for or against a stated position.

The basic assumption underlying the present study is that it is only when they are in contact, actually using texts, that people from different cultures can reach and understand (or fail to reach and understand) one another. In the regrettable but all too common situation of cross-cultural misunderstandings, which often result in or from a breakdown in communication, what is at the root of the problem is invariably a set of misconceptions held by one party about how the other cognitively visualizes and rhetorically/linguistically realizes a variety of communicative goals. Such misperceived notions would then be paraded as truisms about the nature of the language and culture of those on the other side, the textual norms in operation and the rhetorical traditions involved.

In discussing this aspect of 'doing things with texts' within and across cultural boundaries, our ultimate aim is to arrive at a number of conclusions that will enable the language user from either of the two cultures in question to operate felicitously within the rhetorical conventions not only of the target culture but also of his or her own. On a more specific level, the scope of the analysis about to be undertaken is restricted to the kind of interaction that typifies the work of the advanced language user, in a setting such as academic writing or the translation of academic writing.

In the following discussion, a textual example from English is presented which illustrates the kind of reception problems often experienced by Arab readers of English. This is immediately followed by a textual example from Arabic that demonstrates the way an Arab would typically handle the situation depicted by the problematic English text. In fact, when presented in English, the Arabic example will illustrate the kind of production problems that Arab writers of English often encounter.

The two example texts are both argumentative. However, two different contexts, structure formats and sets of texture patterns are in evidence. As we have seen in Chapter 4, this difference reflects deeper differences in persuasive strategy, with two basic argumentative procedures emerging (counter- and through-argumentation), and with each language displaying a particular preference for the use of one over the other.

Both classical rhetoric and modern text linguistics are referred to for a plausible explanation of why Arabs or Westerners tend to argue or counter-argue the way they do, understandably finding the other way alien if not utterly misleading. For a likely explanation, particular focus will be placed on the contextual element 'audience' as this seems to have a great deal to do with the way we go about structuring and moulding texts. In the case of Arabic, a number of interesting factors further complicate matters. At stake is the status enjoyed by the classical language and the position of the vernacular, with the so-called modern Standard Arabic hovering in between. We also have the issue of literacy vs orality, methods of teaching the mother tongue, the nature of hierarchical society, societal mores such as politeness, religious values such as the attitude to truth, political pressures and a host of similar facts of Arab society in the modern age. These will be discussed and illustrated in an attempt to answer the original question hinted at earlier, namely, how viable are textual conventions as transmitters of cultural values?

A Problem of Language Use

Working for quite some time with ESL (specifically Arabic-speaking) students, in fields as varied as language learning, interpreting or translation into and out of English, I have always been struck by one specific problem of text comprehension. This is to do with the inability to appreciate the rather subtle mode of counter-arguing in English. As explained in great detail so far, a counter-argument is, broadly, a text form typically characterized by a fairly opaque re-statement of the opponent's position (claim), followed by a rebuttal (counter-claim). An example of this rhetorical strategy (discussed on a number of occasions from different standpoints throughout this book) is the kind of text in English that typically opens with what rhetoricians call a 'straw-man gambit', paying lip service to a claim advocated by an adversary (in italics):

Sample 1

> Tomorrow's meeting of OPEC is a different affair. *Certainly it is formally about prices and about Saudi Arabia's determination to keep them down. Certainly it will also have immediate implications for the price of petrol, especially for Britain, which recently lowered its price of North Sea oil and may now have to raise it again.* But this meeting, called at short notice and confirmed only after the most intensive round of preliminary discussions between the parties concerned, is not primarily about selling arrangements between producer and consumer. It is primarily about the future cohesion of the organization itself.
>
> From a *Times* editorial

This consummately English textual organization has always proved to be problematical to process, particularly by students of English as a foreign or even second language, in classes of English or translation, worldwide. Sample 2 is a composite rendering concocted from several versions submitted by generations of students taking a translation test over the years. The text is concocted in such a way as to be representative of the kind of problems encountered practically by entire groups of Arabic-speaking translator trainees when given Sample 1 above to translate into Arabic.

Sample 2

> Tomorrow's meeting of OPEC is a different affair since/because [Arabic *idh, fa, haythu*] it is most certainly [Arabic *min al mu'akkad*] about prices and about Saudi Arabia's determination to keep them down. It is also certain [Arabic *min al mu'akkad ayDan*] that it will have immediate implications for the price of petrol, especially for Britain, which recently lowered its price of North Sea oil and may now have to raise it again. This meeting [with *But* deleted], called at short notice ...
>
> (Back-translation from Arabic; insertions in square brackets gloss what went wrong and how)

Note how the thrust of the initial 'thesis' (*Certainly ... Certainly ...*) is turned from one which only pays lip service to pricing and selling arrangements as the primary concerns of the OPEC meeting to one genuinely advocating that these are OPEC's only concerns at the moment. Furthermore, and perhaps more importantly, note how the opposition signalled by *But ...* (which is the cornerstone of the counter-argument) is completely glossed over, simply because it no longer made sense following two *certain[ly]*- statements of categorical commitment. These serious discourse errors are intriguing to say the least. To start with, as already indicated, this kind of error occurs with amazing regularity among foreign learners of English from a huge variety of linguistic and cultural backgrounds. And, perhaps to exacerbate the drama, students committing this kind of error are usually postgraduates with a college degree preceded by no less than six to ten years of schooling in English.

In search of a remedy, the first thing we did was to look for similar discourse signals to, say, the text-initial *certainly* in authentic Arabic texts. Having ascertained that something like this text structure does indeed formally exist in Arabic, the first question to address was: Will the function served be the same as that which the English form fulfils? In response, Arabic may indeed have the same or similar form, but what is served is an entirely different function. To see this in concrete terms, consider the following back-translation of an Arabic text which illustrates the use of what, on the surface, is an equivalent structure to the preamble to Sample 1:

Sample 3a

> No doubt, a distinction has to be made between the Iraqi People and the Iraqi Government, and Security Council Resolution 661, in permitting the provision of Iraq with medical and food supplies, reflects how seriously the world views this distinction.

However, look at how Sample 3b continues:

Sample 3b

> Thus, if the decision-makers in Iraq have committed a heinous crime ... the world would not allow itself to use the same methods as those of the Iraqi regime.
>
> From an Arab newspaper editorial

As used in Sample 3a and 3b, this text-initial element would baffle the English reader. It would set off huge expectations (ultimately, the international community couldn't care less about the distinction), only to be defied when the text continues in the opposite direction to such expectations (this is what the text is about: total concern). That is, the English reader is in a sense thwarted, since he or she could typically see the relevance of the initial citation only in terms of some kind of a subsequent rebuttal. This is not the case in Arabic where the text is not intended to be a rebuttal but rather a whole-hearted endorsement of an initially cited thesis.

At this point, an important caveat is in order. We reiterate an assertion made earlier that rhetorical strategies such as those illustrated by Sample 1 above are not entirely alien to Arabic. As pointed out in Chapter 5, the counter-argumentative strategy was not only known to the classical Arab rhetoricians, but was exhaustively studied and widely practised during more enlightened periods in the intellectual life of the Arabs. Furthermore, such a strategy is still practised in modern Standard Arabic with felicity and utmost effectiveness, albeit almost exclusively by a minority of Western-educated Arabs and those well versed in classical Arabic rhetoric. This leaves us with quite a substantial percentage of users of Arabic today for whom the strategy in question is virtually non-existent in mother-tongue text production and often overlooked in both the reception and the production of texts in the foreign languages with which they come into contact. In modern Standard Arabic, we thus find a tendency towards, indeed a strong preference for, a through-argumentative format as illustrated by Samples 3a and 3b above, and which may be defined as the statement of a given position followed by an extensive defence.

Contrastive Rhetoric

Problems of Arabic rhetoric have attracted the attention of scholars from fields as diverse as the ethnography of speaking, political theory, psychology and applied linguistics. However, before offering insights from Arabic rhetoric proper (*balaagha*) and from more recent trends within Arabic text linguistics, it may perhaps be helpful to summarize what some of these scholars have to say on the kind of problem facing us at this point of our discussion.

We will start with some contentious views often aired regarding the so-called 'mentality' of the Arabs, and entertained mainly from a socio-psychological viewpoint. Shouby (1951), for example, tells us that Arabic is characterized by general vagueness of thought that stems from over-emphasis on the symbol at the expense of its meaning. This, the argument continues, leads to over-assertion and exaggeration as predominant rhetorical modes in the speech of the Arabs. In Shouby's words:

> [Arabs tend] to fit the thought to the word ... rather than the word to the thought ..., the words becoming the substitutes of thought, and not their representative. (p. 284)

Rich in rhetoric, but with meagre corroborative evidence, statements like these have nevertheless been influential and have had a considerable impact on a large portion of the research in this area of contrastive rhetoric. Going by the kind of conclusions reached, quite a number of researchers—linguists, applied linguists, social anthropologists—seem to have uncritically accepted generalizations like Shouby's. Thus, as will become clear shortly, we have the organization of Arabic described as 'circular and non-cumulative', Arabic logic as defying even the rudiments of simple Platonic-Aristotelian paradigms, Arabic writers as confused, coming to the same point two or three times from different angles, while nothing is happening! And so on, and so forth. (For a detailed critique of some of these views, see Sa'adeddin 1989.)

Statements like these, which at best focus on the 'what', and never venture, except perhaps subjectively and anecdotally, into the 'why', have impeded progress in attempting to understand an issue as complex as language in social life across cultural boundaries. That is, unless they are subjected to a critical examination that separates the wheat from the chaff, and salvages those parts of the argument that are usable, such conclusions remain unfalsifiable and therefore practically meaningless. It is precisely such an assessment that we intend to carry out in the following discussion.

The 'Oral' vs 'Literate' Distinction

Most promising in this huge volume of writings is an interesting dichotomy popularized by American anthropologist Walter Ong, namely that of oral vs literate. The distinction is offered as one way of explaining differences in rhetorical conventions which, if it were to be applied to Arabic, would govern the preference in this language for a number of textual strategies such as the through-argumentation opted for in Sample 3. The non-periodic, additive style (commonly attributed to Arabic) is claimed by some to be typically associated with oral composition (e.g. Ong 1971). In the same vein, the high degree of parallelism, the loose, paratactic sentence structure, the predominance of coordination and the paucity of subordination (features which could all be correlated with what we may describe as the 'orate' style of Arabic) are found by a number of researchers to be characteristic of unplanned, spoken discourse, and early and popular writing (Ochs 1979; Turner 1973). (For a review of these views see Johnstone-Koch 1986.) (For an excellent critique of Ong's views, see 'Bible Translation and Primary Orality' by Professor Lourens de Vries 2000.)

Thus, the notion of 'orality', viewed suspiciously by many a native Arab (and understandably so, particularly when exclusively and often pejoratively applied to Arabic), is a potentially useful one. To begin with, the framework of orality, used appropriately to describe an important element in the context of the historical development of Arabic, contributes most positively to the overall picture of Arabic rhetoricity that we are attempting to put together. It tackles head on the question of the different status accorded both to language and to the power of the word by different cultures.

In fact, it is in this spirit that Bauman (1977) explains the function of rhetorical aspects of text such as the predominance of paratactic structures and parallelism. These, Bauman argues, have been found to 'key' (i.e. establish the meta-communicative frame for) artistic verbal performance. While by no means endorsing a reading of this statement which promotes distinctions such as poetic vs non-poetic or literate vs non-literate as the basis of the difference between English and Arabic (taken as though languages could ever be so monolithically dissected), it is nevertheless fair to say that Bauman has highlighted an important sociolinguistic fact that places languages such as Arabic within their proper rhetorical and historical context. This relates to the capacity of any linguistic system of communication to evolve in a way that responds to and copes with the ways its community of users evolves through time.

Viewed in this light, however, orality cannot be an exclusive designation of Arabic or of any other language for that matter. By the above definitions of orality, no English text could conceivably be void of oral features. Nor could any German, French or Spanish text, either. Equally, not all Arabic texts display these features to the extremes depicted. Perhaps more importantly, indiscriminate dichotomization such as this ignores the distinction of 'formal' vis-à-vis 'functional'. That is, while a text may formally exhibit an absence of, say, subordination, the functions of backgrounding, projecting, etc. are nevertheless very much present. For example, consider discourse particles such as sentence-initial *and* in this paragraph-final sentence:

> **And** in Lebanon, at whose citizens' hands the massacres were committed, the parallel enquiry has turned into a charade. (Bold added)

Here, the function of *and*, although seemingly one of coordination, is in fact 'highlighting through subordination' an implicit element that may be glossed by something like: 'Finally, and perhaps most importantly, one should not forget that in Lebanon ...'.

The second point regarding orality, then, is this: having accommodated orality within the general context of the development of Arabic rhetoric, we see no problem in accepting the notion of orality in the case of modern Standard Arabic (and indeed that of current English and other European languages) but only if seen along a continuum: some texts are more oral than others, a statement which is equally applicable to Arabic and to all other languages cited above. But, to make such a statement more meaningful, I suggest that:

> Varying degrees of orality may be seen as a function of text type first, and the specific language in question second.

The 'Presentation' vs 'Proof' Distinction

Orality has been the backdrop against which another distinction is made in examining the differences between Arab and Western rhetorical preferences. This relates to persuasion by '*present*ation'[1] vs persuasion by 'proof'. Johnstone-Koch (e.g. 1983: 55) introduces these terms like this:

> Arabic argumentation is clearly argumentation by presentation [*present*ation]. An arguer presents [v] his truths by making them present [adj] in discourse, by repeating them, paraphrasing them, doubling them, calling attention to them with external particles.

This mode of argumentation which, according to Johnstone-Koch (1991), is essentially paratactic (characterized by heavy coordination), abductive (displaying horizontal reasoning) and analogical (essentially figurative and hyperbolic), is contrasted with Western modes of argumentation which are:

---

1   The segment in italics (*present*) is to indicate that the 'present' in 'presentation' here is taken to mean 'present' (adj) ('not absent'), and not 'present' (v) ('deliver').

based on a syllogistic model of proof and made linguistically cohesive via subordination and hypotaxis. (p. 47)

To put it mildly, it is perhaps a little disingenuous of Johnstone-Koch to heap generalization upon generalization, with little or no evidence. To try to make sense of what this dichotomy (*present*ation vs proof) actually involves, let us briefly cast our minds back to the English-source Sample 1 and the Arabic-source Sample 3. Doesn't Sample 1 exhibit interesting characteristics of so-called *present*ation (e.g. *Certainly it is formally about ... Certainly it will also have*)? Given that the sequence of elements in the entire first paragraph is highly horizontal, wouldn't one say that the text is not particularly hypotactic or paratactic, nor is it particularly deductive/inductive or abductive? As to persuasion by analogy, the reader is invited to browse through the latest Hansard (the verbatim record of debates in the British Parliament) for interesting examples of 'orate' extended metaphors.

Equally pertinently, it could be asked whether Sample 3 has no solid logic of its own which, while by no means corresponding to Johnstone-Koch's Aristotelian model, is nevertheless one that is sustainable in its own right. To illustrate what we mean by logic and proof, let us consider the following use of *Thus, if ...*, an information chunk which follows that initiated by *No doubt ...* in Sample 3. Of course the connection is slightly nebulous, but only if assessed in terms of the counter-argumentative text format in English. As this and numerous other instances clearly show, claiming universality for rhetorical structures which are only valid for given languages is a failing to which many of those working in this field of contrastive rhetoric are particularly prone. In Arabic, given that the *No doubt* is the equivalent of an English text-initial element such as 'There is absolutely no doubt that', there would be no problem accommodating the *Thus, if* element as a conclusion. Within the text conventions of Arabic, therefore, the text is both cohesive and coherent. That is, the argument is logically sustainable and an element of proof is very prominent.

Johnstone-Koch (1991) often cites the phenomenon of repetition as evidence of persuasion by *present*ation in Arabic. In Arabic, however, there are two types of repetition that Johnstone-Koch seems to conflate and deal with indiscriminately, one functional, the other non-functional. Non-functional repetition is that necessitated almost by default by the rules of the linguistic system (***langue***) and, as such, is not necessarily motivated, nor is it necessarily serving a particular rhetorical purpose. When used in this capacity, a given structure would be serving no particular logical function and what is involved would be mere '*present*ation'. Functional repetition, on the other hand, can indeed subsume categories of non-functional repetition, but extends the repertoire to include a variety of forms that are essentially non-systemic (***parole***), and that tend to possess sufficient rhetorical motivation.

The basic difference between the two kinds of repetition, then, is that functional repetition is motivated, serving important rhetorical functions and thus has a place in the overall plan of developing a text. Consider, for example, the textual function of one of the structures which Johnstone-Koch generally cites to illustrate repetition in Arabic, that of the cognate accusative (*al-maf3uul al-muTlaq*):

(1) wa nafa waziru al-kharijiyyati al-suri nafya qati'an an takuna li-suriya ayyata 'alaqatin bi ... (from a news report)

Lit. The Syrian Foreign Secretary denied a categorical denial that Syria has relations with ...

(2) innana narfuDu rafDan qati'an rabta mas'alati al-kuwayt bil-halli al-silmi ... (from a political speech)

Lit. We refuse a categorical refusal any link between the Kuwait issue and the peaceful solution ...

The repetition of *deny–denial* or *refuse–refusal* is intended as a non-functional attempt to convey the adverbial system element in question and not to have any rhetorical effect. Given the genre of the 'news report', the discourse of 'detachment' and the 'narrative' text type which characterize sentence (1) above, the repetition involved in the use of the cognate accusative is non-functional. It is there as a feature of the system whose role is merely to convey the grammatical function 'adverbiality'. If it is preferred to something like *bi shaklin qaaTi3* (lit. 'in a categorical way'), this is only because it is perhaps more idiomatic or collocates better. Sentence (2), on the other hand, is from the genre 'political speech' where the discourse is one of 'commitment' and the text type is 'argumentative'. These features render the repetition involved in the use of the cognate accusative highly functional. When occurring text-initially, as it does here, it signals a 'step' in the argumentative procedure: it formulates a premise to which a follow-up response is required as part of the logic of interaction.

The upshot of this discussion is that, while argumentative texts such as Sample 3 above can be heavy on presentation, though only slightly more so than the inherently less emotive prose of English texts belonging to the same type, presentation is bound to be functional, motivated and always there for a rhetorical purpose. That is, while they do not directly display a syllogistic kind of reasoning to which the English eye is accustomed, Arabic through-arguments nevertheless strike the Arab ear with 'recurring structural cadences' that not only please but also persuade.

There are two points worth underlining in this discussion:

(1) Admittedly, Arabic texts tend to be heavy on *present*ation, but they are no less logical (i.e. proof-oriented) than texts which explicitly observe time-honoured Aristotelian models of logic.
(2) Text type and audience are crucial for general effectiveness and proper 'evaluation'. Regardless of the source language, counter-argumentation will no doubt settle for the minimum of presentation, but, to sustain text coherence, other universal systems of logic are bound to be present, perhaps acquiring prominence and even becoming conspicuously more apparent.

Here again, we may resort to the notion of the continuum regarding presentation and proof, restricting the scope of the latter category to include 'a conventional logical text structure' rather than 'logic' per se. Some texts are more *present*ation-oriented than others, a statement which is equally applicable to both English and Arabic. To restrict the scope of what such a statement might entail and thus make it more relevant:

Varying degrees of *present*ation or proof are a function of text type first, and the specific language second.

The 'Aural' vs 'Visual' Distinction

In the search for features distinctive of each of the two forms of argumentation (e.g. the counter-argumentative Sample 1 and the through-argumentative Sample 3), a more productive line of enquiry to pursue may be that of 'cultures playing to different kinds of audience', with 'audience' used here in the general, more abstract sense of 'audience of receivers' and not in the specific sense of 'the immediate addressees'. In this respect, another dichotomy, which is potentially useful and very much in line with the traditional position on orality, *present*ation, etc., is that of **aural** vs **visual texts** offered by Sa'adeddin (1989). A visual text is one that would ideally be 'a surface orthographic representation of a linearly-developed, logically coherent and syntactically cohesive unit of sense' (p. 39). An aural text, on the other hand, is one that would typically be utilized 'to establish a relationship of informality and solidarity with the receivers of the text' (p. 39). This aural focus on the audience, which Sa'adeddin associates with Arabic, is said to be realized through the preservation of:

> the artifacts of speech ... on the assumption that these are universally accepted markers of truthfulness, self-confidence and linguistic competence, as well as intimacy and solidarity.

However, in closely examining the definition of visual texts on offer and of which Sample 1 could conceivably be taken as an instance, every single term in the above formulation seems to beg a question: 'linearity', 'logically', 'coherent', 'cohesive', 'sense' and so on. Is linearity a sufficient precondition for logicality? Is cohesion a sufficient precondition for coherence? What is non-linear (and hence by implication non-logical) about aural texts (of which Sample 3 could conceivably be taken as an instance)?

An assessment along similar lines could also be carried out of the use of most of the key terms in the definition offered for aural texts. But two important questions may help us make better sense of the present model of Arabic rhetoric. Is aurality tantamount to orality and *present*ation, as redefined above? Can Sample 3 be said to be more aural than, say, Sample 1? If the answer to both questions is in the affirmative, then the categories visual–aural can be accepted and added to the other revised distinctions adopted so far. However, this is to be undertaken only within the notion of something like a continuum: some texts are more aural than others, a statement which is equally applicable to both English and Arabic. To delimit the scope of such a statement, it is suggested that:

> Varying degrees of aurality are a function of text type first, and the specific language and culture second.

A Text-Type Continuum

To sum up and bring together the various strands that have emerged in the discussion of orality, *present*ation and aurality, the idea of a continuum may be generally accepted, as represented in the following manner:

- Regardless of the specific languages involved, some texts are bound to be more oral, more *present*ation-oriented and more aural than others.
- Placed within a text-type framework, this hypothesis could be reformulated to indicate that, within argumentation, and regardless of the source

language, through-arguments tend to be more oral, more *present*ation-oriented and more aural than counter-arguments.
- Here, it may be recalled that Arabic has a particular preference for through-arguments, a statement which can now be taken as tantamount to saying that, on a continuum, Arabic texts tend to swing more towards the more oral, more *present*ation and more aural end.
- But this does not rule out the possibility (slim though it is) that an Arabic counter-argument would nevertheless be less oral, less *present*ation-oriented and less aural than an English through-argument (which is, again, not as common as counter-arguments in this particular language).

Schematically, with reference to Sample 1 (a counter-argument in English) and Sample 3 (a through-argument in Arabic), for example, the orality, *present*ation and aurality continuum may be represented as follows:

Sample 3 or an English equivalent	Sample 1 or an Arabic equivalent
+oral +presentation +aurality	−oral −presentation −aurality

But, to concentrate on the task at hand, namely finding out more about not only what is happening in texts but also why it is happening, the question of audience raised in the discussion of oral, *present*ation-oriented and aural texts calls for a more detailed treatment. As will be most strongly argued shortly, it is the type of status assigned by a given language and a given culture to the type of audience generally assumed that is the crucial factor in accounting for the way context is negotiated and texts developed.

Audience of Receivers and Rhetorical Choice

In most of the discussions of orality, *present*ation and aurality summarized above, reference is constantly made to 'audience' as a contextual factor that influences rhetorical choice. In claiming that Arabic argumentation is argumentation by *present*ation where, in the words of Bateson (1976: 80–81) 'the elegant expression of an idea may be taken as evidence of its validity', Johnstone-Koch (1986) views 'audience' in the general context of a number of factors, including the nature of a hierarchical society, power and authority, even religion and politics:

Argument by presentation has its roots in the history of Arab society, in the ultimate, universal truths of the Quran, and in hierarchical societies autocratically ruled by Caliphs who were not only secular rulers but also the leaders of the faith, and later and until recently, by colonial powers. (p. 55)

Sa'deddin (1989) takes a more pragmatic view of 'audience', relating it to level of formality, solidarity, etc. as determinants of the aural features that he finds pervasive in the Arabic text:

The native Arabic producer intends, by exploiting the informal and casual mode of text development, to establish such relations of solidarity as friendliness, intimacy, warmth, self-confidence, linguistic competence, etc. (p. 43)

Both statements contain a good deal of truth about the nature of the Arabic text and thus take us some considerable way towards answering the question why a text such as Sample 3 above, for example, strikes an English reader as somehow awkward. This awkwardness stems, among other things, from the text producer making his or her argumentative claims linguistically present, by repeating them, calling attention to them, etc. rather than by appealing to some logical proof (Johnstone-Koch: 47). Similarly, Sa'deddin's English reader would feel no less awkward, regarding a text producer perceived as 'trespassing, presumptive, illiterate, haranguing and breathing down the neck of the audience' (p. 44).

Two questions could legitimately be posed at this juncture: How would an Arab audience react to such 'awkward haranguing'? And, if variables of tenor such as informality are invoked, the next question will be: No matter what the particular audience happened to be like in actual fact, how would an Arab approach his or her audience and what kind of assumptions would an Arab be making regarding their likely reaction? Such a line of reasoning would inevitably lead to the following conclusion: for our statements to be ethno-semiotically valid, they have to transcend the immediate here-and-now and generalize on the basis of reactions and assumptions that form an integral part of the discourse of a culture. The receiver must thus be viewed in the abstract, which allows us to pinpoint:

(1) socio-culturally motivated attitudes (semiotic concerns),
(2) how norms can be maintained or flouted in the expression of these attitudes (pragmatic concerns),
(3) how categories such as formality or informality are upheld or manipulated to relay particular effects (institutional-communicative, register concerns).

To put this slightly differently, the receiver may be viewed in terms of general discourse values promoted by a given socio-cultural milieu (e.g. Arab-Islamic society). This has a significant bearing on the way texts are negotiated and text norms established and upheld or flouted. For example, to initiate a text with the utterance 'It is correct to say that ...' is to an Arab text producer an attitudinal expression of commitment to the truth value of the statement (i.e. no ifs or buts!). Now, in the persuasive context I have in mind, the last thing an Arab will think of when uttering this is an audience that is in any way sceptical. They may be totally wrong in this, but, regardless, this is how they would approach the text receiver.

Our Arab speaker may very well be haranguing their Western audience but, to be sure, the same could not be said of what they takes their audience to be—one with whom the establishment of intimacy is an overriding factor. Similarly, intimacy sought and reciprocated will probably be the most likely option entertained by the Arab text receiver. Given appropriate contextual signals, the Western text receiver would have warmed to the argument initiated by 'It is correct to say that ...', only if the text had proceeded in something like the following way:

> *However, the Golan Heights were nothing but a launching pad for Syrian missiles targeting the State of Israel.*

That is, the item 'correct' would be intended to serve a lip-service function and thus imply the expression of a certain attitude that, among other things, always assumes a sceptical audience. To an Arab, by contrast, this argumentative strategy is likely to be shunned on the grounds that the means it employs are devious. Ultimately, both the Western speaker and the Arab speaker are perhaps seeking the same objective, namely that of conveying the truth, as they see it. But the Arab's notion of truth is to reveal it all, as transparently as possible 'to make a potentially available truth actually available to the hearer' (Johnstone-Koch 1986: 53). After all, they feel they owe it to their audience to do just that in return for the faith which their audience have placed in them as arguers, a different kind of demand to that made by a Western audience and responded to by a Western arguer.

Regarding the two modes of argumentation exemplified by Sample 1 and Sample 3 above and said to be typical of English and Arabic respectively, two important points emerge from the discussion of the view that an Arab typically takes of his audience. The first relates to the kind of audience envisaged, the second to the kind of text opted for as most suitable for such an assumed audience. For social, political, religious and other kinds of reasons to do with language in social life, the Arabic language and culture appears to have promoted a unique vision of who is assumed to be the typical addressee. This vision may be summed up by the following conversational maxim:

> On a given occasion, assume that the world is divided into those who vehemently oppose your views and those who whole-heartedly endorse them, but when it comes to whom your contribution is designed to address, talk only to your supporters and be completely oblivious to the opposition.

In short, no sceptics to be entertained, no adversaries to be recognized. Sample 3 above admirably demonstrates this strategy, which brings us to the second important point in discussing audience—the one relating to text type. Two basic rhetorical purposes are distinguished within argumentation—to counter-argue and to through-argue. But the entire argumentative text is originally viewed as one macro-rhetorical purpose in contradistinction to that of 'exposition', a text type which sets a particular scene and presents it through forms such as the description, narration or exposition by induction or deduction, all done in varying degrees of detachment.

The reason why the issue of 'exposition' is raised at this stage is simply to point to a problem inherent in the Arab view of audience as depicted above, namely that the Arab seems to be always almost exclusively talking to his or her supporters. Within this orientation and seen from a Western perspective, the Arab arguer is in danger of losing credibility, with the argument falling short of possessing the necessary persuasive thrust; the text would simply be too bland to have that cutting edge so crucial for argumentation. As though aware of the pitfall, classical Arab rhetoricians tackled this particular aspect of text in context in the manner outlined in Chapter 5.

By the above definition of the kind of audience that an Arab typically envisages, exposition proper would subsume the kind of texts most suitable to use in addressing an audience of non-sceptical, non-adversarial, open-minded receivers. But, as I pointed out earlier, this kind of text is never intended to persuade. As explained in Chapter 5 under defying expectations regarding audience reactions, the Arab rhetorician steps in again and offers the following insight:

> For maximal effect, good orators would be addressing the open-minded as though they were deniers, and the deniers as though they were open-minded. This text-type shift must, of course, be motivated and functional.

Thus, through-argumentation seems to be the answer to the rhetorician's dictum: here, as in Sample 3, we have an expository text in form gradually shifting to serve an argumentative function: an almost indifferent expounding of one's own ideas, addressed to a supportive audience whose support is taken for granted. This exposition, however, is clothed in the kind of texture that only befits a denier. Part of the success of such a shift with an Arab audience lies in the ability of the text, through some process of cathartic identification, to lure the addressees into feeling that they are deniers.

Within this orientation, text types such as the counter-argument (Sample 1) and the through-argument (Sample 3) may be distinguished one from the other in the following way. In counter-arguments, the variable +sceptical −supportive audience would be involved. One would be assuming that the addressee is simply too discerning to accept a text-initial set of sentences such as *Europe is dying, Europe is dying, Europe is practically dead* as descriptive of or calling for the demise of Europe. Given the constraints of a genre such as the editorial and those of a critical kind of discourse such as that of the quality paper, an utterance like this would simply be too irrelevant to sustain a text that continues with more of the same. A change of gear is thus essential; some opposition is expressed ('but, Europe is alive and well'), followed by substantiation ('look at this or that achievement, etc.') and there you have a robust argument.

Through-arguments, on the other hand, would require that the audience be envisaged to be −sceptical +supportive. In Arabic this time, a through-argument initiated by a statement such as *Certainly, the Madrid Conference was a historic event*, all meant absolutely sincerely, would to the English ear sound as nothing but reams of sycophantic discourse. Such a text would assume total endorsement on the part of the audience of the views expressed, an assumption that is most likely to be resented by, say, an English text receiver.

The mode of reasoning illustrated by Sample 3 helps us to appreciate the function of texture phenomena such as repetition, parallelism and paraphrase; the intimacy involved in the liberal use of metaphoric expression, hyperbole, even exaggeration; and the 'fantastic' worlds which emerge from listening to a piece of oratory in Arabic. But, in conclusion, it must be stressed that Western readers, if they are genuinely interested in communication, ignore these seemingly superfluous features of the Arabic text at their peril. These features are all there for a purpose, and while the means of expressing the attitudinal meanings involved may differ from one language to another, the ends are universal values that are globally recognizable. As such, these values are not impossible to relay, whatever the language, and should therefore not be lost sight of.

To Conclude

We are now in a slightly better position to account for the differences between the two modes of argumentation illustrated by Sample 1 and Sample 3 above. We have identified the two kinds of audience that the producers of the two texts assume: counter-arguments would be typically addressed to the sceptical (the 'uncertain' in Arabic rhetorical terminology), while through-arguments typically assume a supportive audience turned into temporary 'deniers' for the purposes of the current persuasive exercise. Within these text-type orientations and re-orientations, variables such as orality, *present*ation, aurality, used as exclusive labels for rhetorical strategy in particular languages, may now have to be reconsidered.

Of course, some texts are going to be more oral than others are, but this is not necessarily an exclusive property of Arabic, English or any other language, but one related to text type alone. Furthermore, some languages would tend to display a particular preference for this or that strategy, but this does not make the tendency in question an exclusive feature of the rhetoric of this or that language. These are merely preferences, tendencies and trends. For example, Arabic tends to prefer through-argumentation. English, by contrast, orients its rhetorical strategy the other way, towards counter-argumentation. Nevertheless, these are no more than general tendencies that may well hold good but should always be taken only as rough approximations in need of further evidence.

18 The Discourse of Alienation and Its Linguistic Realization in a Modern Arabic Novella

The study of the relationship of language to thought, or the way linguistic expression is closely bound up with such discursive spheres as culture and ideology is seen as one of the more promising developments which linguistic stylistics, to name but one specific discipline from within functional linguistics, has in the last few decades ushered in, and which translation studies would do well to consider. While the socio-cultural implications of semiotic structures such as text and genre are no doubt obvious, the impact that discourse has on language as a social semiotic remains uncharted territory. As an attitudinally determined mode of expression, serving such powerful themes as feminism, racism and politics, discourse is particularly privileged as a carrier of ideological meanings and is thus a prime mover of a socio-textual process within which genre or text structures are ultimately assessed for effectiveness, efficiency and appropriateness. As Martin (1985/89) points out, when ideology is challenged, discourse becomes implicated in a number of ways: which discourse (or which genre or text) a group is able to use, and which a group chooses to use, where, when and how, are all matters of immense ideological significance.

In this chapter, the aim is thus to examine the role of language in the expression of ideology and to discuss a number of micro-level aspects of this kind of semiotic analysis. Semiotics is a dimension of context which subsumes the assumptions, presuppositions and conventions surrounding a given utterance and ultimately represents it as sign in constant interaction with other signs. For example, in a speech on immigration into Britain, it was interesting to note how a politician, obviously operating within the dictates of a particular kind of discourse, constantly referred to 'immigrants and their children' as *immigrants and their offspring*. The utterance *offspring* has become a sign (a semiotic entity) in that it no longer simply means 'children' but has in addition taken on discourse values such as 'legalistic', 'de-humanizing', 'racist' (Sykes 1985).

The perspective from which language is viewed as a vehicle for the expression of discourse meanings is essentially prompted by a feeling shared by many in linguistic stylistics that a narrower focus on the language of literary discourse would perhaps shed better light on the nature of literary meaning and thus help to assess it more adequately. Ideology seems to be one of the more salient features of discourse expression, and the analysis of ideological structures and their modes of linguistic expression would therefore not only enrich the analysis of linguistic forms but would also enhance appreciation of linguistic function. It is interesting to note here that, in lexicography an attempt is often made to capture contextual values of word meaning by usage labels such as 'derogatory', 'offensive', etc. Would lexicographers take up the call one day and include in the entry of such words as 'offspring' some of the pragmatic and semiotic values identified above?

To illustrate this socio-cultural angle on literary communication, short extracts from *Qindil Umm Hashim* ('The Saint's Lamp'), an Arabic novella by the Egyptian writer Yahya Haqqi, will be subjected to a semiotic analysis of the kind introduced above. This novella is regarded as one of the most successful examples of prose writing in modern Arabic fiction. In the preface to his English translation (which we shall use throughout as an aid to access the Arabic original), Badawi (1973: ix) observes that the novella is particularly 'rich in sociological significance ... It traces the spiritual development of Ismail [the main character], and the development of his social, moral and mental attitudes'. In a similar vein, Siddiq (1986: 126), who takes a 'deconstructionist' line in analysing the novella, maintains that 'few works of fiction in Arabic or any other language can boast of artistic economy and craftsmanship superior to Haqqi's novella'.

By way of introducing the conceptual framework within which the analysis is carried out in this study, let us consider the following extract from the novella:[1]

At these words *silence* fell on the house, *the oppressive silence of the tomb—* that house where dwelt only *the Koran recitations and echoes of the Muezzin*

---

[1] We shall be using the published English translation which adequately renders both the letter and spirit of the source text and therefore reflects the features under discussion and conveys the points being made. Like all other Arabic source texts used in this book, the source text of this citation will appear in Arabic, with appropriate commentary, in the website companion to the book to be launched immediately after the print edition is out.

announcing prayers. It was as if *they all awoke and grew attentive, then were crestfallen and finally put out*. In their place reigned *darkness and awe—they could not live* in the same house with that *strange spirit that came* to them from across the seas.

The Saint's Lamp, pp. 26–27; italics added

In general, what seems to happen in this type of literary communication is a deliberate and systematic effort to confront, challenge and at times dismantle well-established socio-conceptual structures, and to imbue expression with the unexpected and the unfamiliar, turning the ordinary into the unusual and foregrounding the unforeseen. In the extract cited above, the feeling of powerlessness finds its own discourse, a world view expressed through limiting the action to agents who are non-human and directing it at no one—inanimate non-doers producing only non-events: *Silence fell, dwelt only the Koran, they all awoke, reigned darkness, they could not live, strange spirit that came*. It is this kind of manipulation of linguistic structure to relay discourse functions of various kinds, including that which conveys alienation and powerlessness, which will primarily occupy us in this study.

Literary Context

In the text-linguistic model outlined in this book, literary context (the relevant extra-textual factors and circumstances surrounding a piece of creative writing) is demystified and defined in more or less the same terms as those used for other kinds of contexts (e.g. scientific or legal communication):

(1) The communicative values of register membership. These define the context of situation in terms of the 'use' and 'user' of language. In the above-cited extract from *The Saint's Lamp*, socio-cultural vocabulary or field (e.g. *Koran recitations and echoes of the Muezzin announcing prayers*), the awesome formality or tenor (e.g. *they all awoke and grew attentive, then were crestfallen and finally put out*) and the rhetorical echoes characteristic of narration or mode (e.g. *In their place reigned darkness and awe*) are all communicative aspects of context to which text users, producers and receivers alike, constantly refer.

(2) The pragmatics of intentionality. This subsumes the rules of use governing the appropriateness of utterances, the systems of presupposition and inference at work, and the real-world conditions under which

utterances achieve a purpose and become speech acts through which we 'do things with words'. At one of many levels of analysis, the intention of the author in the above-cited extract is to establish 'silence' as the answer to 'words', to underline a contrast between the 'pure and wholesome' and the 'tainted and defiled'; in short, to underscore a conflict. Knowledge of the world in question, among other things, is vital in order to appreciate, accept or reject this intended meaning.

(3) The semiotics of intertextuality. This regulates interaction within a system of socio-cultural, as well as socio-textual, assumptions and conventions that define an utterance or a sequence of utterances as a 'sign among signs'. Interaction involves:
- a text producer interacting with a text receiver,
- a producer or receiver interacting with a text,
- a text interacting with all other relevant texts (e.g. all 'alienating' language we could conceivably be aware of).

In fact, in the above extract, the 'familiarity' of the 'house' is set as a backdrop of norms (the house, *the tomb—Koran recitations and echoes of the Muezzin announcing prayers*) against which the theme of 'alienation' is played out (*silence fell on the house, the oppressive silence of the tomb—*that house where dwelt only *the Koran recitations and echoes of the Muezzin announcing prayers*). This is all a function of language users' internalization of similar signs making up our knowledge of the genre, which is part of our textual-discursive competence. This is at the text front, as it were. By the same token, the conflict resulting from the juxtaposition of signs like 'the Koran' and 'the Muezzin', on the one hand, and 'strange spirits coming from across the seas', on the other, represents our awareness of different modes of talking (i.e. fashions of speaking, different 'discourses'). Finally, at a very basic level of semiotic analysis, our knowledge of texts, existing in the present, the past or the future, helps through intertextuality to frame and deliver genre signs such as the narrative which threads its way in the extract under discussion.

But, as I have argued elsewhere in this book, discourse semiotics is particularly privileged and must therefore be singled out as particularly relevant to an understanding of the creative act. Certainly, aspects of the communicative or the pragmatic dimensions of context, and the way categories like register or intentionality ultimately find expression in texts, are worthwhile angles from which literary discourse may be viewed and evaluated. The same may be said of the analysis of genre and text, as the implications of these contextual categories for a definition of 'literariness' are only too obvious. But pride of place must go to the semiotic dimension of context and, within semiotics, to the category 'discourse'.

To start with, it is the perception of the utterance as a 'sign', and the appreciation of discourse as 'a mode of talking' characteristic of a given institution (Kress 1985b), that in the final analysis is what enable us as language users to deal with textual occurrences in all their manifestations (intentionality, cohesion, coherence, and so on). The Joycean theme (i.e. the discourse motif) of alienation, of 'dear, dirty Dublin', which finds interesting echoes in *The Saint's Lamp*, runs through the novella and turns both genre and texts into ideological statements on behalf of the 'alienated'. That is, through the discourse in question, the genre materializes as a mega-statement of inner struggle, and texts emerge to serve the higher-level purpose of 'suffering', with both these structures enhancing the narrative with a particular slant on reality that is unique to the inner struggle being depicted.

The second reason for the primacy of discourse relates to our own intuitive feeling that text users usually take a particular stance on reality and can articulate attitudinal meanings only through their discourses. The alienation theme in parts of *The Saint's Lamp* is a statement of (i.e. a discourse of) inner conflict which the anti-hero Isma'il experiences well before his entanglement with the wider, exterior conflict of East and West. This colours the lenses through which we are invited to view the various staging posts on the journey to self-redemption.

Finally, discourse is particularly conducive to the expression of attitudinal meanings in general and ideology in particular. As distinct from genre and text, which are essentially enabling vehicles, mere sites for the expression of what can at times be a number of competing discourses, it is only through our discourse that our attitudes to class structure and class conflict, and consequently our perception of reality and our view of the world, fully come into their own. Alienation is but one among many essentially conflicting attitudinal meanings dispersed throughout *The Saint's Lamp* as signs float, not so much in harmony as in conflict, searching for a resolution. The relationship between discourse and ideology that is vital in this novella will thus occupy us.

Discourse and Ideology

In his analysis of ideological structures, Kress (1985a: 27–28) defines 'discourse' as a 'mode of talking' that he then explains in the following terms:

THE DISCOURSE OF ALIENATION

In essence, it points to the fact that social institutions produce specific ways or modes of talking about certain areas of social life ... That is, in relation to certain areas of social life that are of particular significance to a social institution, it will produce a set of statements about that area that will define, describe, delimit, and circumscribe what it is possible and impossible to say with respect to it, and how it is to be talked about.

But social institutions are rarely static entities. Institutional expression is always imbued with attitudinal meanings, and this can drastically vary as institutions vary. Take, for example, 'alienation' and utter powerlessness as the hallmark of an important discourse which threads its way throughout *The Saint's Lamp*. Through characters like Isma'il, the discourse is there to challenge an entire way of thinking represented by important religious and secular orders in the East or West. Interestingly, this is no different from the alienation and powerlessness depicted by Orwell in *1984* or Golding in *The Inheritors*. To see this from a translation perspective it is prudent to suggest that, since ideological structures tend to make their presence felt within a socio-cultural system of signs, the ideological significance must always be made more transparent (not necessarily overt or explicit) in the translation of a particular discourse. That is, we must be able to 'read off' the ideology in question from the linguistic expression encountered in the text, original or a translation. Language is inevitably implicated when socio-cultural values are involved, as they always are in any work of art.

Both within and across semiotic boundaries, cultures tend to sanction attitudinally determined statements of given ideological positions which themselves become filters through which institutions find a mouthpiece. In other words, ideologies are best viewed as 'systems of ideas' or 'world views' that relate material conditions to linguistic expression. It is small wonder, then, that in literature or non-literature, ideological meaning is part and parcel of the iconicity, indexicality and symbolicity of all texts. This is inescapable and concerns all forms of knowledge, dominant or oppositional.

One way of examining ideological structure, then, would be to consider language, pure and simple. This relationship between language and ideology may be identified at a number of levels. First, language is implicated at the lexical/semantic or the grammatical/syntactic levels. A pioneering study of linguistic function as reflected in the syntax of literary discourse is Halliday's analysis of Golding's *The Inheritors*. The realm is one of 'syntactic imagery' that, in the context of the novel, Halliday (1971: 360) explains as follows:

In *The Inheritors*, the syntax is part of the story. As readers, we are reacting to the whole of the writer's creative use of 'meaning potential'; and the nature of language is such that he can convey, in a line of print, a complex of simultaneous themes, reflecting the variety of functions that language is required to serve ... In *The Inheritors*, it is the linguistic representation of experience, through the syntactic resources of transitivity, that is especially brought into relief.

The Experiential Meaning of Transitivity

A basic property of language is that it enables its users to formulate a mental picture of reality and to make sense of and express what goes on around and inside them. The system of transitivity has evolved to cater for the expression of this kind of experiential meaning. By transitivity is meant the different types of process that are recognized in the language, and the structures through which they are expressed. Essentially, this system seeks to represent (i) the process itself, (ii) participants in the process and (iii) the circumstances associated with the process. These may be illustrated by extracts from *The Saint's Lamp*:

Later my grandfather set up a grain shop in the Square

Here, *set up* is a process, *my grandfather* and *a grain shop* are participants, and *later* and *in the Square* are circumstances.

Predicates like the one illustrated in this example divide into several types:

(i) action predicates, concerned with deliberate action and its consequences that are under the control of the principal noun, e.g.

Ismail set up a clinic in Al-Baghalla district,

(ii) state predicates, which simply attribute properties, mental or material, to objects, e.g.

Though he was not smartly dressed, his clothes were always clean,

(iii) process predicates, or events or changes, mental or material, which happen to things without their control, e.g.

her eye would water.

In proposing the 'mind-style' hypothesis endorsed throughout in this study, Fowler (1986/1996: 157) has this to say:

> [The distinctions within the transitivity system tend to] convey different pictures of what is going on in the world. It is easy to imagine the types of mind-styles associated with a dominance of one sort of pattern: predominant action predicates may go with strong physical activity, foregrounded mental processes with an introspective mind-style, and so on.

In the kind of analysis outlined in this chapter, however, it is the following types of relations that would seem to be of more immediate relevance:

(1) transitive action predicates in which a noun referring to an inanimate object serves as the subject, e.g.

The destructive axe of the town-planning department demolished it together with other old landmarks of Cairo,

(2) intransitive process predicates in which, although people act or move, they do not act on things and they move only themselves, e.g.

He would pause and smile, thinking: if only those girls knew how empty-headed they were!

(3) intransitive process predicates with an inanimate actor, where not only is the action directed at no one, but it is also done by no one animate, e.g.

Gradually the square fills anew with people.

The 'mind-style' hypothesis has had a considerable influence in setting the parameters for a view of linguistic stylistics that basically holds that language is not neutral with respect to discourse and that, therefore, certain syntactic forms will necessarily correlate with certain discourses. In his analysis of *The Inheritors*, Halliday finds intransitive structures to be particularly productive in relaying an atmosphere of 'helplessness': 'people act but not on things; they move but only themselves'. In this kind of 'no-cause-no-effect' discourse, moreover, a high proportion of the subjects are not people; they are either parts of the body or inanimate objects. For example,

The bushes twitched again

This and similar analyses demonstrate that what processes, participants and circumstances feature in a text are ultimately responsible for the text producer's attempt to relay feelings of cognitive limitation, of a diminished sense of causation, of an unexpectedly vigorous objective world.

The Language of Alienation

For the purpose of the analysis presented here, the alienation theme is selected as a discourse ideological structure which, in his brilliant English translation of the novella, M. Badawi (1973: x) aptly describes in the following terms:

> The problem, therefore, is set in social terms. It is not the eternal silence of the infinite spaces that terrifies Ismail, but the silence of the people around him, the absence of communication with his own family, the discovery that he has become deracine, an outsider among his kith and kin.

This sense of loss reflects the trials and tribulations of Isma'il, the main character, on his spiritual journey from beginning to end. This motif is bound to find its own discourse, the emergence of which is facilitated by a careful and appropriate selection of syntactic and semantic imagery. With this in mind, the Square is selected as the vantage point from which to observe Isma'il's outer- and, much more significantly, inner-world, unfolding.

To illustrate how mind-style pans out in portraying alienation, we will now on shift the focus of the analysis from the Arabic source text onto the English target text, and see the process not so much in terms of text producer's intentionality as the effect which the English target text produces on the target reader (i.e. you or the analyst).

The Square is first introduced into the novella in the following way:

Sample 1

> Later my grandfather set up shop in the Square. Thus, our family lived within the precincts of the Saint's mosque and under her protection. The Saint's feasts and calendar became ours and the calls of the Muezzin our only clock. (pp. 1–2)

Notice how, apart from the first clause, the subjects are not people and the predicates are not of the 'action' type: *lived* is an intransitive process, and *became* a transitive process. It is also worth noting how, in the translation, both verbs

THE DISCOURSE OF ALIENATION

are 'ellipted' when a second event comes along: *and (lived) under her protection; and the calls of the Muezzin (became) our only clock*. The ellipsis in the English text seems to further highlight the prevalent atmosphere of ineffectual activity pervading the Arabic source.

Initially, however, the Square is presented to us as a haven of peace:

Sample 2

> ... his greatest pleasure was to stroll by the river, or stand on the bridge. At nightfall, when the heat of the sun had gone and the sharply-etched lines and reflected light changed to curves and vague shadows, the square came into its own, ridding itself of strangers and visitors. (p. 5)

But this peace is short-lived. For one thing, although Isma'il's 'strolling' or 'standing on the bridge' are, strictly speaking, 'movements', they can hardly be said to enjoy a full 'transitive action' status, for they seem to affect the mover only. For another, more compelling reason, the 'going' of the heat of the sun, and the Square 'ridding' itself, through the 'intransitive' and the 'reflexive' respectively, ensure that nothing else changes: a combination of activity and helplessness.

It is the Square 'coming into its own', however, which is perhaps a more significant development. It introduces the necessary element of doubt and foreboding and, through the 'reflexive', signals the ultimate in combining activity with powerlessness and displaying inner strife:

Sample 3

> Gradually the square fills anew with people, weary figures, pale of face and bleary-eyed. They are dressed in what clothes they can afford, or if you prefer it, in whatever they have been able to lay their hands on. There is a note of sadness in the cries of the street-hawkers ... (p. 5)

Here, subjects are not people, even when 'they' are dressed; conceptually *they* refers to the 'weary figures'. Again, none of the subjects is engaged in actions with consequences. In fact, nothing seems to be under the control of the principal subject, which is inanimate in any case: even the clothes are 'whatever they have been able to lay their hands on'. The inactive 'state' is finally ushered in as one of 'sadness'. But conflict escalates and is at its highest in:

Sample 4

> What hidden tyranny have they suffered from and what heavy load weighs upon their hearts? And yet their faces express a kind of content and acceptance of things. How easily these people forget! There are so many hands to receive so few piasters and milliemes. Here there are no laws ... No one really seems to mind much. (pp. 5–6)

There are a large number of clauses in which nouns referring to inanimate objects are used as subjects: 'no one' is in control of his environment, let alone interacting with it:

Sample 5

> Rows of people sit on the ground leaning against the wall of the mosque. Some of them lie asleep on the pavement, a mixed crowd of men, women and children. No one knows where they come from or where they will go. They are like fruit dropping from the tree of life to rot and wither away beneath its boughs. (p. 6)

The peculiar transitivity which imbues this and other passages has cumulatively contributed to what Fowler (1986/1996) labels an 'estranged mind-style'. Throughout, the feeling has been one of total powerlessness. The following extracts make this point clearly:

Sample 6

> When Isma'il came to the square he found it as usual crowded with people, all looking poor and wretched and their feet heavy with the chains of oppression. They could not possibly be human beings living in an age in which even the inanimate was endowed with life. They were like vacant and shattered remains, pieces of stone from ruined pillars in a waste land: they had no aim other than standing in the way ... (pp. 27–28)

The weight is too heavy for words:

Sample 7

> The crowd, like a mass of dead and disfigured bodies, weighed heavily on Isma'il's chest, making his breathing difficult, and straining his nerves. Some of the passers-by collided with him as if they were blind. (p. 29)

And so on. To sum up, in examining the language of Samples 1–7, one particular feature stands out most prominently. This is the predominance of intransitive process predicates that reflects the limitation on people's actions and their world view. In an intransitive structure, the roles of 'affected' and 'agent' are combined. This clearly indicates total absence of cause and effect: people do not act on things around them; they act within the limitations imposed by these things. The frustration of the struggle with the environment is embodied in the syntax.

This pervasive reading may be contrasted with the world of 'cause and effect' outside the Square, particularly in the very beginning and towards the end of the novella, including, most importantly, the period which Isma'il spent in England. As a sample of the 'intruder' theme of 'self-sufficiency', 'total satisfaction', etc. (cf. Siddiq 1986), let us consider the following extract from the very end of the novella:

Sample 8

> Ismail set up a clinic in Al-Baghalla district, near the hills, in a house that was fit for anything but receiving eye patients. His fee never exceeded a piastre per consultation. Among his patients there were no elegant men and women, but they were all poor and bare-footed. Oddly enough, he became more famous in the villages surrounding Cairo ...
>
> He performed many difficult operations successfully using means which would make a European doctor gasp in amazement ...
>
> Ismail married Fatima and she bore him five sons and six daughters ...
>
> (p. 38)

Gone is the world of total powerlessness which allowed for only the momentary hints of potency. This potency, by contrast, dominates Isma'il's world later when he recovers his faith and regains the lost light. As Sample 8 clearly shows, the majority of the clauses are transitive actions with a human subject. The world is organized in a way we can recognize as 'normal'. People may be bare-footed, but they are not hopeless or powerless.

In conclusion, it must be acknowledged that the uniqueness of this text as a statement of an ideological position does not lie merely in the foregrounding of inanimate agents or a predominantly intransitive clause structure. To relay alienation, these patterns interact with other structures in a most intricate way. Lexis encodes this idea of thematic multiplicity. This, in turn, interacts with other estranging structures, including a constant disturbance of sentence structure and sentence sequence. Cumulatively, these features contribute to a topsy-turvy world which is far from neutral or straightforward. An analysis which brings out these elements in their interaction within the text would be extremely instructive and future work on literary discourse, particularly in a language like Arabic, will do well to attend to these and other matters within the framework of ideology and language.

To Conclude

In this chapter, the aim has been to subject *The Saint's Lamp*, a modern Arabic novella, to a cultural/semiotic analysis. This took the form of matching form with function, socio-cultural values with linguistic expression, ideology with discourse. The discourse of alienation, expressing the ideology of inner conflict is found to be pervasive throughout the novella. Intransitive structures, mostly with an inanimate agent, relay an atmosphere of total absence of 'cause and effect', of total alienation.

19 The Translation of Irony: A Discourse Focus on Arabic

The aim in this chapter is to pursue further the thesis that, in terms of underlying textual strategy, the differences between literary and non-literary discourse become of lesser importance than those areas that the two forms of expression have in common (i.e. the communicative potential of register, pragmatic sense and force and the status of the utterance as a sign among signs). In the previous chapter, we saw how our discourse-processing model proved optimally relevant for the analysis of a literary sample, as it would be for any other non-literary variety of language use. In the present chapter, irony, a theme that has traditionally been of interest, sometimes almost exclusively, to the literary critic or the stylistician, is tackled, as an area of language use in non-fictional texts.

In the following discussion, we will continue to argue for the primacy of discourse semiotics as a contextual dimension (i.e. attitude as sign). To demonstrate this, we will offer a discourse-oriented framework for the analysis and description of irony. The specific aim of this practical exercise is to search for a possible solution to problems encountered in translating ironical (even sarcastic) use of language from English into Arabic. Irony is shown to impinge not only on the institutional-communicative aspects of register and on pragmatic meaning but also, and much more significantly, on the three semiotic macro-signs—text, genre and discourse. Texts embody rhetorical purpose (e.g. to report 'tongue-in-cheek'), discourse expresses attitudinal meanings (e.g. to be disparaging), and genre conventionally establishes the appropriateness of particular forms of expression for particular communicative occasions (e.g. the 'send-up' or making somebody or something appear ridiculous by humorous imitation). The problem for the translator arises when different pragmatic and institutional-communicative solutions are offered by different languages in the expression of almost universally recognized attitudinal values which are essentially discourse and semiotic. That is, while almost all languages have at their disposal the potential ultimately to convey, say, a disparaging attitude (a semiotic concern), what constitutes this disparagement in terms of rules of politeness, types of implicature, etc. (pragmatic concerns) and those of register appropriateness, level of formality, etc. (institutional-communicative concerns) can and does vary from one language to another. Given obvious socio-cultural and text-linguistic dissimilarities, English and Arabic are a language pair ideally suited to demonstrate the problematical nature of this contrastive text-linguistic process.

The Perception of Irony

Let us consider the following text sample taken from Edward Said's *Orientalism*, a book noted for its superb polemics. (For the sake of clarity and ease of reference, the sample is presented element by element and these are numbered sequentially.)

Sample 1

[Following an initial (rather tongue-in-cheek) presentation of the basic stance on the issue of the West vs the Orient advocated at the time by Arthur Balfour (Prime Minister of the United Kingdom from 1902 to 1905), Edward Said continues ...]

1. Since these facts are facts,
2. Balfour must then go on to the next part of his argument. (...)
3. Balfour produces no evidence that Egyptians and 'races with whom we deal' appreciate or even understand the good that is being done them by colonial occupation.
4. It does not occur to Balfour, however, to let the Egyptian speak for himself,
5. since presumably any Egyptian who would speak out is more likely to be 'the agitator [who] wishes to raise difficulties' than the good native who overlooks the 'difficulties' of foreign domination.
6. And so, having settled the ethical problems,
7. Balfour turns at last to the practical ones.

8. 'If it is our business to govern, with or without gratitude, with or without the real and genuine memory of all the loss of which we have relieved the population

9. [Balfour by no means implies, as part of that loss, the loss or at least the indefinite postponement of Egyptian independence.]

10. (...) 'If that is our duty, how is it to be performed?'

11. England exports 'our very best' to these countries.

12. These selfless administrators do their work 'amidst tens of thousands of persons belonging to a different creed, a different race, a different discipline, different conditions of life.'

Edward Said, *Orientalism*, pp. 33–34

A number of renderings into Arabic attempted by a group of postgraduate translator trainees were used in obtaining a composite version that we can use as representative of how the above sample is generally perceived, processed and translated into Arabic. The specific issue addressed in this exercise is focused on how Sample 1 seems to be particularly problematical to translate into Arabic, in terms of both understanding and reproducing a crucial aspect of text meaning, namely the use of irony around which the entire text revolves. To ensure optimal contextualization, the students were first given a brief overview of the background to the text, the ideology of the protagonists, and so on.

Initial expectations regarding the difficulties posed by such a text were confirmed by the fact that almost all of those who took the test failed to appreciate or properly handle the ironical meaning threading its way throughout. The questions we shall therefore attempt to answer in the following discussion are: What went wrong for such an important omission to occur? Is language (English or Arabic per se) implicated in such a communication breakdown? How could the communicative process be made more efficient and relevant in such contexts? Could the appreciation of irony be made more effective and systematic? Can text linguistics contribute to this effort under the umbrella of safeguarding appropriateness? How could insights from a contrastive linguistic view of text in context be used to enrich translator-training programmes in this and similar areas of language use?

Before embarking on the details of what constitutes irony pragmatically and how this is processed from a discourse perspective, a comparative statement of what was actually rendered vis-à-vis what could or should have been rendered in the translation test referred to above may be helpful. A representative student version is concocted for illustrative purposes here in back-translation from Arabic.

The following layout is used to present the results:

(1) The linguistic expression of ironical use is underlined, followed by
   (a) the ironical use glossed as intended by the source text, so that we may appreciate fully the erratic nature of the students' rendering,
   (b) a back-translation into English of the students' rendering,
   (c) a gloss of students' erroneous attitudinal meaning. The glosses (in square brackets) are more like a commentary on the limits of discourse expression (i.e. on how far can or should one go with the attitudes relayed by the source text) than anything which could even approximate adequate translation equivalence.

Finally, this, together with the glossing appended, must be read as intended by the students, i.e. not noticing the irony, adopting instead a pro-Balfour stance, with sincere conviction in what is said.

1. Since these facts are facts,
   (a) Since these 'facts' as Balfour blatantly calls them are 'unblemished'
   (b) Since these are indeed facts
   (c) [Since what Balfour has presented is the truth]

2. Balfour <u>must then go on</u> to the next part of his argument
   (a) As though more was needed to prove Balfour's point!
   (b) Balfour feels it is only appropriate to proceed to the next part of his argument
   (c) [Balfour feels a logical necessity to proceed ...]

3. Balfour produces no evidence that the Egyptians and '<u>the races with whom we deal</u>' <u>appreciate or even understand the good that is being done them by colonial occupation</u>
   (a) What he so condescendingly refers to as the races dealt with, and what an unappreciative lot they are for what he unashamedly calls 'the good done them'
   (b) Balfour has no evidence that the Egyptians or the races with whom the British deal appreciate or even understand the good that is being done them by colonial powers
   (c) [It is a pity that no evidence was forthcoming of the gratitude of the natives, as gratitude on the part of these peoples for the great deal

of good done them by the colonizer is expected and wouldn't have gone amiss]

4. It does not occur to Balfour, however, to let the Egyptian speak for himself
    (a) It does not even occur to him ...
    (b) Balfour did not think it was necessary to let the Egyptian speak for himself
    (c) [He simply did not feel that it was 'relevant' to his argument]

5. since presumably any Egyptian who would speak out is more likely to be 'the agitator [who] wishes to raise difficulties' than the good native who overlooks the 'difficulties' of foreign domination
    (a) is more likely to be what he so deviously labels 'agitators' who cannot even cope with normal, everyday 'challenges'. How palpably devious!
    (b) since it can safely be assumed that those who will speak up are likely to be agitators and troublemakers rather than good law-abiding citizens who constructively circumvent difficulties
    (c) [on the grounds that those who will speak up more often than not turn out to be resentful, irresponsible troublemakers, not upright citizens who think positively, taking the difficulties in their stride, as they should]

6. And so, having settled the ethical problems,
    (a) And now that the main ethical problems are 'conveniently' out of the way
    (b) Thus, having solved the ethical problems
    (c) [Thus, having attended to the ethical problems as exhaustively as humanly possible]

7. Balfour turns at last to the practical ones
    (a) As though everything was 'neatly' wrapped up in the preceding argument
    (b) Balfour finally and logically turns his attention to the practical problems
    (c) [To conclude, Balfour finally embarks on a discussion of the practical problems]

COMMUNICATION ACROSS CULTURES

9. Balfour by no means implies, as part of <u>that loss, the loss or at least the indefinite postponement of Egyptian independence</u>
   (a) Conveniently glossing over the fact that 'loss' could only mean loss of such fundamental human rights such as independence, liberty
   (b) Balfour does not of course imply that loss of Egyptian independence is a great loss at all
   (c) [In talking about the loss of which the colonized population have been relieved, Balfour implies that there is nothing sinister about the loss of independence that the Egyptians suffered]

11. England exports '<u>our very best to these countries</u>'.
   (a) How disingenuous—our 'best' is their worst!
   (b) England sends her very best people to these countries
   (c) [The best brains, the best expertise, are all sent to help these countries—what total commitment and self-denial!]

12. <u>These selfless administrators</u> do their work 'amidst tens of thousands of persons <u>belonging to a different creed, a different race, a different discipline, and different conditions of life</u>'.
   (a) Selfless, are they? How dishonest! How racist! Also, what a 'sacrifice' it must have been for civilized administrators to work with gypos, pakis and the like!
   (b) These truly dedicated administrators carry out their duties amidst tens of thousands of men, women and children belonging to a different creed, a different race, a different discipline, a different way of life
   (c) [The ultimate in self-denial for such altruistic servants is to work with people who do not only belong to a different creed but also to a different race, discipline and way of life.]

Ironical Meaning Assessed

Now that the main cause of the problem encountered by our students in the translation of Sample 1 above has been identified mainly as being an inability to appreciate and handle ironical meaning, it is perhaps useful now to review some of the major approaches to the analysis of irony. Through this review, we intend to come up with some form of synthesis of views regarding what actually constitutes this kind of non-literal meaning. In developing this assessment, primary attention will be paid to the kind of analysis that could sufficiently account for what successfully counts as 'saying something and meaning the opposite', attitudinally, both intra- and inter-lingually (i.e. within one and the same language and between languages).

In fact, irony has traditionally been defined as saying one thing and meaning the opposite. Quintilian is quoted as saying that the use of irony involves us in understanding 'something which is the opposite of what is actually said' (IX. II:44). However, this 'semantic' account of irony begs several questions: since 'meaning the opposite' would have to be a 'figurative' process, what is 'figurative meaning'? Similarly, since this figurative meaning depends on what one reads or hears literally, how is figurative meaning derived from literal meaning? Moreover, as Sperber and Wilson (1981: 295) incisively remark, there is always the question 'why [should] a speaker ... prefer the ironical utterance ... to its literal counterpart?'

As an alternative to the traditional view, Grice (1975) proposes a pragmatic approach to irony: figurative meaning is analysed in terms of so-called 'conversational' implicature. Basically, implicatures convey implied meaning and thus tell us how it is possible to convey information implicitly:

A: Is John back yet?
B: The pubs are still open.

Johanesson (1985: 205)

Since, as expected from all implicatures, the reason why John is not back (and possibly the assertion that John may be a bit of a drunkard, an irresponsible individual, etc.) are all left unsaid, the speaker (B) expects the hearer to be able to work out (i.e. infer) the implied meanings through knowledge of the world, the topic of conversation, etc. Grice thus builds his theory of implicature against the background of a powerful theoretical norm, namely that, unless there is a good reason to do otherwise, people tend to be 'cooperative' individuals almost instinctively, always saying what they mean and meaning what they say. Following is how Grices states this **Cooperative Principle** and outlines four sets of rules or **'maxims'** said to enable the speaker to achieve cooperativeness:

> Make your contribution such as is required by the present direction of the conversation.
>
> **Quantity:**
> (1) Make your contribution as informative as is required (for the current purpose of the exchange).
> (2) Do not make your contribution more informative than is required.

Quality:
(1) Do not say what you believe to be false.
(2) Do not say that for which you lack adequate evidence.

Relation:
(1) Be relevant.

Manner:
(1) Be perspicuous.

But the tremendous appeal of Grice's theory to applied pragmaticians is attributable not so much to what happens when people abide by these rules as to what happens when people don't (for a good reason, of course). That is, it is not upholding the maxims, but rather the ways in which speakers can inadvertently break them (i.e. *fail to observe* them), *violate* them (irony intended, but not negotiated properly), or *flout* them (blatantly) that have rightly held so much fascination for the student of communication. In an excellent summary of the Gricean theory, Johanesson (1985: 208) explains the distinction between the different ways of infringing the rules:

> A speaker may accidentally break a rule (this is FAILURE to observe a given maxim).
>
> More interesting than failure is what happens when a speaker intentionally breaks a rule. This is done in two fundamentally different ways: either the speaker breaks the rule in a COVERT manner, never intending the hearer to realize that a rule is being broken, or s/he can break the rule in an OVERT manner, intending the hearer to understand that a particular rule is being broken. In the first case we may say that the speaker VIOLATES a maxim, in the second that s/he FLOUTS a maxim.

Irony is presented by Grice as a case of flouting the first maxim of Quality (namely, 'do not say what you believe to be false'), and the following example is cited (1975: 53):

> X, with whom A has been on close terms until now, has betrayed a secret of A's to a business rival. A and his audience both know this. A says 'X is a fine friend' ...

Crediting Grice with relieving 'semantic theory of the problem of defining figurative meaning and deriving the figurative meaning of an utterance', Sperber and Wilson (1986: 240) nevertheless take the implicature's theoretician to task on the grounds that the theory is as yet unable to account for *why* a speaker should opt for an ironical utterance and not its literal counterpart. However, in examining the alternative theories put forward by Sperber and Wilson, it is difficult to see how their new proposals fill this particular gap, if indeed a gap it is. From the translator's point of view, and by implication that of the contrastive linguist, it may be useful here to reiterate what Hatim and Mason (1990: 98) had to say by way of clarifying where we stand on irony:

> Sperber and Wilson's view of ... irony is not inconsistent with an essentially Gricean view. Thus, ironic understatement, while it may not flout the maxim of quality, does involve apparent flouting of the maxim of quantity ('make your contribution as informative as required').

At this point, a brief account of the Sperber and Wilson model of irony may be needed. The aim is not to recycle what Grice has already said nor indeed to report on the ramifications of the arguments for or against implicature theory. The intention here is merely to reread Sperber and Wilson and highlight those valuable insights that make a case for the semiotic status of irony (i.e. irony as a cultural sign).

An important distinction which Sperber and Wilson draw is one between 'first-order interpretation' and 'second-order interpretation', the latter being exemplifiable by irony. In irony, it is maintained, 'the thought of the speaker which is interpreted by the utterance [e.g. Said's in Sample 1] is itself an interpretation. It is an interpretation of a thought of someone other than the speaker (or of the speaker in the past) [e.g. Balfour's in Sample 1]' (1986: 238). Another related distinction the authors make is between 'use' (involving 'what an expression refers to') and 'mention' (involving 'reference to the expression itself'), with irony properly belonging to the latter category (1986: 303). With this in mind, irony comes to be seen as a case of 'echoic mention':

> By representing someone's utterance, or the opinions of a certain type of person, or popular wisdom, in a manifestly skeptical, amused, surprised, triumphant, approving or reproving way, the speaker can express her own attitude to the thought echoed, and the relevance of her utterance might depend largely on this expression of attitude.
>
> Sperber and Wilson (1986: 239)

Two points emerge from this discussion, which, interestingly, enhance rather than detract from the Gricean account. First, the kind of attitudinal meanings that emerge from uses of irony (e.g. a disparaging attitude), which are beyond a pragmatics of text to identify definitively or describe exhaustively, are in fact semiotic categories (i.e. they are sign systems). As such, pragmatics becomes an adjunct discipline that supplements semiotic description. This explains the many different and varied ways entailed by pragmatic activity in attending to a given semiotic attitudinal meaning.

The second point which emerges from the Sperber and Wilson account relates to the intertextual potential of the various attitudinal meanings. This is made amply clear by subscribing to the notion of 'echoic mention'. Here it would be far more helpful for us to talk about '**intratextuality**' (echoic mentions which span a single, currently evolving text), '**inter**textuality' (mentions which echo other texts) and even '**contratextuality**' (echoes which conjure up earlier mentions only to cancel or contradict them) (Martin 1985; Lemke 1992).

What is being intra-, inter- or contra-textually echoed, then, is an attitude (a sign) held by someone other than the speaker. However, the more important aspect of semiotic meaning is that which reveals the speaker's attitude to the opinion echoed. It is an attitude to an attitude, as it were, and it is commonly one of rejection or disapproval. Sample 1 provides us with a superb demonstration of both the Gricean and the Sperber and Wilson accounts. The overall disparaging attitude is relayed through a number of implicatures, each of which relays a particular attitude not unrelated to the macro-sign 'disparagement'. Although the maxim of Quality, predictably, is the one most at risk in English, other maxims are also being flouted. Here Sperber and Wilson (1986: 240) step in with a supplementary aid to the analyst:

> The recovery of these implicatures depends, first, on a recognition of the utterance as echoic; second, on an identification of the source of the opinion echoed; and third, on a recognition that the speaker's attitude to the opinion echoed is one of rejection or disapproval.

So far, we have seen how it is semiotic systems of signification that ultimately inform both the pragmatics and the register communicativeness of texts. That is, the latter domains of context could most profitably be viewed merely as the means to semiotic ends (signs among signs). It is in this sense that attitudinal meanings can be approached and irony analysed as the implication by echoic mention of such meanings. Nevertheless, before moving on to a discussion of the multi-layered nature of irony which views the manifestation of ironical use as text in context, the problem encountered by our students will be stated specifically, this time purely in Gricean terms.

To Flout or Not to Flout, That Is the Question

When to implicate and how, which maxim to flout and where, all these pragmatic considerations seem to be at the heart of the problem encountered in the translation of Sample 1 above. Of course, the problem is initially one of recognizing and appreciating source-text irony. But, from subsequent class discussion with the students taking the irony test referred to above, a repetition of the exercise with the same and similar groups, and after consulting a number of professionally published translations of the sample in question and similar texts, we are able to conclude that, even when the knowledge is made available regarding what is intended in a particular instance of irony, translators from English into Arabic (and the same holds for a number of other languages) tend to, rather persistently, opt for some literal rendering. Occasionally, this hands-off literal strategy may indeed work, delivering the intended meaning effortlessly. However, this haphazard approach is always a risky strategy. To start with, the literal may simply not deliver source-text intentionality adequately, which is often the case. Secondly, the only way for the translator to know that the literal approach has worked is to work with a correct reading of source-text intentionality and only then to step back and assess the product. This stepping back and assessing the damage is crucial in cases when the literal strategy has not worked and translator intervention is absolutely necessary, which is very often the case.

The inability to handle irony properly (particularly when the literal strategy has misfired) flows from unsound practices in which the translators generally warm up to literal meaning, shunning the extra work involved in the contextual reconstruction necessary for the perception of such subtleties as ironical meaning. Thus, as pointed out earlier, preserving irony becomes a problem not only of reception but also of text (re)production too. The question now becomes simply why the English source text remarkably succeeds whereas the Arabic target text all but fails? Precisely what went wrong in the particular case we are considering, and why did this communicative breakdown occur?

For socio-cultural and linguistic reasons too complex to go into here, English has developed a particular preference for 'understatement'. Irony seems to be one aspect of this multifaceted verbal behaviour which benefits considerably from a penchant for the pithy and the cryptic. In context, the speaker can leave so much unsaid, yet seemingly incomplete utterances can paradoxically speak volumes. In other words, what is unsaid by no means always leaves the utterance incomplete. On the contrary, the utterance could well be 'pregnant' with meaning, witty and memorable. Of course, English in this respect seems to allow some economy with the truth: one is telling a lie, or in Gricean terms, flouting the directive 'do not say what you believe to be false' in as overt a manner as possible. But this is outweighed by the joys of reading between the lines for intention. Sample 1 optimally demonstrates this attitude to truth and the maximal effect that emanates in the process.

For similarly complex reasons regarding this preference in English, Arabic has shown a tendency to move in the opposite direction: one can simply do more by saying more, by being 'present' in the discourse. In the context of Sample 1, for example, it would be virtually impossible for an Arabic speaker, without a heavy dose of context, to declare that 'these facts are facts' and only mean that they are mere humbug. By opting for a literal strategy, some of the translators in our experiment seem to have underestimated how intolerant Arabic is to opaqueness (or absence of what Arab rhetoricians call 'eloquence'—*faSaaHa*). They assumed that a literal rendering of a straightforward statement such as *Since these facts are facts* would suffice, particularly if they preserved the repetition by something like an emphatic device ('indeed').

Thus, the expression of 'disparagement' relayed successfully through flouting the maxim of 'truth' (Quality) in English, must be somehow preserved in translation. But Arabic tendencies are not conducive in this respect. And, here is the dilemma: to keep the English understatement intact would not deliver irony in Arabic, and to go to the extreme of overstatement in Arabic could mean loss of subtlety. What to do? A heightened level of pragmatic awareness should help. Arabic has a particular preference for what the Arab rhetoricians were fond of calling 'useful circumlocution' (i.e. motivated, functional redundancy or *iTnaab mufiid*). This could be the solution to our problem: to overstate for a good reason could relay as sarcastic an attitude as the most cryptic of English styles. Thus, element 1 of Sample 1:

> *Since these facts are facts*

which was literally rendered by the students as: [since these are indeed facts], and could only convey the meaning and relay the attitude: 'since what we have been presented with so far is precisely what has happened', would most effectively preserve the expression of disparagement were it to be recast in Arabic as something like:

> *wa lammaa kaanat haadhihi al-Haqaa'iq fii naZari balfor Haqaa'iqa laa ghubara 'alayhaa*
> Since in Balfour's eyes these facts are facts which absolutely need no proof.

This relays the attitudinal meaning: [Since in the blinkered eye of Balfour these are facts (and the mind boggles to think what non-facts would sound like!)].

That is, what would be at risk in relaying the ironical meaning involved is not Quality but Quantity in Arabic—the maxim which if broken or violated would in a normal world (particularly within Western culture) be penalized as saying more, being over-informative, being verbose. In a creative world of motivated choices in the use of language, however, this verbal excess would be highly communicative in Arabic, telling the reader that there is meaningfulness in circumlocution, ultimately conveying a variety of attitudes over and above the literal meaning. Let us consider how this method of approaching irony could be put to work in translating part of Sample 1 above.

> SOURCE TEXT: 1. Since these facts are facts,
>
> SUGGESTED ARABIC RENDERING: wa lamma kaanat haadhihi al-Haqaa'iq fii naZari balfor Haqaa'iqa laa ghubara 'alayhaa
>
> ATTITUDINAL GLOSS: [Since in the blinkered eyes of Balfour these are facts totally unblemished]

2. Balfour must then go on to the next part of his argument

> yajidu balfor lizaaman 'alayhi an yantaqila ilaa al-juz'i al-aakhari min maquulatih
>
> [Balfour feels as if bound by some 'logical necessity' to proceed]

3. Balfour produces no evidence that the Egyptians and 'the races with whom we deal' appreciate or even understand the good that is being done them by colonial occupation

> wa laa yaflaHu balfor fii al-'uthuuri alaa ma yushiiru qaT'an ilaa anna al-miSriyiina wa 'ala Haddi ta'biirih tilka al-aqwaamu allatii nata'aamalu ma'ahaa yatafahhamuuna aw hatta yafhamuuna al-Sanii'a alladhii manna bihi 'alayhim al-iHtilaalu al-ajnabiyy
>
> [As if gratitude on the part of these peoples should ever be expected, Balfour regrets finding no evidence of this for the great deal of 'good' done them by the colonizer]

4. It does not occur to Balfour, however, to let the Egyptian speak for himself

> ghayra anna balfor la yukallifu nafsahu hunaa 'anaa'a an yatruka li al-miSriyy amra al-taHaduthi bi nafsihi 'an nafsih

[Simply did not think it was worthwhile! After all he is only speaking about the Egyptians and how 'credible' are they!]

5. since presumably any Egyptian who would speak up is more likely to be 'the agitator [who] wishes to raise difficulties' than the good native who overlooks the 'difficulties' of foreign domination

idh thammata iftiraaDHun bi'anna al-miSriyya alladhi yu'abbiru 'an araa'ih maa huwa fi al-ghaalibi illa muHarridun yas'aa li ithaarati al-mataa'ibi 'alaa 'aksi dhaalika al-muwaaTini al-aSiil alladhi yataghaaDHa 'an maSaa'ibi al-sayTarati al-ajnabiyya

[On the grounds that more often than not those who will speak up turn out to be 'resentful, trouble-making agitators' and not 'responsible, upright citizens' who 'think positively', taking the difficulties they face 'in their stride']

6. And so, having settled the ethical problems,

wa hakadhaa wa ba'da an Hasama balfor al-masaa'ila al-akhlaaqiyya

[Thus, and having exhaustively dealt with the basic morality of it all]

7. Balfour turns at last to the practical ones

naraahu yantaqilu wa ba'da Tuuli intiZaar li yabutta fii al-masaa'ili al-'amaliyya

[Balfour at long last turns to the practical problems]

9. Balfour by no means implies, as part of that loss, the loss or at least the indefinite postponement of Egyptian independence

wa yaghiibu hunaa 'an dhihni balfor anna juz'an min tilka al-khasaarati kaana fuqdaana al-miSriyiina li istiqlaalihim aw 'alaa al-aqal t'ajila haadha ilaa ajalin ghayru musammaa

[In talking about the minimal? loss of which the colonized population have been relieved, Balfour simply forgets that part of such a loss was the loss of their independence which the Egyptians suffered]

11. England exports 'our very best to these countries'.

fa haa hiya ingiltara tuSaddiru wa aqTatifu hunaa min maa qaalahu balfor bil Harfi alwaaHid tuSaddiru khiirata ma ladaynaa ilaa haadhihi al-buldaan

[The best brains, the best expertise are all sent to 'help' these backward countries—what total commitment and self-denial!]

12. These selfless administrators do their work 'amidst tens of thousands of persons belonging to a different creed, a different race, a different discipline, different conditions of life'.

> wa ya'malu haa'ulaa'i al-idaariyiina naakiru al-dhaat waSTa ma yaSifuhu balfor wa bi lahjatin ma'saawiyya bi 'asharaati al-alaafi min unaasin la yu'minuuna bi madhhabin yakhtalifu 'an madhhabihim fa Hasb, bal yantamuuna ilaa jinsin mukhtalifin wa yataSarafuuna bi usluubin mukhtalifin wa ya'ishuuna Zuruufan hayaatiyatan mukhtalifa
>
> [The ultimate in self-denial is having to work with a lesser people who do not only belong to a different creed but also to a different race, discipline and conditions of life, what a sacrifice!]

Implications for the Contrastive Linguist

Recast in terms particularly relevant to the contrastive linguist in general and the translator in particular, the hypothesis entertained in this study may be phrased as follows:

> Translation is a sign-for-sign act of transfer which does not necessarily entail (though by no means rule out) the need to preserve the very same pragmatic or register values of the source text. Attitude, however, is a different matter. Attitudes tend to be intrinsic properties of source texts and must as far as possible be retained intact.

Put slightly differently, translation is not necessarily the transposition of a given field, mode or tenor by identical register values, nor is it necessarily the transposition of a given speech act, implicature, etc. by an identical pragmatic manifestation. Translation could by all means be all these things but only if this one-for-one transfer of register and pragmatic values adequately caters for, and ultimately keeps intact, the semiotic sign in question (e.g. a disparaging attitude).

To return to irony briefly, it is safe to assume that the English-source Sample 1 above expresses a pervading disparaging attitude that is propped up by pragmatics through a series of ironical, almost sarcastic, statements. The pragmatic procedure opted for is one of implicature through flouting the maxim of Quality in English (i.e. saying something and meaning the opposite, in both connotation and **denotation**). Disparagement is further supported by an assortment of register-related features exploited specifically to uphold this kind of attitude. These tend to be ideational, interpersonal and textual, rather than mere field-, tenor- or mode-related issues.

The transfer into Arabic, along with many other languages, will confront us with a new set of challenges. At stake is discourse attitude. This must be preserved in its totality. But, as we have seen, although the preservation in Arabic of the semiotics of 'disparagement' (the ultimate sign, and the ultimate goal of translating this text) can, and as far as possible should, be achieved by pragmatic implicature, this may not necessarily have to be leaving unsaid what you really mean. This implicature may indeed be of a different kind to that of the source text: for example, Arabic is more at home with flouting Quantity and not Quality. By the same token, although register considerations are also involved in translating this particular text and attitude (e.g. the interpersonal dimension of level of formality, power and solidarity, etc.), 'implicating' in the way Arabic deems appropriate may entail the exploitation of different register features from those originally and successfully employed in the source text. In short, semiotics may thus be considered as the last court of appeal in translation.

The translator working into Arabic could resort to the principle of 'least effort' and follow procedures similar to those adopted by the majority of those who took the test described above. However, what this means in practice is succeeding in translating the text into admittedly a standard idiomatic variety of Arabic but utterly failing to communicate crucial aspects of source-text meaning (e.g. true intentionality). Whether or not the students in question did this consciously or not (i.e. whether they saw the irony for what it is or failed to do so), those who took the test did produce a product which compromises the pragmatics and general communicativeness of the source text. The transfer of the flouting of Quality, and of source register features as they are, have by and large misfired. Such a transfer could no longer be reasonably expected to convey to the average Arab reader of this text the ironical, disparaging attitude focused on so crucially in the source text.

To end with a word on the likely reasons why Arabic seems to be rather averse to flouting a maxim such as Quality but has no problem sacrificing Quantity, all one can say pending further research is that there seem to be deep-rooted socio-cultural and linguistic and rhetorical-pragmatic grounds for why or why not one opts for this or that kind of flouting. At the risk of oversimplifying what is essentially a complex socio- (and psycho-)linguistic set of issues, we may tentatively conclude that the aversion to 'saying what one knows to be false' has to do with the Arab's attitude to truth and is no doubt related to aspects of the communicative act such as politeness, as well as to more general aspects of language in social life, such as societal and political norms. It is almost embarrassing, even shameful, to an Arab to be seen to be uttering what might be perceived on the surface as a blatant untruth, whether in jest or for real, which is what flouting Quality would be tantamount to.

Interestingly, diachronic criteria may be invoked in attempting to account for the way languages evolve in dealing with aspects of use such as irony. English prose of the eighteenth and nineteenth centuries, for example, shows unmistakable tendencies to flout Quantity in relaying irony, a trend which seems to have died out in modern English. One could here cite the oft quoted *It is a truth universally acknowledged that* by Jane Austin (as though there were two kinds of 'truth', one universally acknowledged, and one not so). Thus, it is not inconceivable that current patterns of, say, ironical use of language in Arabic might change as the years go by.

To Conclude

In this chapter, we attempted to review basic theories for dealing with ironical meaning and focused on the problems of translating ironical use of language into Arabic. Irony was shown to impinge not only on aspects of message construction such as register membership and intentionality, but also on semiotic categories such as genre and discourse. The latter is shown to be particularly privileged as home to attitudinal meanings. Discourse meanings are almost universal and must therefore be heeded and constantly resorted to by the translator, since it is this domain of context that is the last court of appeal for adequacy and equivalence.

20 The Other Texts: Implications for Liaison Interpreting

The aim of this chapter is fairly practical: it is to introduce liaison interpreting (also known as bilateral interpreting or consecutive interpreting) as an interpreting skill that is closely allied to translation (both share 'sense' retrieval as a prerequisite), and to call for its incorporation in programmes of translator and interpreter training. Liaison interpreting (LI) involves the use of an interpreter as an intermediary in situations such as an informal discussion, or a slightly more formal interview/question–answer session, between two speakers who do not speak or understand each other's language, or do so only imperfectly.

It is now commonly accepted in translator training that providing the trainee script translator with basic interpreting skills such as LI serves at least two objectives. First, interpreting helps translators acquire an added skill which will no doubt be professionally useful. The second objective relates to how, albeit indirectly, interpreting skills make translators more aware of what the translation process actually involves, an awareness which will undoubtedly shed more light on the nature of translation itself.

With interpreting in mind, the more theoretical aim of this chapter is to argue that—while by no means downplaying the role of such factors as memory, mental agility, even quick-wittedness in the formation of interpreters, nor the crucial role of linguistic skills such as fluency, breadth and depth of diction, mastery of collocation—the ability to handle the various domains of contextual activity such as register membership (field, tenor and mode) is essential. Nor should we downplay the crucial role of pragmatics and listening for intentions at both the micro-level of utterance and the macro-level of text. And, finally, no less important than either of these contextual domains is cultural semiotics and specifically the mechanism of intertextuality, which all texts must in one way or another utilize: all the 'other' relevant prior texts that the various register-related and pragmatic-textual clues in a given utterance are intended to conjure up for a given language user on a given occasion of use. This argues for the supremacy of the register–pragmatics–semiotics triad or, to put it differently, of the speech act pitched at a particular level of technicality and formality, and treated as a sign among signs.

Throughout this book, we have been dealing with the implications for the translator of register and pragmatics, and have tried to do both topics justice. This chapter will therefore focus on semiotics and, specifically, on the intertextual potential of utterances linking, at a micro–horizontal level or at a macro–vertical level, with other relevant prior texts that, if recalled adequately, become the sites of some indispensable contextual, sign-related work. In addition to horizontal intertextuality (e.g. straightforward reference to Shakespeare's Hamlet *To be or not to be*) and vertical intertextuality (e.g. more opaque references not so much to the Qur'an or the Bible as to the styles of these sacred books), the intertextual potential of utterances is all-pervasive. Intertextuality may be located on any level of linguistic organization (phonology, morphology, syntax, semantics or pragmatics), and at any of the linguistic ranks (word, phrase, clause, text, discourse, or genre). But, it is ultimately both register-sensitive and intentionality-based. (On horizontal vs vertical intertextuality, see Fairclough 1989.)

Multi-Level Textuality

To illustrate the proposals just put forward regarding the primacy of the sign and the role of intertextuality in the analysis of textual register and pragmatic speech acts, and before we turn to the issue of text in context within the specific skill of LI, let us by way of an example consider the following title of a *Guardian* editorial: 'Vanunu Vanishes'. The leading article was condemnatory of 'the act of piracy' committed by Israeli secret agents (Mossad) when, in broad daylight, they abducted a Mr Vanunu from a London street. Vanunu, an Israeli national and a senior nuclear technician employed at some highly sensitive nuclear site in Israel, had earlier talked to *The Sunday Times* and had revealed important information about Israel's nuclear potential.

In the analysis of this utterance, and to avoid getting involved in the intricacies of the reading process and the question of individual differences among readers, we will envisage a model reader and assume some form of idealized linguistic behaviour. The reaction of such a reader and the way he or she would go about gathering the relevant information and feeding this into the process of discovering text are bound to involve justifying 'salience' anywhere this is encountered (e.g. the alliterative repetition of van is 'salient', it stands out). Morpho-phonology would be invoked here and reference would be made to all kinds of relevant actual or virtual texts (Beaugrande 1980) which will, in one way or another, have a bearing on the interpretation of the utterance in question. Involved in this intertextual retrieval exercise would be poetics ('style', a feature of register) and how the intention to go beyond the decorative effect of devices such as alliteration into how the colourful, the flowery, becomes part of doing things with words (a pragmatic consideration).

Also involved, perhaps more significantly, is the expression of a certain discourse: This is the set of attitudinal meanings with which utterances become imbued. Here, we are in the domain of the socio-cultural, semiotic sign, the prime mover of both pragmatic action and communicative register transaction. To be 'comical' (or rather tragi-comical, which we take to be one of the socio-cultural effects conveyed by the alliterative use under discussion) is a sign recognizable by a given community of text users in terms of the attitude conveyed and the linguistic material signalling such an attitude. It is then and only then that the expression of this attitude begins to acquire purposefulness as intended by someone in speaking to someone, and as executed to best effect sometime, somewhere. Here, the universal, attitudinal meaning becomes narrower and more focused (i.e. pragmatic, which is by definition tactical and language-/culture-specific). As texts unfold, intended meanings become even narrower in focus and more specific when, as a rebuttal, the 'tragi-comical' turns into an ideological/satirical weapon through the ideational field, the interpersonal tenor and, ultimately, the textual mode crowning the finished product.

Thus, as we have just seen when morpho-phonology was invoked, the attitude 'tragi-comical' is appreciated only in terms of other relevant texts (other instances of similar registers, other occurrences of similar intentions, other tokens of similar signs). Staying with the same utterance for the moment ('Vanunu Vanishes'), let us see how semantics is brought to bear on intertextual retrieval. At the rank of the word, appreciating the communicative potential of the verb *vanishes* would be that much richer if one were to build on some form of overall attitudinal meaning. This is still the 'tragi-comical' theme that somehow activates in the mind of many the image of the magician, dexterously conjuring up all kinds of tricks out of a hat as part of the 'disappearing act': things 'vanish', 'just like that!' (in the memorable phrase of the late comedian Tommy Cooper). Not in the real world of modern Britain, though, but only in the world of Alice in Wonderland! Intention and register specification will prop up this kind of analysis, and the utterance begins to act purposefully on the textual and extra-textual environment as a sign.

But perhaps even more intertextually potent here is the more concrete 'other' text, that of the title of one of Agatha Christie's better-known novels *The Lady Vanishes*. The entire 'whodunnit' genre, the entire 'brain-cells' discourse of private detective Poirot, and the actual text of the title itself are somehow implicated in conveying the tragic-comical attitude in question and making it pragmatically active within a given register. This, together with the timelessness of the present tense used (involving text syntax), cumulatively adds to the effect of expressing an attitude of someone who, in utter disbelief, simply cannot fully comprehend how in this day and age someone might simply 'vanish', in the middle of the day, in the middle of London.

In theory, the search for 'other' texts constitutive of the context of a given utterance continues unceasingly, but usually a 'situationally determined' threshold of termination is reached and the hunt for signs is called off. The notion of intertextual retrieval as a way of modelling context may be represented diagrammatically as follows:

'Vanunu Vanishes'
phonology | morphology | semantics | syntax
sub-word | word | phrase | clause | text
discourse | genre
actual | virtual
horizontal | vertical
register transaction | pragmatic action
semiotic interaction
ideology | culture

Figure 20.1 Intertextual retrieval

In the maze of the contextual activity which takes place while a given utterance is being processed, intertextuality in both its active (vertical, long-span) and passive (horizontal, short-span) senses thus seems to be the moving force behind 'making sense' of the unfolding text and the restoration of coherence. Underpinning intertextual retrieval is a complex system of meaning-making that relies for its viability on a network of relations that are essentially semiotic. That is, a system of signs is at work, engaging in some form of interaction that may be identified at three basic levels, as we have pointed out on a number of occasions so far:

(a) the interaction of speaker/writer with hearer/reader,
(b) the interaction of speaker/writer or hearer/reader with the text produced or received,
(c) the interaction of text with text.

The Discourse–Genre–Text Triad: Concluding Statements

Text as Macro-Sign

As units of highly intense communicative interaction, signs thus function at the basic level of text producer interacting with receiver, at the more active level of text producer or receiver interacting with the text being processed, and finally at the most engaging of all levels, namely sign interacting with other signs. Part of the privileged level of sign interacting with other signs is obviously text interacting with other texts or intertextuality. It is here that we need to be specific about 'text' as a macro-sign within which various micro-signs would be seen as mutually relevant to the realization of an overall rhetorical purpose. For example, we cite an adversary's 'claim', we then rebut it with our own 'counter-claim' and we support our stance with a 'substantiation', usually closing with some form of 'conclusion'. Four basic micro-signs are thus at work in realizing the macro-rhetorical purpose to 'counter-argue' in English. To illustrate this multi-level structure, let us consider the following text samples:

Sample 1

> Interviewee (English): *Certainly, it is difficult to predict the effect of economic sanctions, when they will begin to bite. **However, the sharpest pain has already started hitting exports. ***Before the invasion, Iraq earned 95% of its foreign exchange from oil. ****Now, its pipelines have been shut and its tankers are stuck in the Gulf. *****With this measure alone, the Alliance is depriving Iraq of some $80 million a day in oil revenues.
> [Asterisks indicate the various micro-signs in succession]

It is perhaps worth noting here that in a practical exercise in LI conducted in a translation class some years ago, the text-type focus of this particular text was drastically misperceived, particularly when the initial 'claim' became an 'assertion': 'There is absolutely no doubt that economic sanctions can ever be predictable'. It was here that coherence all but vanished, with *However* sitting there rather aimlessly, and the statistics turning into meaningless figures.

THE OTHER TEXTS

To appreciate 'counter-argumentation', it is useful to compare this text type with a different kind of text as macro-sign—'exposition'. Here, we normally have no axe to grind and the intention is only to report events in 'time', describe objects in 'space' or explain a concept or a series of related concepts as part of analysis or synthesis, all as these entities are dispassionately portrayed. This expository rhetorical purpose as macro-sign requires a different set of micro-signs from those encountered in a counter-argumentative text. In exposition, we first 'set the scene', then single out the most salient and relevant 'aspects of the scene set', and perhaps wrap up with some sort of 'concluding statement'. Sample 2 below exemplifies this:

Sample 2

> Journalist (English): *How far did you get in your negotiations with Saddam Hussain?
>
> Kurdish Leader (Arabic): **We produced a paper to normalize the situation in Kurdistan. ***We also produced the new law for self-determination. ****Regarding the borders of the self-determined region, here there was disagreement.

There is no doubt that note-taking, a skill indispensable to summary writers in general and to liaison/consecutive interpreters in particular, would benefit from an approach to text which views overall organization in terms of problem-solving and means–ends analysis, as the text typology presented so far clearly does. Furthermore, albeit at a virtual and not necessarily always at an actual level, it is to these macro-/micro-signs (such as the 'claim cited to be countered', the 'scene-setter') that reference is constantly made by the language user. It is on 'sites' of textual activity such as these that context may be crucially mapped out and negotiated. The schemata-like nature of these text signs indicates that they do enjoy a psychological reality, that they are internalized as part of our textual repertoire, and that they correlate with specific cognitive aspects of the way culture, settings and the mind interact.

To illustrate the efficacy of text type as a grid that the language user inter-textually uses to impose order on communication incongruities when these are encountered, let us consider Sample 3a below. The text is a literal translation of an answer offered in Arabic by a government minister in an attempt to dodge a question from a persistent English journalist bluntly asking: 'Are you going to abolish passports and thus facilitate movement among the Gulf States?':

Sample 3a

> Journalist (English): Is it not now time, all these years after the establishment of the Gulf Cooperative Council, to abolish passports ...?
>
> Minister (back-translated from Arabic): Travelling between the countries of the Cooperative Council is the easiest thing to do, and the Gulf citizen doesn't even need a visa. Then [Ar. *thumma*], the passport is considered a proof of identity and as such is indispensable ...

Regrettably, the minister's reply was rendered by the interpreter in more or less the form in which it appears in the above back-translation. This meant virtual loss of coherence. An interpreter more aware of text types would have produced something like the more context-sensitive rendering of Sample 3b:

Sample 3b

> Minister: Travelling between the countries of the Cooperative Council has never been easier, and the Gulf citizen doesn't even need a visa. However, the passport issue is altogether different [and here we draw the line]. The passport is considered a proof of identity and as such is indispensable ...

Discourse as Macro-Sign

Texts do not occur in a vacuum. They occur within discourse, another macro-sign the main function of which is to express attitude, stance and perspective. As the mouthpiece of institutions, discourse becomes the repertoire on which to draw for conveying what one prefers or disprefers, the stock on which to rely for the terms of reference that can elaborate or restrict a given cultural or subcultural code. Structurally, discourse considerations determine the way texts (and elements within text) concatenate (often in sequence, sometimes embedded within each other to form complex hierarchies). Internally, on the other hand, discourse regulates the way the various patterns of texture (theme–rheme progression, lexical cohesion, etc.) are deployed to ensure that texts are purposeful, cohesive and coherent wholes. It is in the latter domain of internal connectivity that discourse may be more fruitfully examined. Key concepts which represent particular world views are inscribed in specific 'cultural codes' that embody ideologies or cumulatively function as statements of some socio-cultural significance (see Fairclough 1989).

Though essentially diffuse, discourse utilizes fairly concrete signals and relays definite statements which provide the text with a variety of 'voices'. At the most general level, we may have overtones that orient the text one way or another (e.g. 'evaluative' discourse typical of 'managing' as a persuasive strategy). More specifically, we may encounter attitudes to specific text worlds such as the didactic, the literary, and the scientific 'code'. Even more specifically, we may come across committed ideological statements, as is often the case with such discourses as feminist, racist or monetarist discourse. All these discourse values may well be fuzzy and negotiable but they are certainly not ad hoc or unpatterned.

To illustrate the crucial role that discourse awareness plays in the pursuit of optimally effective communication, let us consider Sample 4, once again drawn from LI. The English journalist's provocative libertarian discourse fell on deaf ears as far as his Arab interpreter and the government minister interviewed were concerned: the terms he used were intended to carry pejorative connotations and negative values, appropriate for the discourse of Western critics of third-world autocracy. In Arabic and in the Arab world, however, those terms could only carry positive values associated with the discourse of a stable, petro-dollar economy, wealth and prosperity:

Sample 4

> Journalist: Look at Tunisia, despite democratic trappings, power remains *concentrated and personalized*. But perhaps more to the point look at Algeria. Some 180,000 well-schooled Algerians enter the job market every year. Yet a hobbled economy adds only *100,000 new jobs* a year, and *some 45%* of these involve *working for the government*.
>
> (Italics added)

To the interpreter, who happened to be from an oil-producing country with a rich and stable economy, there is nothing wrong with 'power being concentrated and personalized', and it is indeed a privilege 'to work for the government' who can absorb a glorious '45%, no less' of the 'hefty 100,000 jobs added every year'. But, had the interpreter been more aware of the discourse thrust, which in this example is fused into the fabric of the other macro-sign—text ('Some 180,000 ... Yet ...'), he would have had no difficulty in establishing the condemnatory tone. This would have meant retrieving the intertextuality which points to a body of communicative behaviour realized by a variety of discourses and texts as signs known as 'liberal discourse'. We are constantly aware of these as signs among signs. Sometimes they are manageable and easy to pin down, at other times slippery and elusive. But they are there, constituting an important layer of the context enveloping a given utterance.

Genre as Macro-Sign

Texts, then, embody forms of expression appropriate to a given rhetorical purpose in a particular social setting. Discoursal expression is that which is appropriate to a given ideological stance or world view. The third macro-sign, genre, differs from text or discourse only in that it subsumes forms of expression appropriate to a given social occasion or communicative event. The notion of appropriateness in the semiotic analysis expounded here captures the way society and culture tend to sanction particular generic, discoursal and textual structures, assign each of these macro-structures set roles and functions, and police the entire process of partitioning semiotic space. In terms of the mechanisms involved, such a conventional act of 'authorization' is akin to what actually takes place in the process of any semiotic evolution: whether the signifier–signified creating a cumulative effect, or a simple sign which, together with other signs, becomes a bigger sign, and so on, until eventually or even along the way, it develops into myth (Barthes 1957).

Like the other categories of text and discourse, genre has been variously defined. At a very general level, it is useful to be aware of generic structures identified within literary criticism, such as the sonnet, the ballad, the short story, the novel, or even the myth. It is also useful to be aware of the conventions governing other kinds of generic structures such as the academic article, the annual report, even the executive summary. But, from the point of view of contrastive linguistics in general and translating or interpreting in particular, there seems to be ample justification for always focusing on more specific notions of genre. The grounds for doing this, and in effect relegating other more general approaches to secondary place, is simply to do with the fact that within the short story or the academic article, for example, we, as translators or interpreters actually work with numerous kinds of generic structures and feel that these also enjoy the quality of being 'generic' in their own right (the academic abstract, even the summary).

Thus, genre could be used equally appropriately to cover all forms of language use conventionally sanctioned as expressive of what happens in a given communicative event. The smaller these are (hence **'genrelets'**, to coin a new term, e.g. 'New Arrivals' or similar 'signs' in a department store), the more useful and yet more elusive and demanding they prove to be. Genrelets could be as minimal as general performative formulations such as 'the court will rise' or the auctioneer's rapid manner of bid acceptance 'going, going, gone', or more extensive as the formulaic preambles to or concluders of a treaty or a UN resolution.

Though not commonly recognized by mainstream interpreting practice or theory, the fact remains that interpreters do work with generic structures and, unlike translators, tend to require an extremely agile mind to put their cultural awareness and repertory of text schemata or templates to use under pressure. Let us consider Sample 5a drawn from an interview with an Egyptian ex-Foreign Minister and literally rendered here from the original Arabic:

Sample 5a

> Interviewer (English): What line of poetry do you often remember?
>
> Riyad (Back-translated from the Arabic): A hemistich from a line in a poem by the great freedom fighter Al-Sheikh Bashir al-Ibrahimi. I heard him recite the poem which was about the deteriorating situation which the Arab nation found and still finds itself in.
>
> Interviewer: What is this hemistich?
>
> Riyad: **Their constitution ... Do not read, nor write, nor understand** [Ar. *wa dustuuruhunna ... la taqra'anna ... la taktubanna ... la tafhamanna*]
>
> (Bold added)

As pointed out above, awareness of the conventions governing literary genres is an asset in the training of interpreters who could find themselves in situations where this kind of knowledge is called upon, as the example of Sample 5a shows regarding the structure of the poem, parts of the verse, etc. However, the problem in Sample 5a is slightly more complex than this, requiring that the interpreter be more aware of the genrelet as a unit of semiotic analysis.

A number of questions must cross the interpreter's mind in processing this particular text sample: Is genre involved at all? If it is, is the genre involved that of an 'article' from a 'constitution' or that of a 'motto'? If it is the 'motto' that is intended, what structure, forms of expressions, etc. would mottoes conventionally take in English? The answers which have to be provided by the interpreter on the spot with least delay underline the need to be sensitive to generic structures as minimal as the 'motto' and as extensive as legal 'preambles', and to opt for a form of expression appropriate to the social or communicative events or occasions involved. Sample 5b provides a model rendering of the text elements in question:

Sample 5b

> Riyad: And their motto is: **Read not ... Write not ... Comprehend not ...**
>
> (Bold added)

It is the intertextual potential of genres and genrelets that may be utilized in situations such as this. Like the macro-signs text and discourse and the micro-signs subsumed within them, genres enjoy considerable psychological reality, are internalizable as they become part of textual competence and serve as effective controls which impose order on an otherwise unwieldy state of the language.

Micro-Signs: A Final Word

Textual, discoursal and generic constraints are important macro-signals which regulate message construction and ensure that, ultimately, texts are efficient, effective and appropriate. But to operate bottom-up (as opposed to the top-down orientation we have been adopting), the language user needs to be aware of the various micro-signals which help in testing initial hypotheses and making sense of the text as it unfolds (see the introductory Chapters 1 and 2 on decision-making). Micro-signals have been alluded to in passing throughout the above discussion. But it is worth reiterating our views regarding what it is that constitutes these signals, and to conclude with a word on the function of the micro-signal as the carrier of pragmatic and other register specifications while issuing or implementing semiotic/attitudinal instructions.

Within texts, micro-signals are those elements which realize overall structural and textural organization and thus implement the basic rhetorical plan of a given text. Citing an opponent's claim and then rebutting it with a counter-claim are steps in a counter-argumentative routine. But for these elements to convey the necessary rhetorical thrust, they must be seen to carry within them communicative clues (i.e. values) pointing to a particular cultural or subcultural code. It is here that discoursal micro-signals enter text organization through the gateway of texture, which enables us to 'read off' a given ideological stance, a commitment to a cause or simply an attitude to some aspect of the text world as in literary or scientific communication.

Discourse and the texts realizing it are therefore seamless. We have textual demarcation lines, and we have generic constraints that ensure the appropriateness of the way a message is put together to serve both a given rhetorical purpose and a given social or communicative event or occasion. But these textual and generic micro-signals infiltrate discourse through the texture of ideological statements which ultimately convey a certain attitude or perspective.

Now, how does pragmatics and register specification come into all of this, and how do they relate to semiotic meaning posited here to be particularly distinct and truly privileged? While the semiotic domain of attitudinal meaning is home to that which is practically 'universal', pragmatics is the domain of negotiating how best to access and make sense of semiotic values, an exercise in which who is talking to whom, under what circumstances and for what purpose are obviously crucial clues that must be heeded. It is here that register lends us a framework for the entire transaction, providing the vehicle of representing what goes on within us and around us (ideational field), the level at which we can show solidarity or exercise power (interpersonal tenor), and the channel through which communication is transmitted (textual mode).

Wider Implications of Semiotic Analysis

The obvious conclusion to be drawn from the above kind of analysis is that negotiating text in context, with the latter taken *inter alia* to be a function of all the other relevant prior texts surrounding a given utterance, has an important role to play in the training and professional activity of translators and interpreters. More specifically, we suggest that training in skills such as LI contributes most positively to skill development in translator training. Such an awareness of function not only equips these practitioners with the added facility of handling oral or aural interaction, if and when they are called upon to do so, but also makes them more aware of the intricacies of translation as a skill in its own right.

But a less obvious, though perhaps more far-reaching, conclusion of this kind of approach to translation and interpreting, in theory and practice, is that the difference between translation and interpreting is often exaggerated. Of course, the two skills are different in terms of self-evident factors to do with the mode of delivery and reception: Interpreters work under pressure, and there are constraints on perception and storage of information, while recall can be problematic for all kinds of reasons. But in terms of the underlying strategies of approaching context, handling text type and negotiating both the structure and texture of communicative occurrences, the differences are simply too marginal to be worthy of the kind of exclusive treatment the two skills often receive.

Translators and interpreters go about their textual business in more or less the same way. Texts are texts which change only slightly and, to all intents and purposes, negligibly when seen as vehicles of communication, regardless of whether they are destined to be translated or interpreted. To reiterate, there are no doubt differences in mode, tenor, etc. but these are by no means sufficiently stark to justify the setting up of separate 'disciplines' on either side of the professional divide. And each type of professional practice can learn from the other.

The theoretical and practical implications for the profession of the multifaceted position argued for in this book are simply too daunting to be ignored. Leaving aside the extremely uninteresting (indeed tedious) question of territoriality (who is qualified to teach what, and where? And must interpreting be taught only by ex-conference interpreters or poetry translated only by poets?!), one simple question must be posed as it strikes us as relevant to the training of translators and interpreters alike: In the world we live in at present, with cut-backs galore and with higher education facing unprecedented pressures, and with both translation and interpreting still being handled by anyone with a smattering of two languages, can we really afford any artificial over-compartmentalization? Addressing this and similar issues takes on added urgency when we find ourselves sidetracked by interdisciplinary territorial disputes: we should be devoting a little more time to the proper analysis of the texts and discourses of our diplomats, our scientists, our engineers, and our statesmen, and comparing these with other relevant texts and discourses representative of a given target culture. The need for such a wide-ranging contrastive rhetoric must surely make us rethink our priorities and the bulk of received wisdom which we have uncritically accepted for far too long.

To Conclude

The aim was to view LI within a discourse-processing framework and to argue for its inclusion as an important skill in all translator-training programmes. On a slightly more theoretical note, we also sought to demonstrate that, within the various domains of context, semiotics has pride of place by far, and that, within the various micro- and macro-signs, discourse is indeed privileged as a facilitator of semiotic interaction. Texts and genres function as no more than vehicles of communication and carriers of linguistic expression, and it is only when this expression becomes imbued with ideological meaning, and when texts and genres begin to take on added discoursal values that communication truly materializes.

Glossary of Contrastive Text: Linguistics and Translation Terms

ACTUAL: see **Virtual**

ANAPHORA: This is when a linguistic element (e.g. a pronoun) is used to refer backward to antecedent elements in the text (e.g. *The king* spoke. In his speech, *he* said ...). **Cataphora**, on the other hand, is when a linguistic item is used to refer forward to subsequent elements in the text (e.g. In *his* speech, *the king* said ...).

ARGUMENTATION: A text type in which concepts and/or beliefs are evaluated. Two basic forms of argumentation may be distinguished: **Counter-argumentation** in which a thesis is cited, then opposed; and **Through-argumentation** where a thesis is cited then extensively defended. Counter-arguments could be:

    A. **Explicit** (the concession is explicitly signalled by the use of concessives such as *although, while*) (also referred to as the **Concessive argument**),
    B. **Implicit** (the opposition is introduced by the use of adversatives such as *but, however* following the citation of an opponent's thesis) (also known as the **Straw-Man Gambit**),
    C. **Suppressed** (the implicit opposition is introduced without the use of an explicit adversative).

Through-arguments, on the other hand, are basic argumentative formats which could either be 'detached' (objective) or 'involved' (subjective).

ASPECT OF THE SCENE: see **Text Structure**

ATTRIBUTES: see **Element**

AURAL TEXT: see **Visual Text**

BACKWARD DIRECTIONALITY: see **Thematic Progression**

BOTTOM-UP: see **Top-down**

BREAKING A MAXIM: see **Cooperative Principle**

CATAPHORA: see **Anaphora**

CHUNK: see **Element**

COHERENCE: see **Cohesion**

COHESION: The requirement that a sequence of sentences realizing a **Text** display grammatical and/or lexical relationships which ensure surface structure continuity. For example, in the exchange:

A. Where have you been?
B. To the Empire

there is an implicit link between *have been* and *to the Empire* which accounts for the cohesiveness of the sequence.

Coherence, on the other hand, stipulates that the grammatical and/or lexical relationships involve deeper underlying meanings of the various elements of text, and not only continuity of forms. Thus, the ellipsis in the above exchange could conceivably be used to relay 'marital tension'. It is only when contextual glosses such as this are provided that coherence relations may be examined adequately.

COMMUNICATIVE: see **Context**

COMMUNICATIVE DYNAMISM (CD): The phenomenon whereby sentences are made up of **Themes** followed by **Rhemes** and that, in the **Unmarked** case, rhemes are the more communicatively important (i.e. display a higher CD).

CONCESSIVE ARGUMENT: see **Argumentation**

CONNOTATION: Additional meanings which a lexical item acquires beyond its primary, referential, meaning, e.g. *notorious* does mean 'famous' but with negative connotations. **Denotations**, on the other hand, cover the dictionary, 'contextless', meaning of a given lexical item.

CONTEXT: The extra-textual environment which exerts a determining influence on the language used. The subject matter of a given text is part of **Register** and can thus determine, say, the way the text presents who is doing what to whom (**Transitivity**). Three domains of context may be distinguished:

(1) **Communicative**, including aspects of the message such as **Register Membership**;
(2) **Pragmatic**, covering **Intentionality** and **Speech Acting**,
(3) **Semiotic**, accounting for **Intertextuality** among **Signs**.

CONTEXT OF CULTURE: A form of behaviour potential available to the individual text user and yielding a set of options from which to choose. Once chosen, a given option provides the environment for actual selections. To shift the blame from a male perpetrator of a crime onto a woman and dehumanize the latter is a reading which the context of culture makes available. To actually select a particular form of the passive (e.g. *Girl 7 killed while mum was drinking at the pub*), on the other hand, is an aspect of field of discourse related to **Context of Situation**.

CONTEXT OF SITUATION: see **Context of Culture**

CONTRATEXTUALITY: see **Intertextuality**

CONVERSATIONAL MAXIMS: see **Cooperative Principle**

COOPERATIVE PRINCIPLE: The assumption that interlocutors cooperate with each other by observing certain so-called **Conversational Maxims** (also known as **Gricean Maxims**). These are:

Quantity: Give as much information as is needed
Quality: Speak truthfully
Relevance: Say what is relevant
Manner: Avoid ambiguity

However, these maxims may be **Broken** (inadvertently) or **'Violated'** (when the deviation from the norm of adhering to them is not communicated properly). Whether broken or violated, there would no indirect meaning or implicature to be detected. **Implicatures** only arise when the maxims are **'Flouted'** (i.e. not adhered to for a good reason). Thus, to say 'I am voting for Reagan because Carter is the evil of the two lessers' could be

(a) a case of 'breaking' the maxim of manner if uttered by someone who gets the idiomatic saying mixed up, or
(b) a case of 'violation' if said to someone who is not aware of the original idiomatic saying, or
(c) a case of 'flouting', giving rise to an implicature which might be something like 'it is all a sad charade and not worth talking about'.

COTEXT: The sounds, words or phrases preceding and/or following a particular linguistic element in an utterance. This may be compared with the context enveloping that particular utterance.

COUNTER-ARGUMENT: see **Argumentation**

CULTURAL CODE: A system of ideas which conceptually enables **Denotative** meanings to take on extra connotative meanings and thus to become key terms in the thinking of a certain group of text users, ultimately contributing to the development of **Discourse**.

DENOTATION: see **Connotation**

DEVIATION FROM THE NORM: Norms subsume what is conventionally considered appropriate in speech or writing for a particular situation or purpose. These are sometimes deviated from for a 'good reason' mostly to do with pursuing a particular rhetorical aim. For example, instead of an expected **Argument**, the text producer may opt for an **Expository** narrative. Such an expectation-defying choice is normally more interesting and highly dynamic. See **Cooperative Principle** and **Informativity**.

DISCOURSE: Modes of speaking or writing which involve participants in adopting a particular attitude towards areas of socio-cultural activity (e.g. racist discourse, bureaucratese, etc.). The minimal unit in discourse analysis is the discourse statement (e.g. the racism of a remark).

DISCOURSE STATEMENT: see **Discourse**

DISCURSIVE COMPETENCE: see **Textual Competence**

DISTANCE: see **Politeness**

ELEMENT: In dealing with text structure, an element is the minimal unit of analysis and could in compositional terms be a phoneme, a word or a sentence. Within the hierarchic organization of texts, elements make up a **Chunk** and a number of chunks make up a **Text**. One-element, one-chunk texts are not uncommon: *No Smoking*, for example. Elements of an **Argumentative** text are called **Steps**, those of an **Expository Narrative** text are **Events**, and those of an **Expository Descriptive** text are **Attributes**.

ELLIPSIS: The omission (for reasons of rhetorically and/or linguistically motivated economy) of linguistic items whose sense is recoverable from **Context** or **Cotext**.

EVALUATIVENESS: The comparison or assessment of concepts, belief systems, etc. It is the determining factor in distinguishing argumentation from exposition.

EVENT: see **Element**

EVIDENTIALITY: Building on the premise that truth is relative, evidentiality studies the ways in which this relativity is expressed in languages. Put simply, there are some things people are sure of, others they are less sure of and so on. see **Modality**.

EXPLICATIVE: A term used here to refer to languages that tend to express what is intended in a fairly explicit and direct way. In such languages, the relationship between meaning and linguistic expression is fairly transparent. Implicative languages, on the other hand, tend to be less direct, and the lexico-grammar tends to be used less transparently in the expression of communicative intentions. For example, while a clause type such as SVO could be used in English both evaluatively or non-evaluatively (i.e. expressing 'involved' or 'detached' attitudes), in Arabic, the Nominal clause type SVO tends to cater for evaluative functions and another structure, namely the Verbal VSO, seems to be earmarked for the less evaluative, more detached forms of expression.

EXPOSITION: A text type in which concepts, objects or events are presented in a non-evaluative manner. Three basic forms of exposition may be distinguished:
  A. Description, focusing on objects spatially viewed
  B. Narration, focusing on events temporally viewed
  C. Conceptual Exposition, focusing on the detached analysis of concepts and yielding a number of text tokens. Starting with the most detached and moving onto the least detached, these conceptual expository text forms include: the synopsis, the abstract, the summary, the entity-oriented report, the person-oriented report, the event-oriented report. The report can also be formulaic (e.g. the auditors' report), executive (e.g. the company Chairman's annual statement) and reminiscent (e.g. a person's memoirs).

FACE: In the pragmatic theory of politeness, 'face' involves the positive image which one shows or intends to show of oneself. If this image is not accepted by the other participants, feelings may be hurt and 'loss of face' is incurred.

FACE-THREATENING ACT (FTA): see **Politeness**

FIELD OF DISCOURSE: see **Meta-Functions**, **Register**

FLOUTING A MAXIM: see **Cooperative Principle**

FORMAT: see **Text Structure**

FORWARD DIRECTIONALITY: see **Thematic Progression**

FRAME: see **Script**

FREE TRANSLATION: see **Literal Translation**

FUNCTIONAL: Having a role to perform in the realization of context by a **Text**. Functional signals are in contrast with other purely organizational devices whose role is, as the term suggests, merely formal and 'cosmetic' rather than rhetorically motivated.

FUNCTIONAL TENOR: An aspect of tenor or level of formality used to describe what language is used for (e.g. persuading) and is thus very much akin to the notion of text type

FUNCTIONAL SENTENCE PERSPECTIVE (FSP): The assumption that a sentence is to be viewed within a particular communicative perspective, in which, in the unmarked form, whatever is mentioned first (**Theme**) is normally of less communicative importance than what follows (**Rheme**).

GENRE: Conventional forms of text associated with particular types of social occasion (e.g. the news report, the editorial, the cooking recipe). Within a given genre (the **Master Genre**), subsidiary minor genres (sub-genres, **Genrelets**) may be identified. For example, A Letter to the Editor may employ a number of sub-genres such as the 'auctioneer's falling gavel' Genrelet: 'going, going, gone'. Whether the genre is master or minor, the minimal unit of genre analysis is the **Genre Feature** (e.g. the social occasion involved).

GENRE FEATURE: see **Genre**

GENRELET: see **Genre**

GRICEAN MAXIMS: see **Cooperative Principle**

HEURISTIC: A set of analytic principles that rely on variable and not categorical rules in dealing with texts, that help us to learn about and discover things in texts as we go along and that rely on hypotheses and options to be confirmed or disconfirmed in the light of unfolding textual evidence.

IDEOLOGY: A body of ideas that reflects the beliefs and interests of an individual, a group of individuals, a societal institution, etc., and that ultimately finds expression in language. For example, the headline *Girl 7 killed while mum was drinking in the pub* relays a particular ideological stance towards men and women which the newspaper in question adopts and propagates (see **Discourse**).

IDEATIONAL MEANING: see **Meta-Functions**

ILLOCUTIONARY ACT: see **Locutionary Act**

IMPLICATURE: see **Cooperative Principle**

IMPOSITION: see **Politeness**

INFORMATIVITY: The degree of unexpectedness which an item or an utterance displays in some context, see **Deviation from the Norm**.

INSTRUCTION: A text type in which the focus is on the formation of future behaviour, either 'with option', as in advertising, or 'without option', as in legal instruction (e.g. Treaties, Resolutions, Contracts, etc.).

INTENTIONALITY: A feature of human language which determines the appropriateness of a linguistic form to the achievement of a pragmatic purpose.

INTERPERSONAL MEANING: see **Meta-Functions**

INTERTEXTUALITY: A precondition for the intelligibility of texts, involving the dependence of one text, as a semiotic entity, upon another. The 'other' text could be a prior, independent text, in which case intertextuality is the appropriate term. But intertexts could be within one and the same text, and here **Intratextuality** might be a more appropriate term. Finally, the intertextual reference, instead of evoking an image, can preclude it, parody it, or signify its exact opposite, cases which are all subsumed under what is known as **Contratextuality**. This may be illustrated from the tactics of some political speakers using the opponent's terminology for their own ends.

INTRATEXTUALITY: see **Intertextuality**

LANGUE: The abstract system of signs of a language and its principles. **Parole**, on the other hand, is the concrete manifestation of this abstract system of principles.

LIAISON INTERPRETING: A form of oral interpreting in which two speakers who do not know each other's language or know it imperfectly communicate through an interpreter, normally in fairly informal conversational settings.

LITERAL TRANSLATION: A rendering which preserves surface aspects of the message both semantically and syntactically, adhering closely to source-text mode of expression. **Free Translation**, on the other hand, modifies surface expression and keeps intact only deeper levels of meaning. The choice of either method of translation is determined by text properties to do with text type, purpose of translation, etc.

LOCUTIONARY ACT: A distinction is made in **Speech Act Theory** between a locutionary act (the act of saying something, e.g. *It is hot in here*), an **Illocutionary Act** (what is intended by the locutionary act—'please open the window'), and a **Perlocutionary Act** (what the ultimate effect could be said to be—demonstrating who is 'boss' around here).

MACRO-SIGN: see **Sign**

MANAGING: see **Monitoring**

MANNER: see **Cooperative Principle**

MARKED: see **Unmarked**

MASTER GENRE: see **Genre**

MAXIM: see **Cooperative Principle**

META-FUNCTIONS: These are not to be seen as functions in the sense of 'uses of language', but as functional components of the semantic system. They are modes of meaning that are present in every use of language. Thus, the **Ideational Function**, which emanates from **Field of Discourse**, represents the speaker's meaning potential as an observer: language is about something (e.g. *Ten Blacks Shot By Police* and *Police Shoot Ten Blacks* are two different ideational structures, one catering for a white perspective, the other for a black perspective). The **Interpersonal Component**, which emanates from **Tenor of Discourse**, represents the speaker's meaning potential as an intruder: language as doing something (e.g. different uses of **Modality** relay different interpersonal meanings). Finally, the **Textual Component**, which emanates from **Mode of Discourse**, represents the speaker's text-forming potential: how language is made both relevant and operational (e.g. choices of what occupies the slot theme in the text is an orchestrating, textual consideration).

MICRO-SIGN: see **Sign**

MODALITY: Expressing distinctions such as that between 'possibility' and 'actuality', and, in the process, indicating an attitude towards the state or event involved. Modality constitutes one set of means for relaying evidentiality.

MODE OF DISCOURSE: see **Meta-Functions, Register**

MONITORING: Expounding in a non-evaluative manner. This is in contrast to **Managing**, which involves steering the discourse towards the speaker's goals.

MOOD: The basic choice we make between using a statement, a question or a command. This choice is not without significance in the analysis of ideology and the interpersonal meaning.

MOTIVATEDNESS: The set of factors which rhetorically regulate text user's choices, whether conscious or unconscious.

MYTH: The way in which a given sign undergoes a series of transformations until it achieves cultural status in the collective mentality of a community (e.g. the myth 'honour' in the cultural code of a number of language communities around the world).

NEGATIVE POLITENESS STRATEGIES: see **Politeness**

NOMINAL SENTENCE: In Arabic, Subject + Verb + Complement is a word order normally associated with evaluative contexts (e.g. **Argumentation**). The **Verbal sentence**, on the other hand, has a Verb + Subject + Complement structure and is normally associated with non-evaluative contexts (e.g. **Exposition**).

NOMINALIZATION: The condensed reformulation of a verbal process and the various participants involved as a noun phrase. This is an important grammatical resource for **Suppression of Agency** in the expression of ideology as when in saying *The net inflow is* ..., the speaker can get round having to recognize the fact that it is 'immigrants who flow into this country in large numbers', for example.

NON-EVALUATIVENESS: see **Evaluativeness**

OPPOSITION: see **Text Structure**

PAROLE: see **Langue**

PERLOCUTIONARY ACT: see **Locutionary Act**

PLAN: A global cognitive pattern representing how events and states can lead up to the attainment of a goal. To criticize, say, the inefficiency of the educational system, a text producer has to define what the goal is and has then to decide on the most effective way of attaining this. Plans are thus predominantly utilized in putting together argumentative texts.

POLITENESS: A pragmatic theory which is centred on the notion of **Face**, that is, the attempt to establish, maintain and save face during interaction with others. Two main factors regulate the degree of **Imposition** which is ideally kept at a minimum: **Power** and **Distance**. In handling the latter, two basic sets of strategies are in use: **Positive Politeness Strategies** (those which show intimacy between speaker and hearer) and **Negative Politeness Strategies** (those which underline social distance between participants). Any irregularity in handling power and/or distance would result in compromising the degree of imposition in a wide range of what is known as **Face-Threatening Acts (FTAs)**.

POSITIVE POLITENESS STRATEGIES: see **Politeness**

POWER: In the analysis of politeness, tenor or, more specifically interpersonal meaning, two basic types of relationship may be distinguished: power and **Solidarity**. Power emanates from the text producer's ability to impose his or her plans at the expense of the text receiver's plans. Solidarity, on the other hand, is the willingness of the text producer genuinely to relinquish power and work with his or her interlocutors as members of a team. Particular choices within **Mood** and **Modality** are relevant to the expression of either power or solidarity.

PRAGMATICS: The domain of **Intentionality** or the purposes for which utterances are used in real contexts.

PROPOSITIONAL CONTENT: What is involved in saying something that is meaningful and can be understood. Not included here is the function that the particular sentence performs in some specified context. For example, within propositional content analysis, *It is hot in here* would be analysed as a comment on the temperature of the room and not, say, an attempt to get someone to open the window.

QUALITY AS A MAXIM: see **Cooperative Principle**

QUANTITY AS A MAXIM: see **Cooperative Principle**

REGISTER: The set of features that distinguish one stretch of language from another in terms of variation in **Context** to do with the language user (geographical dialect, idiolect, etc.) and/or with language use (**Field** or subject matter, **Tenor** or level of formality and **Mode** or speaking vs writing).

RELEVANCE: Sperber and Wilson (1986) define this in terms of 'expectations' on the part of the hearer that his or her attempt at interpretation will yield adequate contextual effects at minimal processing cost. In this book, we take a rather more liberal view and define relevance both within the Gricean maxims and as part of text-type politeness, thus: Relevance is to do with the compliance by the text producer with **Rhetorical Conventions** regulating what you can and cannot say within the boundaries of a given **Genre**, a given **Discourse** and a given **Text**, a matter which is ultimately regulated by a wide range of socio-cultural factors. For example, relevance is compromised when unmotivated emphasis is used in what is otherwise a fairly detached news report.

RELEVANCE AS A MAXIM: see **Cooperative Principle**

RHEME: That part of a sentence which, in the unmarked case, occurs last and which carries maximal communicative importance.

RHETORICAL CONVENTIONS: A set of variable rules and strategies which conventionally regulate the way a given stretch of textual material is put together (**Text Structure**) and is made to hang together (**Texture**), ultimately contributing to the efficiency of communicative behaviour and to its appropriateness to a given context of situation. In Arabic, for example, almost every sentence of a news report is introduced by a verb of saying (e.g. *he said* ...; *he* *continued* ...; *he added* ...). English news reporting, on the other hand, tends to introduce a whole sequence of sentences with one verb of saying. What is involved here is two different sets of rhetorical conventions.

RHETORICAL PURPOSE: see **Text**

SCENARIO: see **Schema**

SCENE-SETTER: see **Text Structure**

SCHEMA, SCHEMATA: A global cognitive processing pattern representing the underlying structure that accounts for the organization of a text. A story schema, for example, may consist of a setting and a number of episodes, each of which would include events and reactions. Schemata are predominantly utilized in putting together texts of the expository narrative type (see **Exposition**).

SCRIPT: Another term for 'frame'. These are global processing patterns realized by units of meaning that consist of events and actions related to particular situations. For example, a text may be structured around the 'restaurant script' which represents our knowledge of how restaurants function: waitresses, cooks, tables where customers sit, peruse menus, order their meals and pay the bill at the end. Scripts and frames are predominantly utilized in dealing with texts of the expository descriptive type (see **Exposition**).

SEMIOTICS: A dimension of context which regulates the relationship of texts to each other as signs. Semiotics thus relies on the interaction not only between speaker and hearer but also between speakers/hearers and their texts, and between text and text. This **Intertextuality** is governed by a variety of **Socio-Cultural Factors** (e.g. **Politeness**), and **Rhetorical Conventions** (the way news reporting is handled in a given language). These factors and conventions are ultimately responsible for the way the socio-textual practices develop within a given community of text users (see **Genre, Text, Discourse**).

SIGN: A unit of signifier and signified, in which the linguistic form (signifier) stands for a concrete object or concept (signified). When the notion of sign is extended to include anything that means something to somebody in some respect or capacity, signs could then be used to refer to cultural objects such as *honour* (micro-signs), as well as to more global structures such as text, genre and discourse (macro-signs), and to even more global structures such as that of the **Myth**.

SOCIO-CULTURAL FACTORS: see **Semiotics**

SOCIO-TEXTUAL PRACTICES: see **Semiotics**

SOLIDARITY: see **Power**

SPEECH ACTING: see **Locutionary Act**

SPEECH ACT THEORY: see **Locutionary Act**

STEP: see **Element**

STRAW-MAN GAMBIT: see **Argumentation**

STRUCTURE: see **Text Structure**

SUB-GENRE: see **Genre**

SUBSTANTIATION: see **Text Structure**

SUPPRESSED COUNTER-ARGUMENT: see **Argumentation**

SUPPRESSION OF AGENCY: see **Nominalization**

TENOR OF DISCOURSE: see **Meta-Functions**, **Register**

TEXT: A set of mutually relevant communicative functions that 'stick' together (**Texture**) and 'hang' together (**Structure**) in such a way as to respond to a particular context and thus achieve an overall rhetorical purpose. For example, in response to a thesis that the text producer thinks is flawed, he or she may attend to counter-arguing as a rhetorical purpose, which entails the use of particular evaluative forms of linguistic expression with a particular structure format that starts with the citation of an opponent's thesis and moves on to a rebuttal. The minimal unit of text analysis is the text element (e.g. thesis cited to be opposed).

TEXT ELEMENT: see **Text**

TEXT STRUCTURE: The compositional plan of a text. Different **Text Types** exhibit different structure formats. Some of these are formulaic, as in the structure of the Preamble: *X and Y, having met ..., considering ..., re-emphasizing ..., have agreed ....* Other formats are less formulaic, though fairly predictable. For example, a managing counter-argument has the following structure: **Thesis Cited**, Opposition, Substantiation, Conclusion. A managing through-argument simply has Thesis Cited, Thesis Extensively Defended. Whether to be rebutted or defended, the thesis cited always sets a tone. **Monitoring Exposition**, on the other hand, displays the most open-ended of formats: Scene Set, Aspects of the Scene Tackled.

TEXTUAL COMPETENCE: The ability not only to apply the lexico-grammatical rules of a language in order to produce well-formed sentences, and not only to know when, where and with whom to use these sentences, but to know how

GLOSSARY

to make the sentence play a role within a sequence that is eventually part of a well-formed text, discourse and genre.

TEXT HYBRIDIZATION: **Text Types** are rarely if ever pure. More than one **Text-Type Focus** is normally discernible, a situation that is not as seamless as it may seem. In the event that more than one text-type focus is in evidence, one and only one is bound to be predominant, with the others being subsidiary, if not totally marginal.

TEXT TYPE: The way the **Structure** and **Texture** of texts are made to respond to their **Context** and to display a particular **Text-Type Focus**. Three basic text-type foci may be distinguished: **Exposition**, **Argumentation** and **Instruction**.

TEXT-TYPE FOCUS: see **Text Type**

TEXTUAL MEANING: see **Meta-Functions**

TEXTURE: Aspects of text organization which contribute to the overall effect of texts hanging together and reflect the coherence of text structure and the way texts are responding to their context. Texture includes aspects of message construction such as cohesion, theme–rheme organization, as well as text idiom and diction.

THEME: That part of a sentence which, in the unmarked case, occurs first and which normally has less communicative importance than the **Rheme**.

THEMATIC PROGRESSION (TP): The tendency for **Themes** or **Rhemes** to concatenate in particular patterns, relating to text-type focus. In **Exposition**, for example, the tendency is for the discourse to display **Backward Directionality**, that is, themes are redeployed as themes in the subsequent discourse (**Uniform Pattern**). In **Argumentation**, on the other hand, the tendency is for the discourse to have **Forward Directionality**, that is, rhemes are deployed as themes in the subsequent discourse (**Zigzag Pattern**).

THESIS CITED TO BE OPPOSED: see **Text Structure**

THROUGH-ARGUMENT: see **Argumentation**

TONE-SETTER: see **Text Structure**

TOP-DOWN: In cognitive psychology and adjacent disciplines, two different ways in which humans analyse and process language are distinguished. Top-down processing involves the reliance by the text user on contextual information (higher-level knowledge) in actually dealing with the information received (words, sentences, etc.) In **Bottom-up** processing, on the other hand, text users mostly utilize presented information as a point of departure towards the discovery of some contextual knowledge. Needless to say, both types of process are involved in any meaningful act of, say, reading or translating.

UNIFORM PATTERN: see **Thematic Progression**

UNMARKED: The state of certain lexical or grammatical items or structures which are considered to be more basic or common than other structures, **Marked** for particular effects. The cleft sentence *It was John who did it* is a marked form of *John did it*.

VERBAL SENTENCE: see **Nominal Sentence**

VIOLATING A MAXIM: see **Cooperative Principle**

VIRTUAL: A term used to refer to systemic aspects of language structure or *langue* before context is brought in to add another, deeper dimension to meaning. When this happens, and linguistic structures are seen as part of *parole*, we would be in the domain of the actual.

VISUAL TEXT: A text that is put together in such a way as to satisfy the requirements of literate (as opposed to orate) rhetorical conventions at work in societies characterized by literacy (as opposed to orality). In such societies, texts are normally heavily subordinated, possessing minimal unnecessary repetition and being generally tighter (or more complex) in terms of both structure and texture. Orate communities of language users, on the other hand, would be content with so-called aural texts that tend to be heavily coordinated, that exhibit a great deal of repetition and that are generally looser (or simpler) in terms of both structure and texture.

ZIGZAG PATTERN: see **Thematic Progression**

References

Agar, M. 1991. 'The Biculture in Bilingual', *Language in Society*, 20: 167–81.
——1994. 'The Intercultural Frame', *International Journal of Intercultural Relations*, 18(2): 221–37.
al-'Askarii, A. 1952. *al-Sinaa'atayn* ('The Two Crafts: Prose and Poetry'), edited by A.M. al-Bajjawi and A. Ibrahim (Cairo: al-Babi al-Halabi Press).
Austin, J.L. 1962. *How to Do Things with Words* (Oxford: Clarendon Press).
Badawi, M.M. (transl.) 1973. *The Saint's Lamp and Other Stories* (Leiden: Brill; orig. Yahya Haqqi 1944).
Baker, M. 1992/2011. *In Other Words: A Coursebook on Translation* (London: Routledge).
Barthes, R. 1957. *Mythologies* (Paris: Seuil; London: Paladin, 1973).
Bateson, G. 1976. 'A Theory of Play and Fantasy', in J.S. Bruner, A. Jolly and K. Sylva (eds) *Play: Its Role in Development and Evolution* (Harmondsworth: Penguin Books), pp. 79–89.
Bauman, R. 1977. *Verbal Art as Performance* (Rowley, MA: Newbury House).
Beaugrande, R.A. 1978. *Factors in a Theory of Poetic Translation* (Assen: Van Gorcum).
——1980. *Text, Discourse and Process* (Norwood, NJ: Ablex).
——1984. *Text Production* (Norwood, NJ: Ablex).
——1997. *New Foundations for a Science of Text and Discourse* (Greenwich, CT: Ablex).
Beaugrande, R.A., and W.U. Dressler. 1981. *Introduction to Text Linguistics* (London: Longman).
Beeston, A.F.L. 1970. *The Arabic Language Today* (London: Hutchinson).
Britton, J. 1963. 'Literature', in J. Britton (ed.) *The Arts and Current Tendencies in Education* (London: Evans), pp. 34–61.
——1982. 'Spectator Role and the Beginnings of Writing', in M. Nystrand (ed.)

What Writers Know: The Language, Process and Structure of Written Discourse (New York: Academic Press).

Bronowski, J., and B. Mazlish. 1974. *The Western Intellectual Tradition from Leonardo to Hegel* (New York: Harper & Row).

Brown, G., and G. Yule. 1982. *Discourse Analysis* (Cambridge: Cambridge University Press).

Brown, K., and J. Miller. 1992. *The Cambridge Dictionary of Linguistics* (Cambridge: Cambridge University Press).

Brown, P., and S. Levinson. 1978/1987. 'Universals in Language Usage: Politeness Phenomena', in E.N. Goody (ed.) *Questions and Politeness: Strategies in Social Interaction* (Cambridge: Cambridge University Press), pp. 56–288.

Candlin, C.N. 1976. 'Communicative Language Teaching and the Debt to Pragmatics', in C. Rameh (ed.) *Semantics: Theory and Applications* (Georgetown University Round Table on Language and Linguistics, pp. 237–57).

——1985. 'Preface' to M. Coulthard, *An Introduction to Discourse Analysis*. Applied Linguistics and Language Study, 2nd edn (London: Longman).

Carter, R., A. Goddard, D. Reah, K. Sanger, and K. Bowring. 2001. *Working with Texts: A Core Introduction to Language Analysis* (New York: Routledge).

Chau, S. 1984. *Aspects of Translation Pedagogy: The Grammatical, Cultural and Interpretive Teaching Models* (PhD thesis, University of Edinburgh).

Crombie, W. 1985. *Process and Relation in Discourse and Language Learning* (Oxford: Oxford University Press).

Crystal, D., and D. Davy. 1969. *Investigating English Style* (London: Longman).

Daneš, F. 1974. 'Functional Sentence Perspective and the Organization of the Text', in F. Daneš (ed.) *Papers on Functional Sentence Perspective* (The Hague: Mouton), pp. 106–28.

Deyes, A. 1978. 'Towards a Linguistic Definition of Functional Varieties of Written English', *International Review of Applied Linguistics in Language Teaching*, Vol. XVl/4, pp. 313–29.

Emery, P. 1991. 'Text Classification and Text Analysis in Advanced Translation Teaching', *META*, XXXVI, 4, pp. 567–77.

Enkvist, N.E. 1991. 'Discourse Type, Text Type, and Cross-Cultural Rhetoric', in Sonja Tirkkonen-Condit (ed.) *Empirical Research in Translation and Intercultural Studies* (Tubingen: Gunter Narr), pp. 5–16.

——1992. 'Review of Discourse and the Translator by B. Hatim and I. Mason', *Target*, 4(1): 124–26.

van der Eyken, Willem (ed.). 1973. *Education, the Child and Society: A Documentary History 1900–1973* (Harmondsworth: Penguin Education).

Fahnestock, J. 1986. 'Accommodating Science: The Rhetorical Life of Scientific Facts', *Written Communication* 3(3): 275–96.
Fairclough, N. 1989. *Language and Power* (London: Longman).
——1992. *Discourse and Social Change* (Cambridge: Polity Press).
Farghal, M. 1991. 'Evaluativeness Parameter and the Translator from English to Arabic and Vice-Versa', *Babel* 37, pp. 138–51.
Firbas, J. 1975. 'On the Non-Thematic Section of the Sentence', in H. Ringbom (ed.) *Style and Text* (Stockholm: Skriptor), pp. 317–34.
Fowler, R. 1985. 'Power', in T. van Dijk (ed.) *Handbook of Discourse Analysis, vol. 4: Discourse Analysis in Society* (New York: Academic Press), pp. 61–82.
——(1986/1996) *Linguistic Criticism* (Oxford: Oxford University Press).
Francis. G., and A. Kramer-Dahl. 1992. 'Grammaticalizing the Medical Case History', in Michael Toolan (eds) *Language, Text and Context: Essays in Stylistics* (London: Routledge).
Geeraerts, D. 2010. *Theories of Lexical Semantics* (Oxford Linguistics) Oxford: Oxford University Press).
Goodenough, W.H. 1964. 'Cultural Anthropology and Linguistics' in D. Hymes (ed.) *Language in Culture and Society: A Reader in Linguistics and Anthropology* (New York: Harper & Row), pp. 36–40.
Gregory, M., and S. Carroll. 1978. *Language and Situation: Language Varieties and their Social Contexts* (London: Routledge & Kegan Paul).
Grice, P. 1975. 'Logic and Conversation', in P. Cole and J. Morgan (eds) *Syntax and Semantics 3: Speech Acts* (New York: Academic Press, pp. 41–58).
Halliday, M.A.K. 1971. 'Linguistic Function and Literary Style: An Inquiry into the Language of William Golding's *The Inheritors*', in S. Chatman (ed.) *Literary Style: A Symposium* (Oxford: Oxford University Press), pp. 330–68.
——1978. *Language as Social Semiotic* (London: Edward Arnold).
——1985. *An Introduction to Functional Grammar*, 1st edn (London: Edward Arnold).
——2014. *An Introduction to Functional Grammar*, 4th edn (London: Edward Arnold).
Halliday, M.A.K., and R. Hasan. 1976. *Cohesion in English* (London: Longman).
Halliday, M.A.K., and C. Matthiessen. 1999. *Construing Experience Through Meaning: A Language-Based Approach to Cognition* (London: Cassell).
——2014. *Halliday's Introduction to Functional Grammar*, 4th edn (Oxford: Routledge).
Hasan, A. 1975. *al-NaHuu al-Waafii* (Cairo: Daar al-Ma'aarif).

Hatim, B. 1991. 'The Pragmatics of Argumentation in Arabic: The Rise and Fall of a Text Type', *Text*, 11(2): 189–99.
——1998. 'Politeness of Texts', in L. Hickey (ed.) *New Horizons in Pragmatics* (Bristol: Multilingual Matters).
——2005. 'Intercultural Communication and Identity: An Exercise in Applied Semiotics', *Intercultural Communication Studies*, XIV: 4.
——2010. *Arabic Rhetoric: The Pragmatics of Deviation from Linguistic Norms* (Munich: Lincom Europa).
Hatim, B., and I. Mason. 1990. *Discourse and the Translator* (London: Longman).
——1997. *The Translator as Communicator* (London: Routledge).
Hoey, M. 1983. *On the Surface of Discourse* (London: George Allen & Unwin).
Johanesson, N.-L. 1985. 'Pragmatics', *Stockholm Papers in English Language and Literature*, Publication 5.
Johnstone-Koch, B. 1983. 'Presentation as Proof: The Language of Arabic Rhetoric', *Anthropological Linguistics*, 25(1): 47–60.
——1986. 'Arguments with Khomeini: Rhetorical Situation and Persuasive Style in Cross-Cultural Perspective', *Text*, 6: 171–87.
——1991. *Repetition in Arabic Discourse: Paradigms, Syntagms, and the Ecology of Language* (Amsterdam: John Benjamins).
Jones, G., and G.R. Kress. 1981. 'Classification at Work: The Case of Middle Management', *Text*, 1(1): 65–81.
al-Jurjaanii, A. 1987. *Dalaa'il al-I'jaaz* ('Signs of Qur'anic Inimitability'), edited by M.R. al-Daya and F. al-Daya (Damascus: Maktabat Sa'd al-Din).
Katan, D. 2004. *Translating Cultures: An Introduction for Translators, Interpreters and Mediators*, 2nd edn (London: Routledge).
Kress, G.R. 1985a 'Ideological Structures in Discourse', in T. van Dijk (ed.) *Handbook of Discourse Analysis, vol. 4: Discourse Analysis in Society* (New York: Academic Press), pp. 27–42.
——1985b. *Linguistic Processes in Sociocultural Practice* (Victoria: Deakin University Press).
Lemke, J.L. 1992. 'Interpersonal Meaning in Discourse: Value Orientations', in M. Davies and L. Ravelli (eds) *Advances in Systemic Linguistics: Recent Theory and Practice* (London: Pinter), pp. 82–104.
——1994. 'Semiotics and the Deconstruction of Conceptual Learning', *Journal of Accelerative Learning and Teaching*, 19(1): 67–110.
Levý, J. 1969. 'Translation as a Decision Process', in R. Jakobson, *To Honor Roman Jakobson: Essays on the Occasion of His 70. Birthday, 11. October 1966*, Vol. 2 (The Hague: Mouton), pp. 1171–82.

Longacre, R.E. 1979. 'The Paragraph as a Grammatical Unit', on T. Givón (ed.) *Discourse and Syntax* (New York: Academic Press), pp. 115–34.
Lukin, A., A. Moore, M. Herke, R. Wegener, and C. Wu. 2011. 'Halliday's Model of Register Revisited and Explored', *Linguistics and the Human Sciences*, 4(2): 187–213.
Martin, J.R. 1985. *Factual Writing: Exploring and Challenging Social Reality* (Victoria: Deakin University Press).
——(1985/1989) *Sociocultural Aspects of Language and Education* (Oxford: Oxford University Press).
——1992. *English Text: System and Structure* (Amsterdam: John Benjamins).
——2002. 'Meaning Beyond the Clause: SFL Perspectives', *Annual Review of Applied Linguistics*, 22: 52–74.
Martin, J.R. and D. Rose. 2008. *Genre Relations: Mapping Culture* (London: Equinox).
Matthiessen, C.M.I.M. 1993. 'Register in the Round: Diversity in a Unified Theory of Register Analysis', in Mohsen Ghadessy (ed.) *Register Analysis: Theory and Practice* (London: Pinter).
Myers, G. 1989. 'The Pragmatics of Politeness in Scientific Articles', *Applied Linguistics*, 10(1): 1–35.
Nash, W. 1980. *Designs in Prose* (London: Longman).
Newmark, P. 1988. *A Textbook of Translation* (Hemel Hempstead: Prentice Hall).
Nida, E.A. 1969. 'Science of Translation', *Language*, 45(3): 483–98.
Nida, E.A., and C. Taber. 1969. *The Theory and Practice of Translation* (Leiden: Brill).
Nu'aimi A., and D. Kayyal. 1984. *al-Tmlaa' al-WaaDiH* (Baghdad: al-Russafi Press).
Ochs, E. 1979. 'Planned and Unplanned Discourse', in T. Givón (ed.) *Discourse and Syntax* (New York: Academic Press), pp. 50–80.
Ong, W.J. 1971. *Rhetoric, Romance and Technology* (Ithaca, NY: Cornell University Press).
——1982. *Orality and Literacy: The Technologizing of the Word* (London: Methuen).
Palkova, Z., and K. Palek. 1977. 'Functional Sentence Perspective and Textlinguistics', in W. Dressler (ed.) *Current Trends in Textlinguistics* (Berlin: de Gruyter), pp. 212–27.
Peirce, C.S. 1934. *The Collected Papers of Charles Sanders Peirce*, Vol. V: Pragmatism and Pragmaticism (Cambridge: Harvard University Press).
Prince, E.F. 1981. 'Toward a Taxonomy of Given-New Information', in P. Cole (ed.) *Radical Pragmatics* (New York: Academic Press), pp. 223–55.

Qudaama, undated. *Naqd al-Nathr* ('The Criticism of Prose'), edited by A. al-Khafaji (Cairo).

Sa'adeddin, M.A. 1989. 'Text Development and Arabic-English Negative Interference', *Applied Linguistics*, 10(1): 36–51.

Sacks, O. 1985. *The Man Who Mistook His Wife for a Hat, and Other Clinical Tales* (Summit Books).

al-Sakkakii, Y. 1937. *MiftaaH al-'Uluum* ('The Key to the Rhetorical Sciences') (Cairo: al-Babi al-Halabi Press).

Scollon, R., and S.W. Scollon. 1995. *Intercultural Communication: A Discourse Approach* (Oxford: Basil Blackwell).

Searle, J.R. 1969. *Speech Acts: An Essay in the Philosophy of Language* (Cambridge: Cambridge University Press).

Seleskovitch, D. 1968. *L'interprète dans les conférences internationales, problèmes de langage et de communication* (Paris, Minard Lettres Modernes, 2ème édition 1983). Translated into English as *Interpreting for International Conferences* (2nd revised edition, Washington DC: Pen & Booth, 1994). Also translated into German, Chinese, Korean, Japanese and Serbian.

Sell, R.D. 1993. *Literary Pragmatics* (London: Routledge).

Shouby, E. 1951. 'The Influence of the Arabic Language on the Psychology of the Arabs', *Middle East Education*, 5: 284–302.

Siddiq, M. 1986. '"Deconstructing" *The Saint's Lamp*', *Journal of Arabic Literature*, XVII, pp. 126–45.

Simpson, P. 1993. *Ideology and Point of View* (London: Routledge).

Sinclair, J., and M. Coulthard. 1975. *Towards an Analysis of Discourse* (Oxford: Oxford University Press).

Snell-Hornby, M. 1988. *Translation Studies: An Integrated Approach* (Amsterdam: John Benjamins).

Sperber, D., and D. Wilson. 1981. 'Irony and the Use–Mention Distinction', in P. Cole (ed.) *Radical Pragmatics* (New York: Academic Press), pp. 295–318.

——1986. *Relevance: Communication and Cognition* (Oxford: Basil Blackwell).

Stalnaker, R.C. 1972. 'Pragmatics', in D. Davidson and G. Harman (eds) *Semantics in Natural Language* (Dordrecht: Reidel).

Stubbs, M. 1983. *Discourse Analysis: The Sociolinguistic Analysis of Natural Language* (Oxford: Basil Blackwell).

Sykes, M. 1985. 'Discrimination in Discourse', in T. van Dijk (ed.) *Handbook of Discourse Analysis, vol. 4: Discourse Analysis in Society* (New York: Academic Press), pp. 83–101.

Thompson, G. (1996/2014) *Introducing Functional Grammar* (London: Arnold).

——2004. *Introducing Functional Grammar* (New York: Oxford University Press).
Turner, G.J. 1973. 'Social Class and Children's Language of Control at Age Five and Age Seven', in B. Bernstein (ed.) *Class, Codes and Control 2: Applied Studies- Towards a Sociology of Language* (London: Routledge & Kegan Paul).
Venuti, L. 1995. *The Translator's Invisibility: A History of Translation* (London: Routledge).
Volosinov, V.N. 1929. *Marxism and the Philosophy of Language* (translated by L. Matejka and I.R. Titunik, New York: Seminar Press, 1973).
de Vries, L. 2000. 'Bible Translation and Primary Orality', *Technical Papers for the Bible Translator*, 51(1): 101–14.
Werlich, E. 1976. *A Text Grammar of English* (Heidelberg: Quelle & Meyer).
Wienold, G. 1990. 'Typological Aspects of Translating Literary Japanese into German', *Target*, 2(2): 183–197.
Winter, E.O. 1982. *Towards a Contextual Grammar of English* (London: Allen & Unwin).
Young, D.J. 1985. 'Some Applications of Systemic Grammar to TEFL, or Whatever Became of Register Analysis?', in James D. Benson and William S. Greaves (eds) *Systemic Perspectives on Discourse*, Vol. 2. (Norwood, NJ: Ablex), pp. 282–94.

Index

abstract 63, 99, 102, 202, 213, 214, 215–16, 233, 276, 285
acceptability 9, 10, 69, 101, 149, 210
action predicate 244, 245
analytical discourse 76, 79, 92–3
Arabic x, xi, 2–4, 10, 20, 21, 27, 41, 50–3, 54–61, 62—63, 69, 72, 74–81, 88, 89, 106, 109, 118, 120, 124–6, 129, 130, 131, 133–4, 136–7, 146, 148, 151, 153–9, 160–2, 164–9, 172, 173, 177, 179, 180, 181–3, 185–8, 190, 192, 194–6, 198–200, 214–15, 221–37, 238–50, 251–67, 273–5, 277, 285, 288, 290
Arabic rhetoric 52, 53, 54–61, 180, 199, 224, 227, 231
argumentation 27, 28, 38, 41, 44–9, 50–3, 54–61, 68–9, 75–6, 79, 81, 83–5, 89, 93, 115, 121, 124, 141, 143–5, 149, 151–3, 158, 162, 171, 187, 195, 201–2, 205–6, 208, 209, 211, 216–19, 221, 225, 227, 230–7, 273, 281, 283, 284, 289, 292, 293
artificial intelligence 6, 26, 40
audience 37, 39, 84, 89, 94, 208, 209, 210–11, 214, 217, 221, 230–7, 258

background information 124–34, 156, 170, 181
balaagha 55, 199, 224
balance 21, 47, 50–1, 53, 79, 81, 157, 212

Bible 226, 269
bottom-up (text analysis) 17, 24, 29, 65, 100, 101, 142, 278, 282, 293

cataphora 148–59, 165, 168, 170, 281, 282
coherence 8–10, 12, 17, 18, 22, 25, 26, 28, 65, 66, 70, 80, 86, 100, 102, 107, 110, 113, 125, 135, 138, 149, 155, 158–9, 160, 163, 170, 199, 208, 214, 230, 231, 242, 271, 272, 274, 282, 293
cohesion 8–10, 12, 17, 18, 25, 26, 28, 65, 66, 70, 80, 81, 86, 100, 101, 103, 113, 125, 132–3, 135, 139, 147, 149, 155, 158–9, 160, 161, 163, 170, 199, 208, 214, 222, 231, 242, 274, 282, 293
commodification discourse 82
communicative dynamism (CD) 138, 282
communicative transaction 115, 149, 197
conjunction 110, 206
connectivity 9, 10, 274
context of culture 56, 73, 90, 99, 100, 112, 283
context of situation 13, 73, 90, 99, 100, 112, 240, 283, 290
contrastive rhetoric 2, 60, 103, 224–5, 228, 280
contrastive textology ix, 118
Cooperative Principle 257, 282, 283, 284, 285, 286, 287, 288, 290, 294
cooperativeness 4, 257
cultural studies 2

INDEX

decision-making 2, 6–16, 27, 104, 167
deficit 41, 53
description 44, 45, 66, 87, 102, 121, 125, 199, 202, 235, 260, 285
deverbalization 107–8
deviation 50, 152, 173, 283, 284, 286
direct speech 94, 185–8, 190, 192, 194–6, 198–200
discourse analysis ix, 1, 2, 91, 93, 117, 284
distance 4, 12, 87, 88, 188, 189, 203, 209–19, 284, 289

ecological debate 83, 84
editorial 14, 15, 22, 29, 84, 85, 137, 143, 158, 167, 172, 207, 216, 222, 223, 236, 269, 286
effectiveness 15, 32, 49, 59, 118, 224, 230, 238
efficiency 15, 32, 49, 238, 290
ellipsis 176, 247, 282, 284
emotiveness 9, 160, 170–84, 205
emphasis 37, 55, 56, 107, 176, 180, 204, 225, 290
environment (textual) 36, 72, 138, 186, 249, 271, 282, 283
equivalence 22, 71, 72, 157, 160, 161, 188, 193, 254, 267
ethnographical-semantic 71
evaluativeness 24, 44, 49, 55–6, 89, 113, 131, 141, 143, 149, 150, 156–7, 165, 171–5, 177–8, 180–4, 185, 188, 196, 204, 205, 210, 215, 216, 284, 289
explicative 146, 148, 154, 161, 168, 190, 199, 285
explicative language 3, 69, 129, 160, 168
explicit concessive 47, 50–3
exposition 24, 28, 43–4, 45, 48, 49, 50, 53, 56, 57, 68, 82–4, 89, 93, 124, 125, 144–5, 150–5, 158, 162, 171, 195, 201, 202, 205, 211, 213–19, 235–6, 273, 284, 285, 289, 291, 292, 293

Face-Threatening Act (FTA) 208, 213, 285, 289
faSaaHa 262
field 8–13, 15, 17, 23, 25, 32, 33, 35–6, 42, 64–5, 70, 80, 85–8, 100, 115, 136, 145, 188, 190, 201, 240, 265–6, 268, 270, 279, 283, 285, 288, 290
flouting 4, 139, 150, 158, 177, 180–1, 212, 214, 233–4, 258–67, 283
formality 3, 8, 9, 11, 13, 17, 25, 29, 32, 33–5, 63, 65, 67, 70, 82, 86, 110, 114, 115, 190, 231, 233, 240, 252, 266, 269, 286, 290
frame 44, 57, 66, 102, 139, 149, 226, 285, 291
function 8, 9, 11, 14, 15, 25, 34, 35, 38, 39, 42, 49–50, 57–8, 70, 86–9, 91, 92, 95, 96, 100, 103, 104, 109, 114, 119, 125–9, 131–2, 134, 137–8, 143, 146, 152–5, 157–9, 160, 164–6, 170–3, 177, 181–2, 185–7, 194, 196, 201, 215, 223, 226–31, 234, 236, 239, 240, 241, 243, 244, 250, 274, 276, 278, 279, 285–8, 290, 292, 293
Functional Sentence Perspective (FSP) 137, 286
functional tenor 33–4, 286

genre 10, 15–16, 17–18, 22–7, 28–9, 38, 42, 53, 62–4, 67–70, 73–4, 76, 78–81, 84–9, 92–3, 99, 124, 126, 131, 133, 155, 157, 170, 187, 193–5, 197–200, 202–3, 214–17, 219, 227, 229, 236, 238, 241–2, 251, 267, 269, 271–2, 276–8, 280, 286, 288, 290, 291, 292, 293
genrelet 276–8, 286
globalization 3, 53, 62–81
Gricean maxims 212, 283, 286, 290

Hadiith 56, 200
heuristic 18, 49, 117, 121, 144, 286
hierarchy 114, 131, 132, 140
hortatory discourse 92–3
hybridization 48–50, 172–3, 187, 293

ideational   10–12, 15, 17, 23, 25, 35–6, 60, 69–70, 86–8, 90, 93, 112, 172, 266, 270, 279, 286, 288
ideology   3, 8, 10, 16, 17, 38, 48, 63, 92, 98–100, 104–5, 112, 170, 203, 238–9, 242–3, 250, 253, 271, 286, 288, 289
illocutionary   39, 109, 189, 286, 287
implicative   3, 148, 190, 199
implicative language   148, 160, 168, 285
implicature   64, 179, 252, 257–60, 265–6, 283, 286
imposition   43, 207, 209, 211, 213, 215, 219, 286, 289
inference   64, 240
informativity   8–10, 101, 102, 111, 152, 155, 157–8, 212, 284
inside out (text analysis)   10, 17
intentionality   9, 10, 25, 28, 39, 42, 64, 69, 82, 84, 101, 103, 111, 113–14, 123, 134, 149, 157, 159, 168, 179, 187, 189, 191, 206, 240–2, 246, 261, 266–7, 269, 282, 287
interaction   22–4, 26–7, 32–9, 42, 50, 64, 65, 67, 91, 94, 101–2, 110, 115, 144, 149, 163, 173, 189, 193, 197, 203, 207, 209, 216, 220, 229, 238, 241, 250, 271–2, 279–80, 289, 291
interpersonal   10–13, 15, 17, 23, 25, 35–6, 38, 69–70, 86–8, 90, 93–4, 112, 172, 266, 270, 279, 287, 288, 289
interpreter training   2, 268
intertextuality   9–10, 22, 25, 28, 37, 38, 42, 64, 100, 111, 149, 189, 193–4, 241, 260, 268–9, 271–2, 275, 282, 283, 287, 291
irony   3, 12, 59, 96, 168, 179, 212, 251–67

liaison interpreting   108, 268, 287
linguistic competence   231, 233
linguistic stylistics   175, 238–9, 245
literacy   53, 54, 156, 221, 294
literal translation   110, 156, 273, 285, 287
literary context   240
locutionary   39, 109, 286, 287, 289, 292

machine translation (MT)   6
macro-structural   18, 22, 63
managing   28, 37–40, 41–2, 58, 65, 135, 181, 191–2, 200, 275, 287, 288, 292
marked   66, 95, 102–3, 117, 118, 121, 126, 133, 138, 147, 152, 153, 154, 177, 180–3, 196, 215, 216, 217, 282, 286, 288, 290, 293, 294
markedness   95, 152
mediation   1, 105
medical novella   89, 90
micro-structural   18
mind-style   245, 246, 248
modality   11, 17, 94–5, 97, 176, 179, 212, 218, 284, 288, 290
mode   3, 8–13, 15, 17, 23, 25, 29, 32–3, 35–6, 41, 63–5, 68, 70, 76, 78–9, 82, 84–6, 88, 96, 107, 115, 124, 163, 168, 178, 185, 186, 188–9, 190–1, 195, 198, 200, 203, 206–10, 221, 225, 227, 233–4, 236–7, 238–43, 265–6, 268, 270, 279, 284, 287, 288, 290
monitoring   28, 38–40, 42, 49, 65, 135, 143, 191–2, 200, 287, 288, 292
mood   11, 17, 94, 96, 288, 290
motivated   3, 8, 10, 35, 48, 50, 101, 118, 125, 131, 133, 150, 152, 153, 158, 173, 180, 183, 207, 212, 215, 216, 219, 228, 229, 233, 235, 262, 263, 284, 285, 290
motivatedness   288
motivation   4, 48, 66, 102, 152, 168, 211, 212, 215, 229
myth   28–40, 276, 288, 291

naming   180
narration   38, 44–5, 50, 121, 124, 129, 130, 132, 133, 141, 145, 187, 195, 199, 202, 235, 240, 285
news report   24, 128, 131, 133, 167, 173, 181–4, 186–7, 194–5, 197, 212, 229, 286, 290
Nominal sentence   146, 156, 181, 288, 294
nominalization   17, 94, 96, 176, 289, 292

orality 53, 54, 78, 104, 156, 178, 187, 221,
    226, 227, 230–2, 237, 264, 294

paragraph 3, 113–23, 124, 140, 178
passivization 17, 93, 96, 177
performance 50, 63, 93, 226
perlocutionary 39, 109, 287, 289
persuasion 45, 60, 209, 227–8
plan 22, 25–6, 29, 44, 65, 66, 81, 89, 102,
    113, 125, 131, 132, 135, 148, 172, 206,
    229, 278, 289, 292
politeness 3, 48, 54, 78, 201–19, 221, 252,
    267, 284, 285, 288, 289, 290, 291
pop-academic 62–5, 76
power 8–9, 11–12, 25, 31, 35, 38, 48, 67,
    70, 73, 83, 86–7, 92, 93, 105, 170, 176,
    188, 203, 209–19, 226, 232, 266, 279,
    289, 290, 292
pragmatic action 115, 189, 200, 270–1
pragmatics 2, 26, 32, 39, 40, 41, 64, 65,
    82, 101, 107–8, 111, 112, 114, 139, 192,
    201–19, 240, 260, 265, 266, 268–9,
    278, 279, 290
presupposition 37, 64, 238, 240
process 1–4, 6, 10, 27, 28, 30, 37, 42, 64,
    70–1, 73, 87, 96, 103, 106, 108, 126,
    128, 142, 146, 154, 167, 194, 204, 206,
    219, 238, 244–6, 249, 268, 276, 294
process predicate 244–5, 249
progressive directionality 1
proof 60, 175, 227, 228, 230, 233
propositional 131, 179, 193–4, 290
punctuation 187, 196, 198–9
purpose 3, 14–16, 17–18, 22, 25, 26, 28,
    31, 38, 39, 67, 68, 71, 81, 82, 88, 89,
    90–2, 97, 98–109, 113–14, 123, 125,
    128, 130, 131, 135, 139, 141, 148,
    149–54, 168, 170–3, 177, 180, 185–6,
    188, 194–6, 199, 201, 204, 209–11,
    214, 215, 220, 228–9, 235, 237, 241,
    251, 270–4, 276, 278, 279, 284, 287,
    290, 291, 292

rebuttal 14, 15, 21, 54, 58–9, 69, 92, 121,
    143, 149, 151, 162, 205–6, 216–17, 222,
    224, 270, 292
reference switching (*iltifaat*) 200
referentiality 175
register membership 9, 25, 64–5, 69, 70,
    82, 85, 149–50, 188, 240, 267, 268
regressive directionality 144, 145
relevance 13, 18, 207, 283
repetition 10, 36–8, 55–6, 66, 97, 101–5,
    214, 228–9, 236, 263, 270, 294
report, reporting 23, 24, 29, 35, 38, 40,
    89, 96, 124, 126–8, 131, 133, 162, 167,
    172–3, 177, 181–7, 194–5, 197, 207, 212,
    213, 229, 251, 259, 273, 285, 286, 290
resolvers 83–5, 93
rhetoric 1–3, 52–3, 54–60, 62, 103, 155,
    157, 158, 180, 199, 221, 224–5, 227–8,
    231, 237, 280
rhetorical purpose 14, 16, 17–18, 22, 26,
    28, 38, 67, 68, 81, 82–92, 98–101,
    113, 114, 123, 125, 128, 131, 135,
    141, 148, 149–50, 152–4, 168, 171,
    173, 185–6, 195–6, 201–4, 211, 220,
    228–9, 235, 251, 272–3, 276, 278, 291,
    292

scenario 19, 21, 26, 66, 78, 102, 291
schemata 26, 44, 66, 102, 273, 277, 291
script 26, 268, 285, 291
semiotics 2, 15, 26, 33, 34, 36, 39, 53, 65,
    68, 70, 82, 90, 112, 114, 139, 149, 172,
    200, 238, 241–2, 251, 266, 268–9,
    280, 291
sense 18, 32, 63, 91, 98, 99, 107–12, 195,
    199, 230–1, 251, 268, 284
signs 15, 32, 35–7, 40–2, 65–6, 69–70, 115,
    131, 141, 149, 150, 152–3, 189, 193,
    201, 238, 241–3, 251, 260, 269, 270,
    273, 275, 276, 278, 280, 282, 287, 291
situationality 9–10, 100, 102, 111
social institutions 35, 69, 243
social processes 35, 69, 188

socio-textual practices   27, 62, 64, 67–9, 73–4, 76, 79, 81, 205, 291
solidarity   8, 9, 11, 12, 17, 25, 35–6, 70, 86–7, 188, 203, 231, 233, 266, 279, 289, 290, 292
speech acts   25, 39, 64, 73, 110, 172, 179, 191–2, 241, 269
staging   135, 162, 242
state predicate   244
stirrers   83–5, 90, 93
straw-man gambit   14, 19, 58, 74, 89, 122, 222, 281, 292
structural (organization of text)   26, 113, 116, 117–18, 120, 121, 123, 124, 131–3, 135, 230, 274, 278
style   23, 32, 54, 105, 107, 110, 155, 178, 181, 198, 202, 225, 226, 245, 246, 248, 270
subordination   178, 226–8
subtitling   99, 100, 106–7, 109–12
systemic-functional   87

tenor   8–13, 15, 17, 23, 25, 32–6, 64–5, 70, 86–8, 115, 188, 190, 233, 240, 265–6, 268, 270, 279, 286, 288, 289, 290, 292
text processing   2, 6, 13, 17–27, 28, 32, 64, 87, 90, 107, 141, 148, 151, 172
text receiver   23, 31, 32, 39, 55, 56, 101, 113, 142, 152, 168, 171, 179, 180, 184, 207, 209, 210–12, 234, 236, 238, 241, 289
text structure   2, 3, 21–2, 25, 27, 28, 30, 52, 113–15, 117, 122, 124, 126, 128, 134, 135, 141, 147, 149, 150, 152, 162, 196, 198, 212, 223, 230, 281, 284, 285, 289, 290, 291, 292

text type   2–3, 15, 22, 26, 28, 38, 41–53, 54, 56, 57, 60, 62, 82, 92, 98, 113–15, 121–3, 124–5, 132, 134, 135, 141, 142, 145, 147, 148–59, 160–8, 170–3, 179, 187, 201–19, 227, 229–31, 235–7, 272–4, 279, 281, 285, 286, 287, 290, 292, 293
textual competence   2, 6–16, 26, 32, 152, 207, 278, 284, 292
textual transfer   1
texture   2–3, 10, 22, 26–7, 28–30, 36, 64–5, 70, 76, 116, 122, 124–5, 131–4, 135–47, 148–52, 160–9, 170, 175–7, 180, 183, 187, 194, 198, 208, 221, 236, 274, 278, 279, 290, 292, 293, 294
Theme-Rheme   139, 146, 274, 293
Thesis Cited   14, 45–6, 75, 120, 162, 196, 292, 293
top-down (text analysis)   24, 29, 100, 142, 278, 282, 293
transitivity   176, 244–5, 248, 282
translation theory   1

universe of discourse   17, 37, 90, 145–6, 205

variation   28–32, 124, 141, 146, 148, 160, 190, 201, 213, 214, 290
verbal sentence   136–7, 146, 156, 181–3, 289, 294
visual text   230–1, 281, 294

word order   3, 4, 103, 138, 177, 180, 182, 288

www.ingramcontent.com/pod-product-compliance
Lightning Source LLC
Chambersburg PA
CBHW031706230426
43668CB00006B/129